CW00738435

A Scottish Blockade Runner in the American Civil War

A SCOTTISH BLOCKADE RUNNER IN THE AMERICAN CIVIL WAR

Joannes Wyllie

OF THE STEAMER *AD-VANCE*

JOHN F. MESSNER

Whittles Publishing

Published by

Whittles Publishing Ltd.,
Dunbeath,
Caithness, KW6 6EG,
Scotland, UK

www.whittlespublishing.com

in association with
Glasgow Museums

© 2021 Culture and Sport Glasgow (Museums) 2021

ISBN 978-184995-482-2

Printed and bound by CPI Group (UK) Ltd, Croydon, CR0 4YY

All rights reserved.
No part of this publication may be reproduced,
stored in a retrieval system, or transmitted,
in any form or by any means, electronic,
mechanical, recording or otherwise
without prior permission of the publishers.

To Heather, Martha and Sadie

and

George Zepik, a true lover of all things Civil War.

CONTENTS

ACKNOWLEDGEMENTS

The story of Joannes Wyllie could not have been told without the support of a multitude of people. Like those of the ships that Wyllie commanded during the Civil War, my crew has been made up of contributors from both sides of the Atlantic – from Scotland, England, Ireland, Bermuda, and the United States. The combination of their knowledge, skills and unending willingness to assist has made much of the research for the book seem like a smooth day's sailing.

I am grateful to Carol McNeill, whose help was essential in discovering Wyllie's personal family history in Fife. She gleefully took the wheel to steer me in the right direction towards the history of the Wyllie family. She admitted with no hesitation that before my initial contact she'd had no knowledge of blockade running or of Wyllie, yet now she, like me, has become obsessed with the topics. I thank her for all her help, and salute her as founding member of the Joannes Appreciation Society.

I tip my hat to Lorna Hyland, assistant curator at the Merseyside Maritime Museum in Liverpool, for her eagerness to assist with my queries regarding maritime records from that port. Wyllie was associated with Liverpool for his whole maritime career. Every query regarding the archives was answered with speed and enthusiasm. If only all of us were as helpful and enthusiastic as Lorna, research would be a doddle.

Almost all of the archival history of the steamer *Ad-Vance* as a blockade runner can be found in the state archives of North Carolina. Contained within the collection of the papers of Governor Zebulon Vance can be found letter books and telegrams relating to the purchase and operation of the steamer during the war. Also in the archives are disbursements for the voyages of the steamer and the only known records of payments made to Wyllie while master. I offer my thanks to Vann Evans, audiovisual materials archivist, who went above and beyond the call of duty as he located a cargoholdful of documents that offered me the chance to create a full history of the vessel and Wyllie's role on it.

Throughout my research I was able to identify only one living family member of Joannes Wyllie. It was my great fortune to be contacted by Mary Akerman, Wyllie's great-grandniece, during the writing of this book. She enthusiastically gave me new insights into the Wyllie family as well as providing very kind assistance during my research. My heartfelt thanks go out to her for all her help.

I offer my thanks to Barry Sullivan, archivist of D.C. Thomson and Company in Dundee, for combing through the records of *The People's Friend* and other titles published in Dundee. It is within the pages of publications printed by this company that three of the four known images of Wyllie can be found.

The records of the capture of both of Wyllie's blockade runners are held by the National Archives in the United States. Special thanks to: Carey Stumm, archivist, National Archives at New York City and Joe Keefe, archives specialist, National Archives at Boston, for their assistance and the provision of the full archival records for both cases; Gregory O'Connor, archivist (higher) at the National Archives of Ireland for helping with crew and passenger lists of Wyllie's ships that passed through Ireland; Angus Wark, reference services team supervisor at the National Library of Scotland who provided from its archive a complete copy of the article *Risen from the Ranks: Captain Wyllie, the Great Scottish Blockade Runner* as found in *The People's Friend*; Elizabeth Walter, records assistant at the Bermuda Archives, for locating and providing copies of the customs records for Wyllie's steamers that passed through the ports of Bermuda during the Civil War. And she having provided details and larger scans of the only known photograph of the steamer *Ad-Vance* as a blockade runner, I would like to offer my thanks to Lisa Crunk, photographic archivist at the United States Naval History and Heritage Command, Washington.

To the staff at Glasgow Museums, without whose support this book would not have been possible: Emily Malcolm, curator of maritime history; Susan Pacitti, publications manager; Martin Bellamy, head of research; Niamh Johnston, collections access assistant; Rosemary Watt, research manager; John Westwell, designer; and Enzo di Cosmo, photographer.

The following individuals and groups provided me with much appreciated information on topics related to the histories of Scotland, maritime trade, art and the Civil War: Chelsea Grayburn, registrar at the South Carolina Confederate Relic Room and Military Museum; Barbara Johnston at the Borders Family History Society; Grahame Ramsay of Lodge St Clair of Dysart 520; A.S. Davidson (deceased) author of the book *Samuel Walters: Maritime Artist*; Jillian Lewis of Fife Museums and Archives; Mariam Touba, reference librarian; the New York Historical Society's Patricia D. Klingenstein Library; Karen Emmons, archivist/librarian at the Historic Charleston Foundation; Sharon L. Gee, PBA Galleries, San Francisco; Bob Surridge of the Southport Historical Society of North Carolina; Dr Stephen Wise, author of *Lifeline of the Confederacy*; Rick Burton, owner of the painting of the *Frolic*; Catriona Foote at the University of St Andrews; Tom Barclay, reference and local history librarian, Scottish and Local History Department at South Ayrshire Council; Daniel E.

Sutherland, expert on Anna McNeill Whistler, University of Arkansas; and Cathy Wright, curator at the American Civil War Museum.

To my great friend, Hugh Hornby, thank you for your advice and encouragement.

To the many more individuals from museums, archives and historical societies who have helped with the research. I humbly thank you all. Thank you also to Dr Stephen Wise for your foreword to this book and for your assistance in researching the history of the blockade. Your book, *Lifeline of the Confederacy: Blockade Running During the Civil War*, is the most detailed and informative description of the blockade that has yet been published.

To my family, friends and colleagues who have put up with my constant nattering on about Joannes Wyllie, blockade running and the Civil War, I thank you for your patience.

FOREWORD

It has been said the best vessels and the best captains that challenged the United States blockade of the Confederacy during the American Civil War came from Scotland. John F. Messner provides an excellent case that this thesis is true.

Joannes Wyllie and the *Ad-Vance* were both of Scottish birth, and together constituted one of the war's most successful teams of captain and ship to test the blockade. Neither Wyllie, also known as John Wyllie, nor the *Ad-Vance*, once known as the *Lord Clyde*, had started their careers with the intention of becoming blockade runners. Indeed, Wyllie came to experience a life at sea as an escape from the role of well-educated teacher. In 1852, he reversed course and took to a life at sea. As he had risen through the ranks of academia, he too advanced his standing at sea: he progressed from apprentice seaman to, at the age of 34, the sailing master/captain of the *Ad-Vance*.

Like Wyllie's, the *Ad-Vance*'s pre-war career did not suggest its future role as a wartime blockade runner. Originally named *Lord Clyde*, it had been built in 1862 by Caird & Company, a family business located in Greenock, on the Clyde. The vessels produced by Caird and other Scottish firms were known as Clyde steamers, and became the prototypes of the Civil War's most successful blockade runners. These rakish vessels combined a long iron hull, a narrow beam, a powerful engine and a shallow draft for tremendous speeds.

The *Ad-Vance*, née *Lord Clyde*, and other Clyde river packets and their successors became part of a vital Confederate supply system designed to support the Southern military against the larger and more industrialised North. However, at the start of the American Civil War no one had envisioned a fleet of specialised ships running munitions and supplies through a cordon of enemy warships.

When the United States established a blockade of the Southern coastline, the leaders of the Confederacy initially adhered to a theory known as King Cotton, based on the notion that Great Britain, whose textile industry was dependent upon the South's cotton, would immediately intervene on their side or face economic ruin. In support of this concept, Southerners stockpiled their cotton at the start of the war, and the Confederate government bought up 400,000 cotton bales to assist the planters. But in the event Great Britain did not intervene, and Southern military leaders, realising the war would be long and hard fought, began to construct factories to manufacture their own munitions, uniforms and accoutrements. However, it would take time to bring these industries on line and as a stopgap measure, until the factories were up and running, the leaders of the Confederate war effort turned to acquiring 'articles of prime necessity' brought in by ships running through the growing Northern blockade.

To pay for the supplies it needed, the Confederacy discovered a new use for its cotton. Once seen as an instrument of foreign policy, it was now employed as a medium of exchange. Following the lead of the Navy Department, the government began to use cotton to finance its overseas ventures by issuing a variety of cotton bonds. There were two ways for a holder to make a profit from the bonds: they could receive monthly interest payments then redeem the bond at face value after a certain length of time, or they could bring the bond to the Confederacy and receive cotton. It was the latter method that made the bonds so popular. Using the bonds, cotton could be obtained in the Confederacy for 10 cents a pound and sold in Great Britain for the equivalent of 50 cents, thus making a $50 cotton bale from Wilmington, North Carolina, worth $250 in Liverpool. The value of Southern cotton allowed the Confederacy to fund its overseas operations and pay for vital munitions.

Early in the war the North Carolina legislature, believing it could do a more efficient job in outfitting its state units than could the Confederate government, requested from it funds that would normally have been used by the nation's Quartermaster Bureau to purchase clothing for the North Carolina troops serving with the army. This was granted, and the state officials used the money to buy raw materials that were turned into uniforms by the state's growing textile industry. However, by the end of 1862 North Carolina was facing a severe shortage of leather, cotton and wool. The crisis was such that the state's adjutant general, James G. Martin, suggested to Governor Henry Toole Clark that a blockade runner should be purchased to bring in the necessary material from Great Britain. Clark apparently felt that he did not have the authority for such action, but his successor, Zebulon Vance, agreed to sponsor a state-operated blockade runner.

The state issued $1.5 million in bonds backed by North Carolina cotton, which Vance despatched to Great Britain in the custody of John White and Thomas Crossan. The two were to purchase materials, plus shoes and blankets for North Carolina soldiers, plus a vessel to deliver the supplies. Vance and Martin had chosen their agents carefully, giving each a specific role. John White, an established dry goods merchant, was in charge of purchasing and shipping supplies. Thomas Crossan, a former lieutenant in the Confederate Navy, was in charge of choosing and outfitting the blockade runner.

The steamer chosen by Crossan was no ordinary vessel. It was the iron-hulled sidewheeler *Lord Clyde*, which had been operating for six months between Dublin and Glasgow. It was sold to North Carolina for $175,000 (or £34,000), and in less than one month, loaded with vital merchandise, it was on its way to Bermuda, under the command of Joannes Wyllie.

On 28 June 1863, Wyllie brought the *Lord Clyde* safely to the wharf at Wilmington, loaded with, among other items, dry goods, cloth, shoes and cotton cards, used for turning cotton into thread. The cloth was sent to Raleigh, the North Carolina state capital, where state-operated factories turned it into blankets and uniforms. The cotton cards were distributed to households throughout the state; the resultant thread could then be used by the families and the surplus taken by the state for uniform production.

The strength of Messner's work is his compilation and explanation of the accounts detailing Wyllie's blockade-running exploits on the *Ad-Vance*. While Wyllie was known in his personal sphere and home location, his accounts of his actions are not well known in the general historiography of Civil War naval and maritime history. Reminiscences by blockade-running captains, often recorded decades after the war, are often flawed, but Wyllie's recollections, presented through Messner's careful analysis of events and people, are accurate and mesmerising.

Wyllie compiled an impressive record while on the *Ad-Vance*, making it the war's tenth most successful blockade runner. Yet he has been overlooked by most blockade-running chronicles. This is partially because credit for the *Ad-Vance's* success was usually given to the North Carolina officers who accompanied Wyllie on board the runner. Officially he was merely the sailing master, but to all intents and purposes he was the ship's captain, in charge of day-to-day activities and the manoeuvring of the vessel as it ran the blockade. The North Carolina officers were there as supercargoes, the individuals representing the interests of the ship owner, in this case the State of North Carolina. It was Wyllie who captained the ship when it was most in danger, but because of the presence of the North Carolina officials, former naval officers, it was often they, instead of Wyllie, who were acknowledged for the *Ad-Vance*'s success . It is to Messner's great credit that this historical oversight is now corrected.

Wyllie and the *Ad-Vance* were part of a massive system that had profound effects on both sides of the Atlantic. One-third of all steam-powered blockade runners, nearly 120 vessels, came from Clyde shipbuilders. Throughout the war 20 Scottish firms, employing some 20,000 workers, continued to produce specialised vessels, built specifically to run the blockade. Ship technology leaped forward, and the profits that flowed into Glasgow companies, combined with workers' high wages, produced an economic boom that was felt not only in Scotland but throughout the British Empire. However, the greatest effect of the blockade running was felt by the Confederacy's forces.

Wyllie's and the *Ad-Vance* were vital cogs in a logistical system that brought supplies to the Confederacy, allowing the nation to properly outfit its armed forces. During the war, just under 300 steamers tested the blockade. Out of approximately 1,300 attempts more than 1,000 were successful, giving the runners a near 80 per cent success rate. These ships brought in 60 per cent of the Confederacy's modern arms; 30 per cent of its lead for bullets; 75 per cent of the nation's saltpetre needed to make gun powder; and nearly all the paper required to make cartridges. Artillery of all sizes was run through the blockade. The majority of cloth for uniforms; leather for shoes and accoutrements; metal for manufacturing war materials; medical supplies; and chemicals and canned foodstuffs all arrived on blockade runners. Because of the blockade running the South was never without the means to fight, and had an opportunity for victory.

The Ad-Vance is well-known as a blockade runner, fabled in story, photographs and pictures. In comparison to its cohorts, its 15 successful trips ranked it tenth in successful runs through the blockade. While many masters moved between vessels, Wyllie's career is impressive because he was on that particular ship, fulfilling a pivotal role, during all of its successful runs. In the hierarchy of captains, Wyllie is among the top five masters who so often evaded capture to deliver cargoes to the Confederacy.

John Messner has done a fine and commendable job in bringing to life the varied and fascinating career of Joannes Wyllie. Messner's comprehensive account will stand as an example of excellent research blended into a well-crafted narrative that brings to Civil War historiography an important book. Wyllie's close friend, the Reverend Peter Anton, declared of Wyllie that in comparison to other, better known, Scottish blockade-runner captains, Wyllie need not 'yield the palm' of accomplishment to anyone. And in his work John Messner has ensured that Wyllie's palm is held high for all to see.

Dr Stephen Wise
author of *Lifeline of the Confederacy: Blockade Running During the Civil War*

INTRODUCTION: THE GREAT SCOTTISH BLOCKADE RUNNER

> There is no better, no more genial, no more highly respected gentleman of our district.
>
> – From an advertisement in the *Fife Herald* of 16 November 1901 for an upcoming lecture by Joannes Wyllie on his time as a blockade runner.

The Earl of Rosslyn was late. The other members of the organising committee were busy looking at their watches while the attendees were filing into the hall. The members of the audience, escaping the cold rain of the late autumn Scottish evening, made their way through the lobby into the fine grandeur of the Adam Smith Theatre. It was a large audience, there for an evening's entertainment – but the show would not start until the earl appeared, and the news making the rounds was that when his train had stopped at the station he had been nowhere to be found. Until he arrived, the audience must wait, as he was to be in the chair that night – and the show could not start without its chairman. The wait would be no problem, however, for the assembled crowd, as they all were there with great anticipation, and a hopefully brief delay would not, like the chill of the rain outside, dampen their spirits.

The earl had specially arranged to attend the night's programme. He was the laird, with a large estate and business interests in Fife, the county on the east coast of Scotland just north of Edinburgh. He had accepted the invitation from the Lord Provost of Kirkcaldy to chair the session at the Adam Smith Hall; named after the famous economist, another son of the area, it was the largest and grandest venue in town. The earl, a close friend of that night's performer, had mentioned to the lord provost that he'd had alternative plans for that evening; he had passed up the chance to dine with Lord Rosebery, the former prime minister, because he, the earl, had deemed his presence on the stage in Kirkcaldy more important.

LECTURE

BY

CAPTAIN WYLLIE, OF MITCHELSTON,

ENTITLED—

"REMINISCENCES OF SEA LIFE AND RUNNING THE BLOCKADE,"

IN

ADAM SMITH HALL, KIRKCALDY,

ON

WEDNESDAY, 27th November, 1901.

You should hear Miss MARGUERITE BURNETT Contralto Vocalist, in her rendering of the "Death of Nelson." Sea Songs by Local Artistes.

The Chair will be taken by The Right Hon. The Earl of Rosslyn at 7.45 prompt.

Advertisement for Captain Wyllie's lecture at the Adam Smith Hall, Kirkcaldy – one of the 26 he delivered to his captivated audiences in Fife.

Newspaper image © The British Library Board. All rights reserved. *With thanks to The British Newspaper Archive* (www.britishnewspaperarchive.co.uk)

The local papers had been running advertisements for weeks in the lead-up to the evening. The event was to be held on the evening of 27 November 1901, and excitement had been building in the town for what looked like the must-have ticket of the season. We might wonder why the earl was going to lend his august presence to this event: was it for the arrival of the latest soprano from Europe, or for a heated debate on temperance, or for a celebrated vaudeville comedy act?

No, this excitement was all for Joannes Wyllie, a 73-year-old local farmer. What, surely, could this man have to offer in terms of entertainment that could fill a hall with 1,600 people?

When the earl did arrive he claimed he had been having a nap on the train, so had missed his stop. Some audience members sniggered, knowing the earl's habits of imbibing, but all were happy that the evening's entertainment would now begin.

The earl wasn't there to introduce Wyllie's thoughts on the latest techniques of animal husbandry or the best potatoes to plant for the Scottish climate. He was there to present and endorse one of the most well-known, most well-loved and most entertaining sons that Fife had ever produced – even if that reputation didn't seem to extend past the boundaries of the county. For before Wyllie ploughed the fields of his farm at Mitchelston he had ploughed the waves as a mariner.

He had started as a mere apprentice seaman and had risen through the ranks to become a captain. But many men in the coastal town of Kirkcaldy could claim similar histories. How was this man different from any other ship captain?

Over the years he had enthralled his neighbours, friends and local groups alike with tales of the high seas, of danger and cunning, of love and death, of shipwrecks and foreign lands. But mainly, Wyllie would delight his audience with tales of the chases that he had once been involved in as captain of one of the most successful blockade runners during the American Civil War. This jovial, eloquent man, who had tilled the land for the past 35 years, had once been master of the *Ad-Vance*, a Scottish-built paddle steamer which had crossed the Atlantic in 1863 in order to take cargoes of arms, food, clothes and merchandise of all sorts from the ports of Nassau in the Bahamas and St George's, Bermuda, to the Cape Fear River, North Carolina, there to unload at the port of Wilmington. But at that time the Southern ports were surrounded by the forces of the Union Navy flying the Stars and Stripes, attempting to prevent the import of vital supplies for the rebellion that had been started by the Confederate States of America two years previously, when they had declared independence from the United States.

'The captain was frequently applauded during the course of the lecture, his description of the various scenes, interjected with a fine spice of humour, keeping his audience always in the best of spirits.'

Newspaper image of the Adam Smith Hall © The British Library Board. All rights reserved.
With thanks to The British Newspaper Archive (www.britishnewspaperarchive.co.uk)

Running the blockade involved not only evading the Union forces but being able to navigate your ship in the unpredictable Atlantic on the eastern seaboard of the Southern states. It was a dangerous task, but was also a potentially highly lucrative endeavour. Able seamen and captains alike would share in the huge profits that would come from shipping in the armaments necessary for the war effort of the Confederacy, foodstuffs for the people of the South, plus medicines, building materials such as lead and iron plate, and chemicals. But along with these necessities flowed luxury goods from Europe: perfumes, the latest fashions, liquor and housewares.

Many in the crowd in the Adam Smith Theatre that winter's night would have heard Wyllie speak before; ever since he had returned to the land he had told of his tales at sea. While introducing himself at the many lectures he gave across the county of Fife, under the title 'Reminiscences of Sea Life, and Blockade Running', he would often refer to the romantic and adventurous tales of Sir Walter Scott, the famous Scots author who had lived near Wyllie's birthplace.

Wyllie's talks were always given in aid of a local charity or to support a member of the community who had fallen on hard times. Never did he offer his service for a fee. But on that day in November 1901, in the biggest hall he was ever to speak in, and in front of what must have been his largest ever audience, Wyllie was himself the recipient of the funds raised by the ticket sales. He owned no property, his farm being rented from the Rosslyn Estate, and now, at the age of 73, he found himself in need of the aid of those who could give it.

Born in 1828 in the small village of Nenthorn, near the Scottish/English border, after his father had moved there for work, Wyllie had spent his youth and early adulthood in Fife. His father was a gardener who rented his home from the Earl of Rosslyn, and Wyllie seemed bound to follow in his father's footsteps until chance led him to a new life at sea. His maritime story did not began as a blockade runner, nor did it end when he was captured by the Union Navy after a successful 17 months on the steamer. His career at sea spanned over 15 years, taking him across the globe from New Zealand to the harbours of Burma (Myanmar) and India and South America, and through the Mediterranean to the Black Sea.

But it was on the *Ad-Vance* that Wyllie made his impact. Wyllie's role on this famous runner has never before been fully examined. The established history of the steamer makes only brief mention of his time on board. He was sometimes listed as the sailing master, other times as captain. His nationality was confused in various contemporary documents, listed as Scottish in some, but in others as English. His name, too, was often confused, spelled in various sources as Wylie or Willie.

My research for this book started with a simple question: Who was Joannes Wyllie? The reason for this question was that an oil painting of the *Ad-Vance*, by the renowned English maritime artist Samuel Walters, was put on display in an exhibition about blockade running at the Riverside Museum in Glasgow. On the painting I discovered a small brass plaque

Running the blockade, from atop a British-built paddle steamer. A successful run could bring a fortune to all the crew. It was this opportunity that led many British sailors to cross the Atlantic.

Illustrated London News

stating Wyllie's name as master of the steamer. The painting had belonged to Joannes Wyllie and had been donated to Glasgow Museums in 1917, some 15 years after his death. The history of the paddle steamer and its use as a blockade runner has been well documented over the years, but Wyllie's story was almost a complete mystery. A look through published histories revealed little about his role during the Civil War and nothing about his personal history, his origin or his later life. Even a book with a focus on the Scottish role in the conflict, *Clyde Built: The Blockade Runners, Cruisers and Armoured Rams of the American Civil War* by Dr Eric Graham, contains almost nothing about Wyllie, noting only that he commanded the runner *Deer* on a single failed attempt into Charleston towards the end of the war.

My next step was to enter "Joannes Wyllie" into the search bar of the British Newspaper Archive. This led to a few definitive hits. From the first ten mentions Wyllie's life story began to unfurl. It was from these that his life as a farmer in Fife was discovered, that before his time at sea he had been a student at the University of St Andrews, and that he had initially sought to become a teacher. Details of his life after his maritime career started to trickle in, and a complete story of his life could begin to be told. From these initial anchor points, the story of Wyllie's life and career expanded. In addition to research into his life in Scotland, I undertook a re-examination of his role in the Civil War.

This research revealed that far from being a bit player on this important vessel, Wyllie was key to the success of the *Ad-Vance* from the very day it left Scotland. Diaries, court reports and official histories offer insights into his career. From these sources it became clear that he was well liked by both crew and passengers, and greatly respected by the North Carolina state officials and the private owners of the vessel.

Wyllie was also a respected member of his community. He was a member of local agricultural groups, was active in his church, represented his fellow tenants in the business of local politics and business, and was for 30 years a member of the local school board. He took part in local sporting events, from hosting horse races on his farmland to setting up a local cricket club and attending curling matches in the winter. He was a man of action, once saving a couple from an attack from a rabid dog, while also being an amateur thespian, taking part in local dramatics.

The details of the life of Joannes Wyllie came from three main sources: merchant and naval records held in the United Kingdom; contemporary articles and mentions in newspapers on both sides of the Atlantic; and documents charting the history of the of Civil War found in several institutions in the United States, primarily North Carolina.

Just over a decade before his last major lecture on that evening in November 1901, the July 1889 edition of *The People's Friend* ran the feature 'Captain Wyllie: The Great Scottish Blockade Runner'. It was part of an ongoing series focusing on Scots who had bettered themselves, made it, and become famous in various walks of life. It was written by the Reverend Peter Anton, a well-known and prolific author of such biographies of famous Scottish worthies, and a good friend of Joannes Wyllie.

Their connection had begun in 1875 when at the age of just 25 Anton had been selected as the minister at Wyllie's local church. The search committee for this post had been led by Wyllie himself, and after Anton's appointment the two men struck up a friendship that would last the rest of their lives. Anton first wrote about the American Civil War in 1887, when he penned an article in *The People's Friend* on the famous blockade runner Augustus Charles Hobart-Hampden. In a promotional piece for this article he wrote in the *Fife Free Press* that although he was writing on the famous English lord turned runner, his exploits would, of course, pale in comparison to those of their own neighbour, Captain Wyllie:

> It will be eminently satisfactory to all Scotsmen to know that in the matter of blockade running the renowned Hobart has to yield the palm to the accomplished gentleman who spends the evening of his days in the quiet retirement of Mitchelston.

JAMIE'S VENTURE,
OR
THE SCOTTISH BLOCKADE RUNNERS.
By the Author of "The Lass of Udny," &c.

The blockade runner was a regular character in British magazines and novels after the war. Few blockade-runner captains ever shared their own histories, so more romanticised stories appeared – Jamie's Venture being just one such example.

Newspaper image © The British Library Board. All rights reserved.
With thanks to The British Newspaper Archive (www.britishnewspaperarchive.co.uk)

Tales of blockade running during the Civil War, even a quarter of a century later, were still often seen as near-fictional adventurous tales, and were popular throughout Britain. The previous December the first chapter of a serialised story entitled 'Jamie's Venture, or the Scottish Blockade Runners' had appeared in the *Dundee, Perth, Forfar, and Fife's People's Journal*. Over the next three months, 21 chapters of danger, romance, war and intrigue would thrill the journal's readers. It was billed as 'a story to please everybody' – but to Anton its content must have appeared thin in comparison to the real-life exploits of his friend.

The People's Friend was – and still is – a mass market magazine, available to many people across Scotland, and with a reach to at least the north of England. This meant that for the first time Wyllie's story could thrill people across the nation. Yet even with this publication his exploits failed to reach beyond the shores of Britain. The article does not appear to have travelled across the Atlantic, and after his death in 1902 his important role in the history of the American Civil War was all but forgotten.

Joannes Wyllie was, however, no mere footnote to the history of the *Ad-Vance*. On the contrary, he was the ever-present member of crew, a trusted sailing master and ultimately commander of one of the most successful blockade runners of the Civil War. This was the highpoint of his maritime career, during which he served on 12 ships.

RISEN FROM THE RANKS.

CAPTAIN WYLLIE:

THE GREAT SCOTTISH BLOCKADE-RUNNER.

A SKETCH OF HIS LIFE AND ADVENTURES AT SEA.

BY THE REV. P. ANTON.

The article that introduced Wyllie's story to the wider public. The publication of 'The Great Scottish Blockade Runner' in the July 1889 edition of The People's Friend *spread his exploits across Scotland and England. Sadly, just this single illustration accompanied the article.*

Reproduced by permission of the National Library of Scotland.

The audience on that cold night in November 1901 came to see a man whose life had begun as the son of a gardener but who became one of the most important members of the crew on one of the most successful of all blockade runners during the American Civil War. But although his tales entertained and delighted the crowd in the hall that night, his fame as a blockade runner was contained during his own lifetime to Scotland. The history of his role and the impact he had during the Civil War then continued to lie undiscovered for over a century. Only now can the full story of this great Scottish blockade runner be revealed.

1

'JOHN' WYLLIE'S EARLY LIFE, 1828-1852

> He is a young man, and promises to become highly useful ... We believe he is yet destined to fill some office of no mean rank.
>
> – From a review of Wyllie as teacher by the leaders of Strathmiglo Subscription School, 1846.

The Scottish Borders is an area steeped in mystery, intrigue and history. It is home to fierce families with rivalries spanning centuries, its landscapes and local myths inspiring some of Scotland's most famous poets. Its medieval monastic abbeys, once centres of both religion and commerce, lie today in ruins as symbols of the violent histories that have passed over this land.

Even with its rich history this region is not well known outside Britain. The wider region, historically speaking, stretched from the Solway Firth on the edge of the Irish Sea in the west to Berwick-upon-Tweed on the North Sea in the east. It was the scene of many battles and skirmishes between Scotland and England, even after the Act of Union of 1707 had joined the two nations. It was home to families who maintained their castles and tower houses for the kings of Scotland, or indeed sometimes those of England. Feuds between these families led to arguments, while cross-border raids for cattle or other goods – known as reiving – became an image associated with the inhabitants of the area to this day.

It is a green land of forest, hill and moor, with rivers host to salmon and trout running towards both the North and the Irish Seas. The Borders always has been an area off the beaten track: few major roads run through it and even when the railways arrived in the 1840s it remained an area that many travellers simply passed through when making their way north or south.

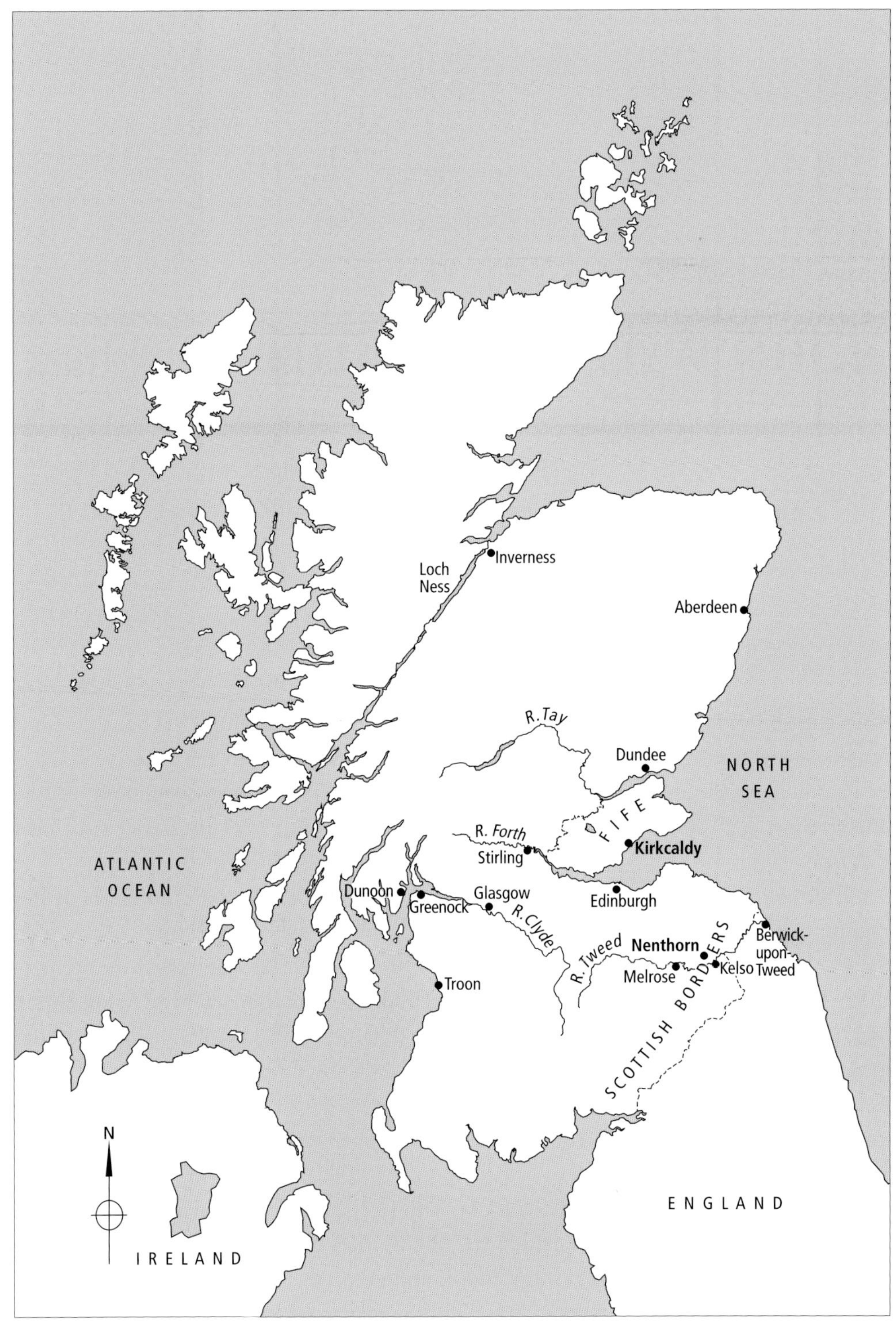

Scotland: important locations in Wyllie's life

The market town of Kelso on the banks of the famous River Tweed. It was near here that the story of Joannes Wyllie began.

Courtesy of the Library of Congress

It is here that the story of Joannes Wyllie begins, in the village of Nenthorn. No more than a few houses and church, it is nestled amongst rolling low hills in a corner of Berwickshire a few miles north of the market town of Kelso. With under 400 inhabitants in the district in 1834, the population was described as 'almost wholly agricultural, and partakes of the general habits of that class; but the local attachment is not strong. Not a single farmer in the parish is a native of it.'[1] There was one inn in the village, the toll house on the road from Kelso to Dalkeith (south of Edinburgh), and there was a school for the 30 children of the area. Several large country estates surrounded the village, and still do now; the closest, just to the south-east, is Newton Don, its large country house built in the 18th century and set in 3,300 acres, described in 1800 as 'a remarkably pretty, cheerful place, fine single trees scattered over a beautiful, sloping lawn – all unfinished.'[2] In 1817–1818 its owner, Alexander Don, greatly altered the house to the designs of the renowned English architect Sir Robert Smirke, at considerable expense. This included plans to improve the grounds of the estate as well: Don sought to create a modern, fashionable estate with both beautiful aesthetics and profitable commercial sites like mills and forests for timber. This ambitious plan required the necessary labour – mainly experienced gardeners who could level the lawns, plant the avenues and dig the water features to make the grounds as fine as the house itself.

One of these gardeners who had come to the district in the early 1820s to work at the estate was Alexander Wyllie, a native of the small coastal town of Dysart, near Kirkcaldy in the county of Fife. Alexander came from a family of gardeners, his father being employed on a nearby estate belonging to the Earl of Rosslyn, whose family held several estates in Fife. What motivated Alexander to make this journey of over 60 miles can only be speculated: it could have been that he had heard of the work going from his laird, the Earl of Rosslyn, who would have heard of the work from Alexander Don himself from conversations held in Westminster; Rosslyn was a member of the House of Lords and Don was the MP for Roxburghshire.[3] Whatever Alexander's motivations were, the work at Newton Don would have been an exciting opportunity for him as a bachelor in his mid-20s, and he would spend the better part of a decade in the Borders. It was a time not totally devoted to work, though, as Alexander found love while in Nenthorn; in 1823 he married a local woman, Janet Smith. Over the next five years the couple would have three children: Margaret in 1824, James in 1826, and John in 1828.[4]

Although too young himself to recall his life there, Wyllie would later tell how his father, Alexander, met the famous writer Sir Walter Scott, whose large country house, Abbotsford near Selkirk, was not far from Newton Don. Alexander would tell of seeing the great man during his frequent visits to the Don estate; his most memorable recollection was of a walk near Sir Walter through the gardens:

> One beautiful evening, when the rays of the setting sun were filling all the valley with a golden haze, he had a rare experience which he often recounted to his friends. When he was engaged about the garden he saw Scott coming out of the mansion house all alone. Making his way slowly through the

The country estate of Newton Don, located just north of Kelso, was where Alexander Wyllie went to work in the early 1820s.

© CSG CIC Glasgow Museums Collection

> garden, evidently enchanted with the beauty of the evening, he at length took his stand on a terrace overlooking the landscape beneath. After looking about him for a time in silence, for there was not a creature near, and Sir Walter was wholly unaware of the gardener's presence, our hero's father at length heard him repeat these words –
>
> 'The curfew tolls the knell of parting day,
> The lowing herd winds slowly o'er the lea,
> The ploughman homeward plods his weary way,
> And leaves the world to darkness and to me.'
>
> The gardener listened. Scott went on with his recitation in a deep, low-noted, and impassioned voice, and without slip or hesitation of any kind continued until he had concluded the 'Elegy.' He then, quietly as he had come, left the terrace and gained the festive party assembled in the mansion.[5]

With stories told to them of his encounters with this famous Scottish writer, Alexander's children would find a love for the stories and legends of Scotland told by Scott in his novels *Waverley*, *Rob Roy* and *Ivanhoe*, to name but a few. The family would spend seven years in the Borders, but from the 1831 census it is clear that Alexander and his family had returned to Dysart by the time their daughter, Helen, was born that year.

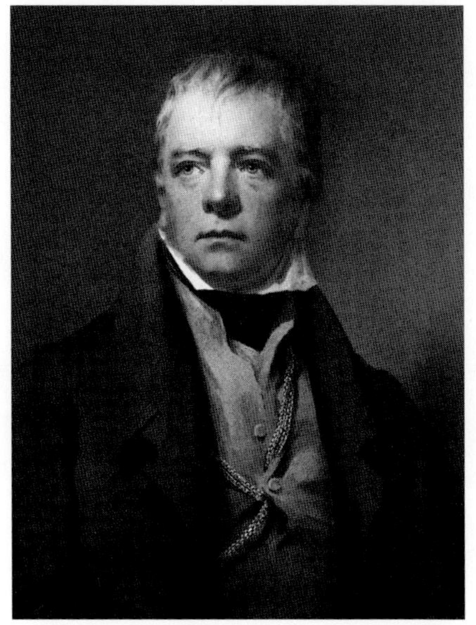

The famous Scots author and poet Sir Walter Scott (1771–1832) was an inspiration to the young Wyllie. Alexander told the young John tales of seeing and hearing the great man when he visited Newton Don.

© CSG CIC Glasgow Museums Collection

After Alexander returned to Fife he found work again on the Earl of Rosslyn's estate. In the 1830s Dysart had a small harbour, home to a fishing fleet, as well as a large hinterland filled with farms and coal mines. The population of the town and surrounding area was listed in the 1831 census as 7,104 inhabitants, described as of being of 'industrious habits … and upon the whole, they are contented and happy with their situation and circumstances. There are a great number of very intelligent individuals amongst them, and not a few who are distinguished both for religious principle and good moral practice.'[6] Wyllie's boyhood in Dysart would have been spent learning the family trade as a gardener, tilling the soil and maintaining his cuttings and plants through the bitter Fife winters. By 1841, the Wyllie family, now made up of just Alexander and his five children, lived in a house on The Green in the centre of Dysart. There is no listing for Janet Wyllie in that census, and she is believed to have died sometime after the birth of her third son and last child, William, in 1836. Wyllie recalled that he attended the local parish school, and that at this very early age he was filled with a love of literature.

He would work in his father's garden during the day – which was renowned in the area as a model example – and he attended school in the evenings. He soon found the daily tasks of the gardener's profession to be repetitive and became 'insufferably wearied' of the

The port of Dysart on the Fife coast, home to a small fleet of fishing boats. It was near here that Wyllie spent his early years working the fields of his father's garden.

© CSG CIC Glasgow Museums Collection

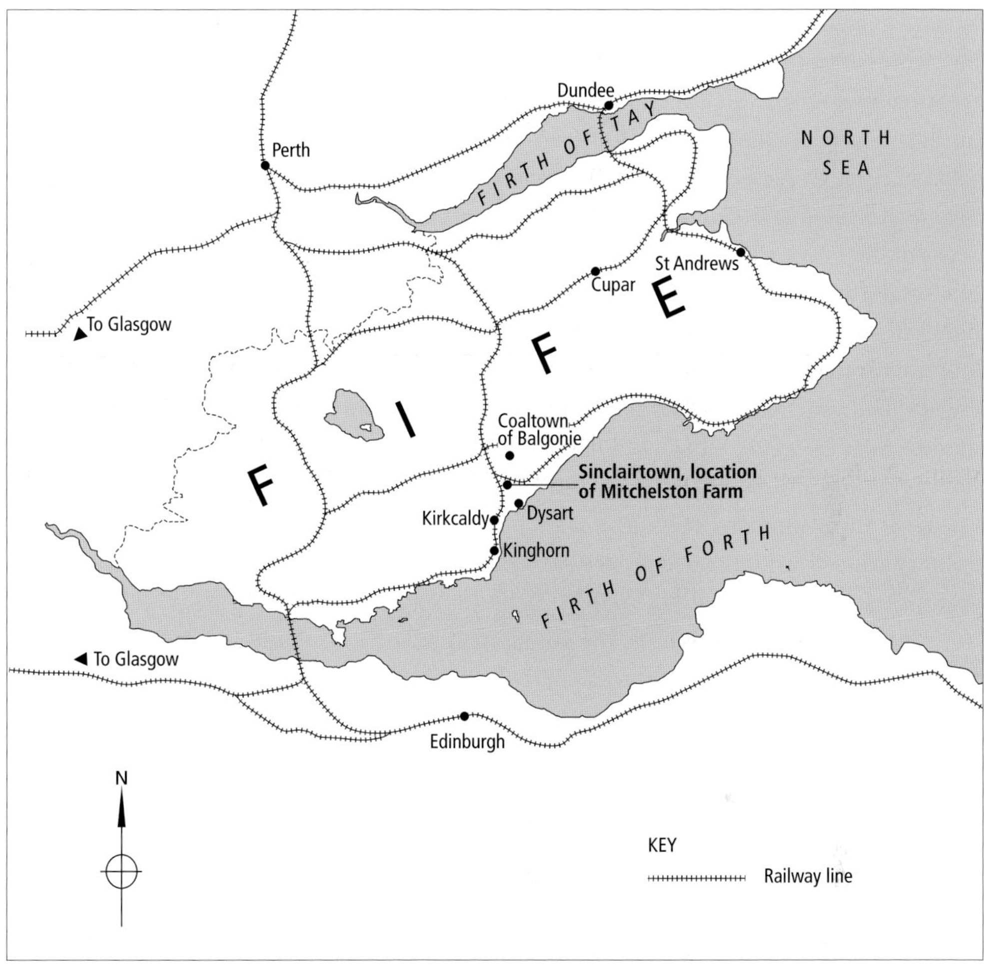

The county of Fife, including Kinross

routine. So along with a friend he decided to set off on an adventure: to make for an English port and there to join the crew of a merchant ship or enlist in the navy.

The excursion to England took its toll on the two young men, who would have been aged no more than 17. Their exact destination is not known, but the ports of Newcastle and Hartlepool would have been home to the ships they sought. After a month of wandering, the boys became quite despondent. Wyllie noted, though, that while in England they luckily came into contact with a friend who offered them shelter; this was possibly an acquaintance that Wyllie had made while his family lived in Nenthorn, which is less than 10 miles from the border.

Both boys then decided that their quest for a maritime adventure was at an end, but rather than returning straight home to their families they made for the nearest army barracks, intent on enlisting.[7] Wyllie recalled that he was then despatched to Ireland, but no records exist that can locate him positively there at any time in the early 1840s. The one recorded memory of his time in the army was of extreme displeasure as he recalled that his 'heart seems to have sickened at the sight of the floggings administered to delinquent soldiers'. Though records of Wyllie's brief military career do not exist, reports of the regular flogging of soldiers were common in the newspapers. Just one example, coming from the pages of the 17 March 1845 edition of the *Dublin Monitor*, noted 'We allude to the torture of a soldier named Patrick Rice … sentenced by order of a Court Martial to receive one hundred lashes, for an unpardonable breach of military code, i.e., making away with his kit'.[8] This practice was a standard punishment in the Army and continued until 1888. This cruelty made such an impression on the young man that he decided to desert. After six months away he made it back to Fife and his family home. It would seem that an offence such as desertion would have warranted considerably more than the 100 lashes dished out for the theft of uniform, but fortunately for him Wyllie faced no repercussions for this military crime; he might have given false details on enlisting, thus giving him cover for his eventual escape.

Whatever the circumstances, the young man once again found himself in his father's garden. But his education in the local school had given him another idea for a profession, and it would not be long until he 'turned his thoughts to the occupation of a teacher, as likely to give him relief from a kind of work which he felt so uncongenial to his nature'.[9] Although he had no formal training he answered an advertisement for a teacher at a school in Strathmiglo, a village 10 miles north of Dysart. He took up the post in the late summer of 1845, making him just 17 years of age. Over the next year it would seem that his first foray into education had been a successful one because at the end of the school term, in August 1846, the *Fife Herald* noted that the scholars at that Strathmiglo Subscription School were examined by the local committee, and noted the 'great attainment of the children'. Their teacher, Mr Wyllie, was noted to have great character and, as he was bound for college, was given the warmest of wishes and thanks.[10]

After just one year as the teacher at Strathmiglo he had sought to formalise his choice of profession by qualifying as a parochial master. He had set his sights on higher education, and was accepted at the University of St Andrews, starting his studies in October 1846. St Andrews is the oldest university in Scotland, founded in 1413, and is one of the four ancient universities of the nation.[11] It is located in the town of St Andrews on the north-east coast of Fife. It has a harbour, and was at the time one of a number of towns along the coast with fishing fleets and coastal trade vessels. In 1831 it had a population of 5,621.[12] By the mid-1840s the university was attended by between 100 and 200 students and had a staff of one principal, eight professors and one lecturer. Wyllie matriculated in February 1847, students being required to have registered and been a student in at least one class before the formal ceremony could occur. Each new student signed the handwritten matriculation roll, which had started listing names in 1747; they would sign in alphabetical order according to their first name. The roll itself was written in Latin, the language of academia, and many of the students chose to Latinise their names on the roll, so William became *Gulielmus*, Andrew *Andreas*, Peter *Petrus* and John *Joannes*. John Wyllie, however, chose not to perform this act of classical acclamation and chose instead to sign just as John. The history of the St Andrews Matriculation Roll notes that some incoming students at this time would not have known their latinised name, and so signed their Christian name instead.[13] Although records show that he would continue using his given, or Christian, name of John for several more years, Wyllie would now have been bestowed an alternative name, one that he would go on to use fully later in life.

Wyllie now found himself immersed in the world of a classical university education, steeped in tradition and formality. First-year students, known at St Andrews as bigants, took classes in Greek and Latin, and were also expected to undertake mathematics classes as soon as possible. Next would be courses in logic, moral philosophy and natural philosophy. In total, students were expected to compete a four-year *quadrennium*, during which they would be encouraged to take courses in history and chemistry in addition to language and philosophy.[14]

The records from the university show that John Wyllie took classes entitled Greek 1 and Latin 1 in his first academic year of 1846/47. The records do not list him enrolled in courses for the following year, but do show that in 1848/49 he attended classes in Logic, Mathematics 1 and Sens. Philosophy (philosophy of the senses).

University education at that time was not free of charge, and the son of a gardener would struggle to cover his costs. In October 1848 the Rev. John Landall Rose wrote in support of John Wyllie receiving a bursary of £10 (amounting to almost £1,000 today: see Table 1) for the upcoming year. Wyllie's relationship with Rose stems from his first job as teacher. As a member of the local clergy, Rose would have taken part in annual inspections of the schools in his area, so he would have known of Wyllie's qualities from his work at Strathmiglo from his 1846 inspection, the young teacher apparently making a good impression on his observer. This request for funds could explain why Wyllie does not appear in the university records for the 1847/48 academic year.[15]

Wyllie's name disappears from the university records after the 1848/1849 year, indicating that he did not complete his *quadrennium* in four years. But the university offered students, once matriculated, the option to pause their studies and resume them after any lapse of time. Wyllie recounted in *The People's Friend* that after two years of college life he once again sought to resume his professional career. The financial stress of more years at university might have been the reason for him to leave St Andrews before his studies were complete, or maybe he had a yearning to resume his role in the schoolhouse.

In the 26 July 1849 edition of the *Fife Herald* there appeared an advertisement 'TEACHER WANTED FOR THE SCHOOL at COALTOWN of BALGONIE'. This post was offered with a salary of

St Andrews University's United College was where 'John' Wyllie was enrolled for two years in 1846–1849. Here he was taught the traditional curriculum of Greek and Latin as well as mathematics and natural philosophy.

© Special Collections, Glasgow University Library. Licensor www.scran.ac.uk

£10 and a free house, garden and schoolroom. Testimonials would need to be lodged with a member of the search committee, and term would commence in late August. Coaltown of Balgonie, as the name might suggest, was a town linked to the coal mining industry. Fife was one of the centres of coal extraction in Scotland, and in the early part of the 19th century many villages and towns had grown around the mines, which attracted workers and their families. The school at Coaltown, endowed by the laird's wife, Lady Nina Balfour, had an enrolment at the time of 100 students. Fresh from his time at university, Wyllie took up this role with energy and enthusiasm, staying at the school for the next three years. It was a successful appointment and one which Wyllie would relish and make his own. Even before the end of his first year he had already made a significant impression on his pupils. He was gifted a 'handsome silver snuff box and a school knife' by the scholars, and it was noted that 'We are glad to see the youth of this place now beginning to appreciate, what has hitherto been valued at too low a rate by the generality of individuals, the valuable services of an efficient teacher.'[16] In addition to teaching the 100 or so students, Wyllie went on to found a circulating library at the school, being commended once again in February 1851.

TEACHER WANTED,

FOR SCHOOL at COALTOWN of BALGONIE, MARKINCH, FIFE. £10 Salary is given, with Free House, Garden, and Schoolroom. The Scholars (1848) upwards of One Hundred in number. Entry immediately. Testimonials to be lodged with Mr BALLINGAL, Sweetbank, Markinch, on or before the 6TH AUGUST next.

Wyllie found a job very soon after leaving university; he took the post of teacher at the Coaltown of Balgonie school. Endowed by a local landowner, it educated the children of nearby millworkers, miners and farmers.

Newspaper image © The British Library Board. All rights reserved.
With thanks to The British Newspaper Archive (www.britishnewspaperarchive.co.uk)

The gift had the following inscription 'Presented to Mr. John Wyllie, by the members of the Coalton (*sic*) and Square Circulating Library, for his gratuitous services as librarian, 1851.' The members of the library remarked 'Long may we enjoy the services of such an active public benefactor and efficient teacher of youth amongst us.'[17]

Wyllie's burgeoning career as a teacher appeared to have been both enjoyable and beneficial, he being recognised twice for his hard work in his two years at Coaltown. His time at St Andrews, and his self-professed love for literature, must have endeared him to the local populace; by September 1851 his library had over 400 volumes 'in all departments of literature, and by many of the best authors of the day'.[18] The growth was directly attributed to his activities as he embraced every opportunity to increase funds for the institution. His skill in oratory, which must have been learned and tested while at university, first became manifest in a speech given to his pupils in January 1852. Over 40 minutes, Wyllie offered up the importance of religion, industriousness, punctuality and in all things being truthful. A key excerpt was recorded:

> You may be industrious, persevering, emulous, and punctual, but you cannot be true friends, or worthy members of society, unless you are truthful. Truth lies at the foundation of all well constituted, and well-regulated societies, as well as at the bottom of every truly great and noble character.[19]

This was the first recorded instance of Wyllie delivering a public lecture. His gift for oratory that began in this small schoolroom would one day fill grand halls with guests in the thousands. Yet that day he was focused on this small group of young children, seeking to inspire and motivate them to bigger and better things, himself being an example of such hard work.

At the end of the 1852 spring term, during the examination of the students, Wyllie was once again commended by the elders of the school, stating: 'The whole proceedings testified alike to the progress of the pupils, and to the diligence and qualifications of the teacher.' He had obviously made a positive impact on his students and local community, and it would seem the start of a promising career – but a strange turn of events would lead Wyllie to turn to another calling.

In the 2 January 1851 edition of the *Fife Herald* there appeared an article about the melancholy death of the able teacher at the Coaltown of Balgonie school, one Mr John Wyllie. He was reported to have been returning home from a convivial meeting of friends at a local public house on Friday night. It went on to state that halfway home he was seized with pain in the bowels and accompanying sickness. As he lay down upon the road to recover, a cart came along and its driver, not seeing the prostrate man, ran him over. From injuries he received he died the following morning. The article then went on to describe his time in the village, his role as teacher and the loss to the community.[20]

This news must have come as a shock to Wyllie as he flicked through the pages of the *Herald*, as at that time he was fit, in good health, and decidedly not dead. Where had the paper received such information from? He was the only teacher at the Coaltown of Balgonie school and the only Wyllie employed there. The next edition of the *Fife Herald* noted that their report of the previous week had been based on the details of a letter sent to the newspaper by a 'very respectable person'; however, they had now learned, possibly from the fact Wyllie had made it known to the newspaper's staff that he was still alive, that this letter was a fiction. The signature on the earlier letter was now deemed to have been a forgery. The *Herald* urged its readers to assist in uncovering this foul deed and 'that this precious piece of blackguardism may be exposed and traced to its proper source, we append a *facsimile* of the handwriting.'[21] To print that copy of the letter, illustrating the handwriting, the newspaper would have needed to create a bespoke printing block, as precise as could be done, so that the evidence for identification would be as clear as possible. This itself would have been a significant and costly item to publish, since images or drawings of any kind, especially bespoke ones for single use, were rare in newspapers. In fact, other than the masthead on the front page of the paper that appeared on every edition, no other drawings/ etchings/ illustrations featured in that edition of the *Herald*. But even with the quick correction by the newspaper the damage was done. Like many shocking news stories, it was picked up and repeated within the pages of other newspapers around Scotland, from Edinburgh to John o' Groats.

The act of 'blackguardism' was never exposed within the paper: no other articles were published in the wake of the appeal. Who had sent the letter, and what their motives had been, remained a mystery. To many outside his local area, the schoolteacher John Wyllie was now deceased through what appeared to have been the misfortune of a drunkard. Wyllie later went on to recount that he had for a time when he was a teacher been made the 'butt of merciless ridicule', but he failed to name the party who had been responsible nor why indeed the badgering had been committed. This fake death report in the local paper would appear to have been an ultimate act of treachery.[22]

Later, Wyllie himself recalled the event, and explained how he then went on to seek retribution from the guilty party. The episode appeared as part of the article in *The People's Friend*, with its author recounting Wyllie's actions.

> He terminated his connection with Coalton (*sic*) by a practical joke. A party took advantage of his youth and inexperience to bring him into ridicule and do him what harm he was able, and was quite unaware of the kind of individual he was dealing with. Wyllie resolved to be quits with him at the close.

Whatever had caused this rift – the words spoken between Wyllie and this mysterious foe, or the acts taken by each party – the falsification of his death was to be the last straw for Wyllie. What might have caused this row? Could it have been a professional dispute? The emotion might lead one to think it was more visceral: an affair of the heart perhaps? Whatever the cause, Wyllie's plan to get even with his adversary was recounted later by Anton:

> By a dexterous, bold, and well-executed plan, he got the gentleman duly imprisoned in an empty well. Having done this, he placed his hat and coat by the side of a mill-dam. Much suspicion arose from the absence of the gentleman and the finding of the discarded garments in the immediate vicinity of deep water. The most obtuse minds came to the conclusion that the dam contained a dead body. Ingenious raking appliances were discovered, and much fruitless labour was expended by an agitated community.[23]

Kidnap and imprisonment seem quite an extreme riposte, but there is no evidence to corroborate that this actually happened. Wyllie continued as teacher at the school until 1852, at which time it was reported that his management was excellent and that the examiners found that he was 'a careful and painstaking teacher'. If Wyllie had indeed committed such actions they would surely have painted him in a far more negative light to the locals and governors of the school. So Wyllie's revenge might have been a dish best served cold, being acted out in May 1852 after he had finished the school year with the examinations at the Coaltown of Balgonie school.[24]

This date is important to Wyllie's story, as it was soon after this point that he would give up his post as teacher. It would seem that the drama of the fake death and his plan for revenge was a turning point in his life. He put some distance between him and these events. He travelled to Glasgow and, at the comparatively mature age of 24, signed on as an apprentice on a sailing ship. He would now fulfil his dream of seeing the world from the deck of a ship, thwarted previously during his failed attempt to join a ship at an English port. Whether he intended this to be a brief sojourn away from his home or a longer endeavour is not known. But from 18 May 1852 Wyllie was no longer a teacher. He was a mariner, bound for incredible adventures across the globe.

2

WYLLIE'S CAREER AT SEA BEGINS

What he underwent during that voyage was enough to have made many lads cut and run at the first port, but the Captain is true grit.

– From a newspaper description of Wyllie's first voyage, from a lecture he gave in December 1888.

Broomielaw is a word synonymous with Glasgow's industrial heritage. It is the Glasgow quayside where the city's international trade began. It is where the Customs House stood, a central hub of trade always bustling with excise officers taking note of all the cargoes coming and going. Here you would find ships unloading tobacco and cotton from the Americas, sugar from the British colonies of the Caribbean, spices and rice from India, and raw materials from every other corner of the globe. Out would go the manufactured goods like printed cotton cloth, glass, ceramics and machines of vast variety and size. The export of such items in the mid-19th century had made Britain the most powerful economy in the world.

The quay was always busy. Passengers could be seen waiting to board paddle steamers for day trips to the resort towns along the Clyde coast and around western Scotland, and sleek mail steamers ready for the fast crossing to Ireland, and then there were the larger cargo vessels departing for ports across the globe. The Broomielaw was in fact a gateway to another world. It was a place that took you away from the grime of the Victorian city to the fresh air of the countryside or the deep water of the oceans. It was a place where fortunes could be made – or lost. Where a man could find a calling, a new trade or profession. Where an old life, with its mistakes and transgressions, could be left behind.

It was here that John Wyllie came in May 1852. He had travelled from rural Fife, a distance of 50 miles, to the growing industrial city that was fast gaining the reputation as the workshop of the world. It was not just geographically that it was far from the pastoral

The Broomielaw was the busy quay at the centre of Glasgow. Ships arrived from across the globe while paddle steamers took trippers to the Highlands and Islands of Scotland.

© CSG CIC Glasgow Museums Collection

lands of his home county: Glasgow was a centre of industrial innovation, with its shipyards, engine works, potteries and mills producing high-quality goods that found markets across the globe. As this international trade developed, the city's quays and docks rapidly expanded to accommodate the ever-growing fleets of steamships and sailing vessels that carried this transatlantic and colonial trade. Wyllie was just one of the hundreds, if not thousands, of people who came to the city every day seeking new employment or escape.

Glasgow's shipping companies were always looking out for eager or desperate men, whether qualified or not, to crew their ships. The newspapers in the city ran dozens of advertisements for ships leaving soon for destinations near and far: 'Saturday afternoon pleasure sailing to Renfrew', 'Steam from Glasgow to London', 'Emigration to America', 'Steam to Calcutta in sixty four days'. All these ships needed a full complement of crew. They required everyone from masters and seaman to carpenters, pursers, doctors and engineers.

Although a university-educated teacher, Wyllie had no experience as a sailor. Could he even tie a knot? What he did have was a willingness to work hard and, as shown by his time as a teacher, enthusiasm and drive, always looking to better himself. So he would have had a plethora of options for his first voyage. Would he look to join the crew for the short trips to Dublin or Belfast, or a European trader making regular voyages to the Mediterranean, or a clipper heading for the antipodes? With all these options set before him he made the bold decision to seek adventure far from Scotland, and signed up for a voyage that would take him to the other side of the world. Turning the pages of the *North British Daily Mail*, he would have seen the list of vessels loading for foreign ports: the *Ceylon* for Buenos Aires, the *Royal William* for Quebec, the *Elizabeth* for Alexandria, as well many ships heading for other exotic destinations. Not all of these vessels would require more crew, of course, but his options would have appeared both varied and enticing. On 18 May he found a ship that was taking on more men, including even a teacher like himself, with no nautical skills. He signed on to become a member of the crew of the *Hope*, which would sail within the week for the great British colonial possession of India. It was a barque of 515 tons, built in 1839 in Saint John, New Brunswick, Canada. Its complement was the master, two mates, a carpenter, a steward, a cook, nine able seamen and four apprentices. Wyllie signed on as an apprentice. It was the bottom rung of the ladder, taken by those with no experience at sea and eager to learn the trade.

ABOARD THE *HOPE*: SUNSETS, SHARKS AND STORMS

The agreement made by the crew members with the master listed all the particulars expected for such a contract. Wyllie was signing up for a period of no more than two years, and the *Hope* would be making for Bombay and from there, 'if required, any other ports in the Indian or China Seas, or wherever else freight or employment might offer'. Provisions for the crew were listed in detail: one pound of bread per day per sailor, ¼ oz (ounce) of tea, ½ oz coffee, two oz sugar and three quarts of water. Meat was listed as rotating between beef and pork on various days, along with three servings of peas a week. One half-ounce of lime juice per ounce of sugar was issued daily, to combat scurvy. It was noted that no spirits were to be allowed on board, and if a seaman was found not to be sober the master was at liberty to terminate the agreement and seek other crew.[25]

A young man signing on as an apprentice was nothing unusual, but the crew list of the *Hope* noted that Wyllie was 'not registered'. And indeed, I cannot trace any surviving apprentice record matching John Wyllie either of Dysart or as born in Nenthorn, Berwickshire. No other note of explanation is found in the document with regard to this situation. An unregistered apprentice of a slightly older age than usual, who had never been employed at sea before, was now set to begin his first voyage. It was the start of what would turn out to be four years of global exploration aboard the *Hope*.

A week after Wyllie joined the crew, the *Hope* sailed down the Clyde on 24 May bound for Bombay (now Mumbai).[26] Its master was John Smith, a native of Saltcoats, Ayrshire. A

John Smith (1825–1915) a fellow Scot, was Wyllie's first captain as he set off on his career at sea on the barque Hope. *Smith, though just four years older than Wyllie, was an experienced mariner. Wyllie recalled that Smith treated his crew fairly, especially those who were new to the labours of the ocean.*

© CSG CIC Glasgow Museums Collection

man of just 28 years, he had recently returned from a voyage on the *Cordelia*, his first time in command of a vessel. Having gone to sea in 1842, Smith would go on to have a long and successful maritime career, ultimately ending as a ship owner.[27] He worked for many years for the City Line, a shipping company based in Glasgow. In 1908 he wrote a history of the company, and in it he recounts his own career at sea, giving details of his first voyage on the *Hope*. Captain Smith's youthfulness was remarked upon by fellow masters as it was making its way down the River Clyde: one master shouted out, 'Man, you are a young man to be captain of such a large ship,' with Smith responding 'That's not my first ship I've had charge of.'[28]

Over the next four months Wyllie began his education as a seaman. The *Hope* sailed along the established British colonial trade route: first making for the South Atlantic, then rounding the southernmost tip of Africa at Cape Agulhas, finally sailing north through the Indian Ocean towards the subcontinent. An apprentice would be expected to learn the basic daily routine of a sailor, including tough physical tasks such as maintaining the sails and rigging, and swabbing the decks, as well as beginning his training in navigation.

The *Hope* arrived at Bombay on 20 September with no events of any note recorded during the voyage.[29] Even such an uneventful voyage must have been an eye-opening experience for a first-time sailor: in the lectures Wyllie gave after his retirement from the sea he made frequent mention of his first ship and its captain. His love for the barque and for its master, only four years his senior, was noted in Anton's account of Wyllie's time at sea:

> His captain, however, was an exemplary seaman, and took the greatest interest in the temporal, intellectual, and spiritual wellbeing of his crew. Every dog-watch he called his men to worship. The deep bass voices of the sailors blended in many a holy psalm. The choir was wholly bass, and the singing pretty much in a monotone, but what of that? They tuned their hearts, by far the noblest aim. The captain also taught ignorant Jacks to write and cypher. He had a great stock of patience, and there was a benign and gracious smile continually lighting up his honest face. The young man soon learned to entertain for his first captain the greatest respect, and he never afterwards sailed under one he loved so much.[30]

The *Hope* stayed in the port for over a month, allowing Wyllie the chance to explore the city. The impact of the city on its first-time visitors was described in the book *Life in Bombay*, published the year he arrived:

> for upon landing, the immediate impression which strikes every mind, is not only the immense population of the island, but the unceasing variety of costumes and complexions, betokening the natives of the Asiatic, and of several European nations. Parsees, Mussulmauns, Hindoos of every caste, Persians, Armenians, Portuguese, and Indo-Britons, literally swarm under the horses' feet as you drive through the bazaars; and it requires no small portion of nerve, as well as dexterity, to steer one's course in safety through streets and roads absolutely alive with human beings, to say nothing of the numerous vehicles, horses, buffaloes, and bullocks which impede one's progress on all sides.'[31]

The *Hope* was then loaded with its return cargo of cotton bales, which were brought out to it at anchor by the small boats of the port. On 15 November it set sail for Liverpool.[32] This was where the majority of the British cotton trade was organised: into it came the raw cotton from India, Egypt and the Americas; it was then sent to the nearby Lancashire mill towns, which specialised in the spinning and weaving of the fibre.

After passing through the Indian Ocean and rounding the southern tip of Africa, the *Hope* called at the remote island colony of St Helena, which at that time was where many ships stopped to replenish stores and water. Just a day was spent there, after which the *Hope* set sail again, heading north, and by 5 April had docked at Liverpool.[33] Its cargo was noted as 2,534 bales of cotton, 1,227 bundles coir yarn and 1,262 bags of galls (used for making ink). After unloading the *Hope* made its way on up the west coast of Britain towards Glasgow, where it would again take on cargo for a voyage towards the east.

Wyllie's first round trip at sea was now complete. It had entailed 11 months away from Britain without any exploits of note beyond seeing the wide expanses of the open sea, exposure to different cultures, and days upon days of learning how to be a sailor. His experience at sea must have proved to be favourable, as he decided to continue his training by signing on for another voyage on the *Hope*, one that one would prove far more memorable than his first. This time the ship was bound for the port of Moulmein (today, Mawlamyine) on the banks of the Salween River on the coast of Burma (Myanmar). Moulmein was the chief city of the British colony of Burma, and a centre of maritime trade in central Asia, linking the trade from the east – China and Australia – to the ports to the west of it, in the Bay of Bengal and the Arabian Sea.

The voyage started in late May, when the *Hope* was recorded as leaving Troon, on the Ayrshire coast. Its cargo was not recorded, but Troon was a well-known stop for ships loading coal from the Ayrshire coalfields for ports across the British Empire. The voyage proceeded without incident down the Irish Sea and on towards the coast of Africa. All was fine until the *Hope* passed just north of the Canary Islands, at which point it was found that the ship's pumps, which were worked every four hours or so, could not keep pace with incoming water. The crew shifted the cargo and pumped harder, and finally the leak was discovered and mended, Wyllie recalling: 'The leak was put to rights by the carpenter, and glad the men were to find themselves relieved of the labours of the pumps, and once more at sea, their sails bellying to the favourable breeze.'[34]

As the barque sailed south the crew took part in one of the great nautical traditions, crossing the line. This event takes place as a ship crosses the equator (and continues in one form or another on some vessels today): crewmen, and sometimes passengers, crossing the equator for the first time were obliged to participate in a rite of passage that was part ridicule and part baptism into the mariner's trade. Wyllie, crossing for at least the fifth time, so exempt from victimhood, was able to recall his captain taking part in the ceremony on the *Hope*. 'Ship Ahoy! Are there any on board not my sons?' and from the bow of the ship Neptune, seated in state, came along; all that Wyllie could recollect was that his face and head were towsy' (dishevelled or shaggy).[35]

A much more detailed account can be found from the diary of the great scientist Charles Darwin, who recalled such an event as he first passed the equator in February 1832:

> In the evening the ceremonies for crossing the line commenced. The officer on watch reported a boat ahead. The Captain turned 'hands up, shorten sail,' and we heaved to in order to converse with Mr. Neptune. The Captain held a conversation with him through a speaking trumpet, the result of which was that he would in the morning pay us a visit.

> We have crossed the Equator, and I have undergone the disagreeable operation of being shaved. About 9 o'clock this morning we poor 'griffins,' two & thirty in number, were put altogether on the lower deck. The hatchways were battened down, so we were in the dark & very hot. Presently four of Neptune's constables came to us, & one by one led us up on deck. I was the first & escaped easily: I nevertheless found this watery ordeal sufficiently disagreeable. Before coming up, the constable blindfolded me & thus lead (*sic*) along, buckets of water were thundered all around; I was then placed on a plank, which could be easily tilted up into a large bath of water. They then lathered my face & mouth with pitch & paint, & scraped some of it off with a piece of roughened iron hoop: a signal being given I was tilted head over heels into the water, where two men received me & ducked me. At last, glad enough, I escaped: most of the others were treated much worse: dirty mixtures being put in their mouths & rubbed on their faces. The whole ship was a shower bath, & water was flying about in every direction: of course not one person, even the Captain, got clear of being wet through.[36]

Such frivolities at the equator were to be short-lived. Soon afterwards, as the *Hope* entered the southern hemisphere, the leak once again appeared. The crew 'pumped and better pumped, but they could not gain an inch on the water. Their situation was sufficiently perilous, for it was either pump or sink.' They were not far from the port of Bahia on the coast of Brazil, and Captain Smith ordered that the *Hope* make for safety to make repairs. But unbeknownst to Captain Smith, Bahia was being ravaged by yellow fever. The *Hope* made port on 19 July, where in quick fashion it was surveyed and lightened, and had its seams caulked, from its underwater copper sheathing to the gunwales.[37] While the repairs were being made the devastation in the port caused by the disease was vivid, as Wyllie noted:

> Entering the fine harbour of Bahia was only leaping from the frying pan into the fire. 'Black Jack' was working devastation on all hands. Some ships had lost every one of their crews. None could be got to bury the dead. Glad as they had been to get in, they were gladder still to get out.[38]

Leaving Bahia as fast as it could, the *Hope* then made for the Cape of Good Hope, entering the Indian Ocean and sailing towards India. It was here that Wyllie witnessed an event that would remain with him for the rest of his life. It was a sadly frequent occurrence at sea: the death of a sailor on board would be mentioned by him again and again when he recounted his maritime career.

> Dysentery seized on one of their seaman, a bright and lively young fellow from Glasgow. It was sad to see the young life wasting away. Sadder still, in the wanderings of his mind, to hear him recall his bird-nesting experiences, the name of his mother, and 'Mary,' the name of another still nearer and dearer than every other. Soon life fled. The body was sewed in his hammock, some iron bars were placed at his feet, and then came the most solemn of rites – a burial at sea. They day was fine, without a breath of wind. There was only the long, soft ocean swell. The muffled bell tolled all hands aft. Bareheaded and footed they gathered round the capstan. Tears ran down weather-beaten faces as the captain read these words of the Service:- 'We therefore commit his body to the deep to be turned into corruption looking for the resurrection of the body (when the sea shall give up her dead), and the life of the world to come through Jesus Christ our Lord.' The Union Jack was removed, and the body glided through an open port. Bolt upright it sank, down, down, through the clear, deep, blue water, till it seemed no larger than a shell on the shore. 'The sea and him in death they did not dare to sever, it was his home when he had breath, 'twas now his home for ever.'[39]

Later in life, when Wyllie spoke about his time at sea he would inevitably return to this occurrence, speaking of the great risks that men put themselves through to sail the seas. It would form one of the key narratives of his story, one that he obviously could never forget. Wyllie never mentioned the name of this poor friend, but it is believed to have been William Thompson, as his death from cholera was recorded as taking place aboard the *Hope* on 19 October 1853.[40]

Next, the crew were faced with a new danger: it was found that the water tank had almost completely run dry. It meant that the crew had to ration their supply and were forced to survive on just one wine glass of water per day. For three weeks the men had to endure 'pangs of thirst' as well as an outbreak of scurvy. Wyllie commented that the ship became a floating hospital before they were able to reach their destination.[41] Their salvation came when they finally made land at Amherst (Kyaikkhami) on the coast of Burma on Christmas Day, reaching Moulmein five days later.

The city of Moulmein was renowned for its famous golden-topped pagodas. The town and port were described in the book *Burma Under British Rule*; the

> hills are almost entirely covered with pagodas, some in ruins, with shrubs and trees springing from fissures in the bricks, others all white or covered with gold-leaf. The neighbouring monasteries are particularly rich in carved teak. The view over the town from these hills in the centre is perhaps one of the

The iconic golden pagodas of Moulmein in Burma were one of the first wonders that Wyllie visited during his time at sea. Coming from a small village in Scotland, the apprentice seaman must have been intoxicated by the sights, smells, tastes and local traditions.

Courtesy of the Library of Congress

> most attractive in all Burma … the whole neighbourhood is picturesque in a spacious way that is seen nowhere else in the ports of Indo-China.[42]

This trip to an exotic eastern city must have been an immersive, visceral experience for Wyllie. Once again his senses would have been assaulted by the smells of spices, the sounds of the shouting voices in the markets and the sight of peoples and goods from across Asia and beyond.

The *Hope's* crew, with assistance from local labourers, unloaded the coal and loaded teak, and then began preparations for the voyage home. Unlike the outward voyage, the homeward one would prove calm and uneventful. The *Hope* once again called at St Helena, then made a brief stop at Shannon, western Ireland, for provisions, before docking in London in the first week of October 1854. Sadly for Wyllie, he was to lose his beloved captain while the ship was in the capital: John Smith signed to take the barque *Prince Charlie* to Colombo in Ceylon (Sri Lanka). This was not enough, however, to deter Wyllie;

he promptly signed on for yet another voyage on the *Hope*, under a new captain, heading west across the Atlantic and towards the Americas.

Under the command of the new captain, J. Davies, the barque first made for Newport, Wales, to load coal for the British colonies of the Caribbean, and from there to Jamaica, arriving on 25 June 1855.[43] By now, Wyllie was no longer a mere apprentice. His merchant seaman records show that after his first voyage he had been promoted to able seaman and then to boatswain – a rapid rise for one so new to the trade.[44] After leaving Jamaica, Captain Davies navigated to Patuca on the northern coast of Honduras, to load a cargo of mahogany.

There was no port at the mouth of the Patuca river, so the ship anchored offshore and the logs had to be floated to it over the sandbar and through the breakers. Wyllie found himself on one of the barque's boats making the runs back and forth, and working with local labourers to move the wood. All went successfully until the last run. As the boat was rowed back to the *Hope* it was hit by a squall and capsized, sending Wyllie and the five other occupants into the water. All held onto the overturned boat for dear life, splashing, shouting and banging the hull in order to gain the attention of the ship's crew. But this activity also led to ill-wanted attention, as they were soon surrounded by several sharks. The other men trod water for an hour – for some reason not attacked by the sharks – but Wyllie, unable to swim, held tight to the boat, then began to feel his strength slip. When another boat from the *Hope* finally reached the desperate men, Wyllie was 'at the point of giving away' and before he was lifted from the waves had become unconscious. He recalled, however, that 'A kind Providence and pure Jamaica (rum) went hand in hand with his splendid constitution in soon making him his old self again.'[45]

Once they had loaded the ship, they set sail for Liverpool, but after running through the Straits of Florida just north of Cuba the *Hope* struck the Bahama Banks several times, resulting in the resumption of the vessel's old leaky condition. The leaking was one thing, but then came an ill omen as the *Hope* sailed with the Gulf Stream off the east coast of the United States: a favourite cat died. Wyllie remarked that sailors are 'deeply tainted with superstition, and all these little things set agoing in their minds all kinds of horrid presentiments'. Next, the *Hope* was hit by a hurricane ripping away the masts, washing over the boats, and smashing the stanchions and bulwarks.[1*] The *Hope* became a hulk, its rudder ineffective, at the mercy of the waves. After a few days the situation became even bleaker. What happened next was described by Wyllie:

> We could do nothing. The provisions ran down, and we were far out of the track of vessels. Having been for several days without food, the last fearful resort of the seaman was before us. Someone must be sacrificed if the life of the others was to be saved. With what baleful looks we regarded each other.

1 * No hurricane is on record towards the end of 1855, so more than likely this was a violent storm.

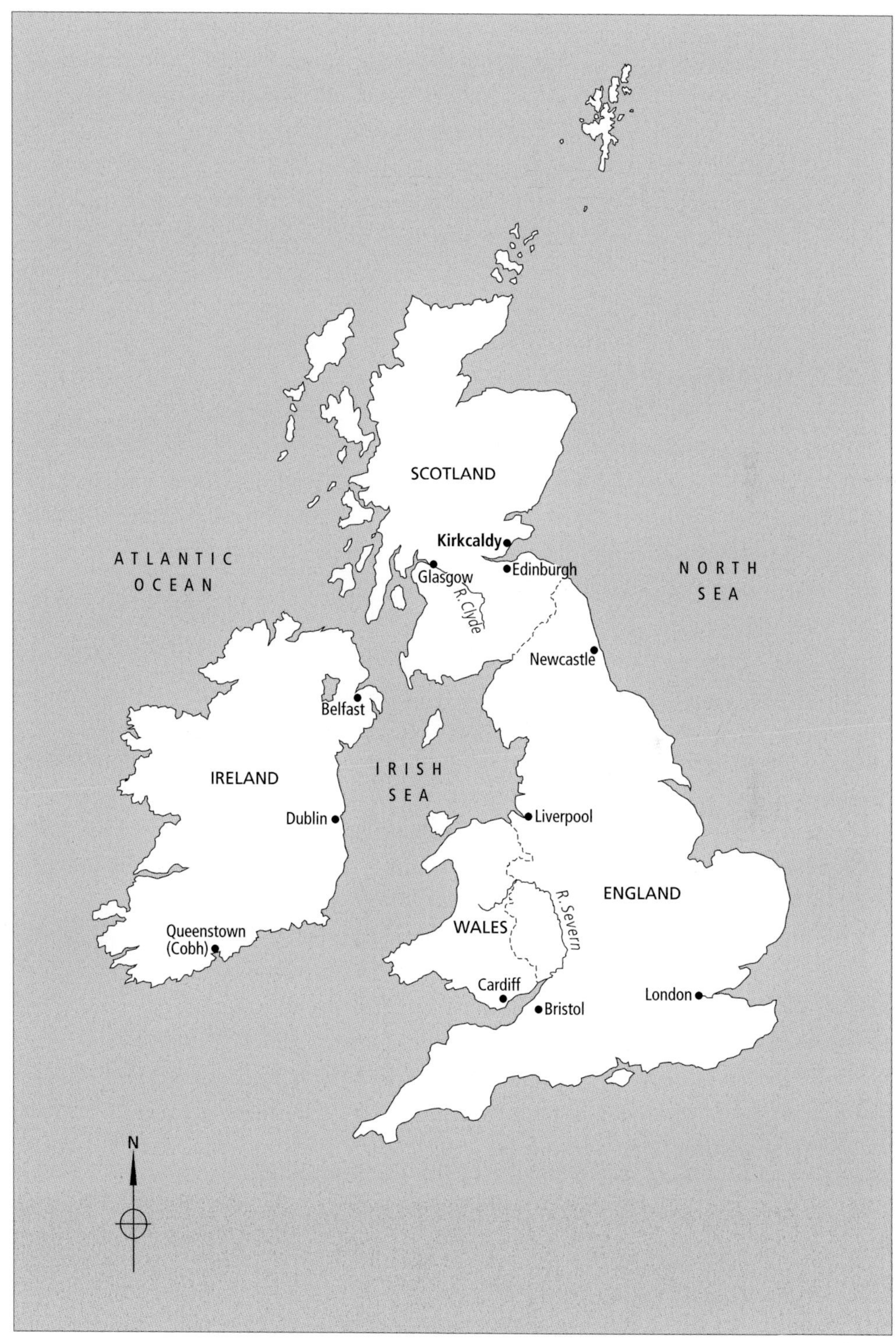

The British Isles: relevant ports and cities

But just as the crew were contemplating resorting to the dreadful 'custom of the sea' to save most of themselves, they spotted a ship and made distress signals. The vessel came to their rescue; their saviour was the *Samuel M. Fox*, out of Le Havre and bound for New York. Its crew supplied provisions, pump leather and materials to jury-rig the *Hope's* masts. The *Fox*'s log stated that it had come across the *Hope* on 30 January 1856, so for *Hope* that was 56 days out from Honduras.[46] Wyllie wrote that 'providence saved them from these ultimate horrors of the sailor' and, of the *Fox*'s crew, that 'their benevolence was princely'.[47]

After the repairs were complete and provisions transferred, the *Hope* made for the closest European port, arriving at Kinsale, in south-west Ireland, on 1 March, where its condition and the cause of its distress was reported locally and in the shipping press. The date of striking the Bahama Banks was reported as 20 December, and the date of the disastrous gale as 7 January.[48]

After a stay in Ireland the *Hope* completed its voyage by arriving at Liverpool on 2 April.[49] As the mahogany logs were brought up from the holds and lifted onto the docks Wyllie finally said goodbye to the *Hope*. After almost four years aboard and three blue water voyages, he now decided it was time to find a new ship; he was eager to win promotion – and perhaps find a more seaworthy vessel.

Aboard the *Indian Queen*: Loss, Love, and Poisoning

In the spring of 1856 the major nations of Europe were entering the third year of what is considered to be the first modern war. The forces of Britain, France, Russia and Turkey were fighting over control of the Crimea, the small peninsula on the north coast of the Black Sea. In reality they were involved in a conflict to establish which empire would dominate the vital trade routes to India and the East.

The previous year, thousands of British soldiers had been shipped out there, along with cannon, supplies, munitions and other military equipment. Then on 30 March 1856 the warring nations signed the Treaty of Paris, ending the conflict and thus requiring the combatants to leave the field of battle. The British government chartered some of the largest and fastest ships available, to make for the Crimea to complete this withdrawal: clipper ships, usually found plying the tea trade between London and China or on the migrant service to Australia, set sail for the wartorn peninsula. It was on one of these that Wyllie would next find himself, on a voyage that would hopefully prove less eventful than the previous one.

The *Indian Queen* was a sleek ship of 1,041 tons built four years earlier in New Brunswick, Canada, intended for the Australian trade.[50] It was a part of the famous Black Ball Line of Liverpool and was captained by David Frederick Jobson, a Scot who had worked the Australia and South Pacific trade for the previous five years. It arrived at Liverpool on 22 May from Hobart Town, Tasmania, with a large cargo of wool and a large number of passengers. The voyage from the antipodes had taken 89 days, and the conduct of the crew and speed of the trip were commended by the thankful passengers in letters to the local newspapers.[51]

The *Indian Queen* was quickly chartered by the government to become part of the flotilla heading for the Black Sea. The clippers bound for Australia usually set off in early autumn, to take advantage of prevailing winds and to time their journeys with the tea harvest in China, so a trip to the Crimea would not only suit the government but also the ship's owners looking to fill the dormant months and make a quick profit. Notices were posted in the local papers and a new crew was taken on, including Wyllie as third mate. He had yet to pass any official competency test, as required by the Board of Trade, but as he had been promoted to bo'sun aboard the *Hope*, his knowledge and skill earned him the temporary position on board the *Indian Queen*.[52] The clipper sailed on 10 June 1856, making for the port of Balaclava. The Battle of Balaclava had taken place between the forces of the Imperial Russian Army and a combined force of British and French soldiers in October 1854. The Russian forces had been trying to capture the port, which was key to the supply lines of the allied armies. Two of the most famous phrases in military history, the 'Charge of the Light Brigade' and the 'Thin Red Line', are associated with this battle. The events had been widely reported in Britain, and the crew of the *Indian Queen* would have been well aware that their destination, previously a little-known port on the Crimea, was now world famous.

Balaklava harbour was crowded with troopships and armaments ships in the summer of 1856. It was Wyllie's first experience of sailing into a war zone – one that he would repeat seven years later during the American Civil War.

Courtesy of the Library of Congress

When the *Indian Queen* arrived in Balaclava the harbour was bursting with vessels, and much of the material and many of the soldiers had already sailed for home. The apparent lack of planning by the government in sending out vessels that were not in the event required was noted in the Liverpool press, and would form part of a wider public outcry over the perceived waste of resources and poor planning of the war.[53] The *Indian Queen* returned loaded with some stores but no troops. It arrived at Portsmouth on 17 September, and after unloading returned to the Mersey to resume its usual role in the emigrant trade to New Zealand and Australia.

Passing the Test

Arriving back at Liverpool on 23 September 1856, after this one short voyage as third mate Wyllie prepared for his examination of competency for second mate. He didn't have much time. The *Indian Queen* was set to sail on 31 October, bound for New Zealand. The test, set by the Merchant Shipping Act of 1854, required the applicant to have been at sea for no less than four years. As his first voyage had been in 1852, he was looking for promotion at the earliest possible opportunity. He would need to have a 'legible hand' and understand 'the first five rules of arithmetic' as well as being able to understand and use logarithms. He also needed to understand basic navigation through the use of sextant and visual observations, had to give satisfactory answers on the rigging of ships and the stowing of holds, and had to be conversant in the rules of the road.[54] The arithmetic and maths would surely have been easy for Wyllie, given that his university education had given him a firm foundation in that area. His nautical skills, having been learnt and practised over the past four years, would have been fresh and up to date. He duly passed his examination in Liverpool on 3 October.

His application and certificate bear some interesting details regarding his career. First it is the first recorded instance known of his use of the moniker Joannes. The previous documents on which he had been listed – census returns, newspaper reports and the apprentice documents for the *Hope* – had recorded his name as John. Wyllie never explained the reason for this change, but whatever the reason, he was now officially known as Joannes for the rest of his life.

The second mystery from this certificate relates to his age. On both application and certificate he lists his date of birth as 22 May 1832 and his place of birth as Kelso. The day and location are both correct – but the date, four years off, made Wyllie 24 years of age, rather than his true age, 28. As a former university student and teacher, it would seem odd for him to mistake his own date of birth, and so it was perhaps a deliberate ploy to mask the comparatively mature age at which he had become an apprentice.

The newly qualified second mate, Joannes Wyllie aged 24 from Kelso, signed up again on the *Indian Queen*, this time for a voyage to the East Indies. The destination for the loaded clipper was to be Wellington, the capital of New Zealand, with Wyllie as third mate on wages of £5 per month, with £5 paid in advance. Though he was now qualified as a second mate, it seems that Wyllie might not have yet gained the confidence of his new master and thus had signed on at one level below his newly acquired rank. The crew was made up of 35 men, and on board they would take 437 passengers, of whom many were migrants, including families with young children. The advertisements in the local press promoted the fact that the vessel 'sails very fast, and has magnificent accommodation for all classes of passengers'.[55]

The clipper left Liverpool on 31 October and began a very quick passage to the antipodes. The log of the *Indian Queen*, kept by the captain, was published once the vessel had arrived in New Zealand. It not only recorded dates of arrivals at maritime landmarks but also mentioned the onboard condition of the passengers, primarily the sickness of many of the children, who, the captain noted, suffered from the combination of 'tropic light airs … conjoined with the effects of the vertical sun'. After the clipper had passed the Cape of Good Hope an outbreak of measles occurred. Captain Jobson recorded that there were no fewer than 67 cases amongst the passengers on board.[56] All told, 22 died during the 87 days of the voyage, 12 from the measles and the others from pneumonia or diarrhoea. But as well as those sad losses there were also six births.[57] The measles outbreak, pregnant passengers and the usual onboard health conditions would have kept the ship's doctor busy. John Batty Tuke, a 21-year-old new graduate from the Royal College of Surgeons in Edinburgh, was travelling to New Zealand to serve as surgeon and a senior medical officer during the ongoing conflict with the native peoples. Tuke would later return to Scotland and become an innovator in the field of psychiatry while working at the Fife and Kinross Asylum.[58]

After arriving at Wellington on 31 January 1857 the vessel was feted in the local press. The arrivals of the fast clippers from Britain were regularly noted, especially the duration of the voyage: the competing shipping companies would then use that information in their advertisements, boasting of their speedy travel and comfortable conditions on board. After disembarking its passengers the *Indian Queen* stayed in port for almost two months. During this stay Captain Jobson and the crew hosted a grand party on board on 4 March. Invited were citizens of Wellington along with officers from the garrison. A large awning was spread over the deck, and the guests were rowed out to the clipper to be treated to supper, song and dance. The band from the 65th Regiment, at that time stationed in Wellington, came aboard to provide the music. After the usual toasts to the health of the queen and the success of the Black Ball Line, the captain and officers, including the newly promoted Wyllie (he had been promoted to second mate on 26 January), were graciously thanked by the guests. The evening ended with the launching of fireworks from the vessels at anchor in the port.[59]

The return journey started on 27 March, the initial destination to be Hobart Town on the island of Tasmania, where the ship arrived a month later. Leaving Wellington, it carried no significant cargo, being listed as arriving in ballast, and put in at Hobart in order to resupply its water tanks for the long return voyage to Britain. It was here that Wyllie would

The port of Wellington, New Zealand, at the time of the Indian Queen's *visit in spring 1857. On what would be Wyllie's longest ever journey the clipper carried hundreds of migrants to the booming colonial town.*

Courtesy of the Museum of New Zealand, Te Papa Tongarewa

witness yet another of life's poignant moments. The *Indian Queen* arrived on 27 April, and after just three days in port he noted that Captain Jobson had found himself a bride. Wyllie recalled:

> But in the affairs of life comedy and tragedy lie very close together. At Hobart Town their captain landed a bachelor, with disengaged affections, and before three days were gone he brought aboard as his wife one of the best, prettiest, and handsomest ladies he thought he had ever seen.[60]

This beauty was Jane Henry Gow, the only daughter of James Gow, a merchant from Hobart Town.[61] Was it love at first sight? Cupid's arrow striking when Jobson passed by the fair lady as he walked the streets of city? Or was it that the two might have met in the early months of 1856 when the *Indian Queen* had been in port for six weeks during its last voyage to Australia? The two might have awaited the chance to see each other once again when the *Indian Queen* returned. Either way, the captain had found his love and married her, and she then sailed with her groom to England, where she made her home until her death in 1921.

On its return from New Zealand the Indian Queen *stopped at Hobart Town, Tasmania, to replenish supplies.*

Courtesy of the Allport Library and Museum of Fine Arts, State Library of Tasmania

With the quick stop at Hobart Town concluded, the clipper cleared the port on 6 May, bound for Moulmein.[62] This stay would not be as peaceful and scenic for Wyllie as his first.

ARGUMENT, REVENGE AND POISONING

The *Indian Queen* sailed northward through the Indian Ocean, first making for Bombay where it spent the month of July, and then heading round Cape Cormorin and east for Moulmein. The voyage was uneventful, and when it arrived at Moulmein the clipper would load a cargo of rice for its return to Liverpool. While in port Wyllie was part of a party that was invited for dinner aboard another ship in harbour. The group included Captain David and Jane Jobson, several members of the crew and an old friend of the captain. This friend was a superintendent of a local wood yard in the port. Wyllie recalled that they had dined 'not wisely but too well', and the party then set back for the ship on the ship's gig. But for some reason, the captain's friend became agitated and insulting. This was enough for Captain Jobson, who ordered Wyllie, the steersman of the gig, to pitch his friend overboard.

> This Wyllie did in a trice, but still held a good grip of him, to see if his feet would touch the bottom of the river, as they were inshore. Wyllie then pleaded the captain to have mercy, and the man's wife – a Creole – also pleaded strongly. After he had been well ducked the Captain relented, and the woodyard man was pulled in. He was cured. Not a word was spoken again till they parted.

Whatever the yard superintendent said that had made Captain Jobson so wrathful is not known, but this slight and his embarrassment was not soon to be forgotten by his erstwhile friend – nor his wife. A plot was hatched by the two to seek their revenge. Several days after the events on the gig, Wyllie and the ship's purser were invited to visit the man's house for a meal. Wyllie's impression of this man had not been a good one and he initially refused to attend, but the purser was keen, and so Wyllie agreed to accompany him. The invitation was part of the plot against Wyllie! Anton recalled his fate:

> When they were leaving the house the Creole took them into her apartment and treated them to a parting glass of brandy. Wyllie thought he saw the very tempting serpent in her eyes as she filled the glass. And he was not wrong; the liquor was drugged. The Creole had been stung by the outrage committed on her husband, and had resolved on revenge. They were driven rapidly to the ship, but by the time he reached it our Joannes was delirious. His friends thought he was a dead man. A doctor was got, luckily without a moment's loss, powerful emetics were administered, and his verdict was that his patient had partaken of a powerful Indian poison.[63]

Wyllie remained in a critical condition aboard the *Indian Queen* as it left Moulmein. He would not recover until the vessel made it to St Helena on 17 November. While still suffering from the after effects of his own poisoning and recuperating on board the *Indian Queen*, Wyllie learned from fellow crew members of the tragic death of the doctor who had cured him. Anton recalled:

> It was strange coincidence that the doctor to whom Wyllie owed his life, being at that time somewhat ill himself, had the wrong medicine given him that day by an hospital servant, and was dead in less than an hour after taking the draught. Instead of the mildest of medicines he had got the fatalist of poisons.[64]

The doctor's name was James Charles Kelly Bond; he was the assistant surgeon on the Madras Establishment, and civil surgeon of Moulmein. He was 35 years of age and only recently married.[65] After returning home from a christening party at a friend's house on the night of 27 October, Bond retired to his bed and intended to take two 'blue pills' he had prepared in an attempt to help with an illness he had been suffering. But his servant mistakenly gave him two strychnine-laced pills that had been prepared months earlier, intended for the destruction of local stray dogs. Although medical aid was called, Bond died just three hours after taking the poison. The sad story was made even more lamentable in that his wife gave birth to their first child just two days later.[66]

Soon after arriving back in England, on 22 March 1858, the officers of the *Indian Queen* found themselves in front of a Liverpool judge charged with cruelty towards one of the clipper's seamen, John McAllister, who had joined the crew during the brief stop at Hobart Town. Several weeks after their arrival in Liverpool he died at the local workhouse, having been found in a seriously ill state at the city's Prince's Dock. McAlister, who years earlier had been sent to Hobart Town as a convict, was returning after paying his debt to society. He had told the governor of the workhouse that he was severely mistreated by Captain Jobson and the two mates. Testimony lodged at the coroner's court indicated that he had been beaten and kicked by the officers, but the coroner would state that death was caused by bronchitis and congestion of the lungs, a purely natural cause. The jury returned a verdict of death by natural causes, but also presented that a vote of censure be passed on the captain and officers for their gross ill-treatment of McAlister.[67]

Now back in Liverpool Wyllie decided to leave the crew of the clipper and look for new employment. On 25 May he sat his examination for a certificate of competency as first mate, less than two years since his last successful examination. Again his date of birth was listed as 1832, still making him four years younger than his real age. It was once again his first opportunity to apply for such a promotion, again revealing his dependability as a mate and his eagerness to continue his rise towards command.

HOME WATERS: HONING HIS CRAFT IN THE STEAMER TRADE 1858–1860

The next few years would be spent in calmer waters and much closer to home. Wyllie joined the crew of the *Tamaulipas* and then the *Nemesis*, both Clyde-built screw steamers operated by the firm of J. Moss & Company of Liverpool. When he joined the *Tamaulipas* it was the first time he served aboard a steam vessel. As first mate on both of these steamers, he spent a 'goodly number of quiet and enjoyable years in trading between Liverpool and Bordeaux. Many a pleasant trip he had down the Channel, passing Ushant, across the Bay of Biscay, skirting Gibraltar, hugging the Levant, piercing the Bosporus and coasting the Black Sea.'[68] Cargoes on these steamers were varied: wine, oil, brandy and fruits. It was a regular trade, with a return voyage once a month. Nothing of note occurred until a fateful voyage on the *Nemesis* in September 1860.

The *Nemesis* left Liverpool bound for its usual destination of Bordeaux on 11 September, with a crew of 18. On board were seven passengers, including several of the steamer's part-owners along with their wives. The captain was Samuel Morrish, a master with three years' experience on the Mediterranean trade. Two days after departure, after a fine run down the Irish Sea, disaster struck as the *Nemesis* was transiting the tricky narrows of the Raz de Sein, off the coast of France to the south-west of Brest. Wyllie's own recollections of the event were:

> The weather was beautiful, the sea smooth, the wind just sufficient to fill the sails, and the month was September – pleasantest month in all the year. It is half-past ten in the morning ... In passing through the Bec de Rez Passage on the French coast at dead low water the ship struck a sunken rock, and remained fixed. The captain found himself rudely stretched on the middle of the cabin floor. The passengers were all promenading on deck. Soundings showed that all round the vessel there was deep water. Abreast the engine room, both starboard and port, they found only thirteen fathoms. They were evidently poised on the pinnacle of a great rock. Sounding the hold seven feet of water was found. 'Clear away the boats' was the captain's order. The crew and the passengers were then divided equally amongst them. The ladies behaved splendidly. They never uttered a scream. When they were clear away they looked more like a pic-nic party than a shipwrecked crew and passengers. The flood tide beginning to make fast, they saw the doomed vessel slip from the rock, and, with all sail set, and as if in mockery of the crew who had deserted her, continued her course, as if directed by an invisible helmsman. It was the beautiful creature's last touch of pride. Soon her jib began to dip to the water it had so often nodded in its heyday of life. Lower still it stooped, till they seemed tenderly to kiss. Then the ocean opened his glassy arms and took her to himself. In a minute the sea was as smooth as ever. 'Time writes no wrinkles on thine azure brow, as at creation's dawn thou rollest now.' They were twenty-five miles from Brest, and, after a long, steady pull, they reached that place about midnight. They were in most perilous circumstances and if a gale had arisen it is questionable if one of them had survived to tell the tale I am telling now.[69]

The sinking of the *Nemesis* was reported in Liverpool by 17 September 1860, confirming Wyllie's recollection that all passengers were saved and the ship was a complete loss.[70] Like today, any such event at the time would be investigated in order to ascertain the cause of the sinking and whether any activities might have been effected to stop the loss of the steamer.

So in October a Board of Trade inquiry was convened at St George's Hall, Liverpool. Captain Morrish and First Mate Wyllie were called to answer for their conduct during the events of the voyage. The weather was noted as having been fine on the day, and the captain had chosen to take the Raz du Sein route in order to save some time rather than taking the longer, more westerly, route around the Ile de Sein. Captain Morrish testified that he had taken his chosen course many times before; but he only had English charts, not French ones, and the rock the *Nemesis* had struck was not mapped. Wyllie then testified that immediately after the collision with the rock the steamer took on water and after just five minutes it was 18 inches deep. The engines were ordered reversed in order to try and free the *Nemesis*, but it was stuck fast. The crew and passengers abandoned ship and were loaded into three boats. In just 15 minutes the *Nemesis* disappeared beneath the waves – a complete loss. The owners of the steamer had confirmed that it was insured for £8,800, and went on to present statements that they had confidence in Captain Morrish and he 'was always steady, sober, and attentive, and the only fault he had to find with him was his extreme caution'.[71]

After all the evidence had been presented the board adjourned to review the details and deliver a verdict. A fortnight later it ruled that Captain Morrish and the *Nemesis*'s crew were not responsible for the sinking, but noted that Morrish, although an experienced captain in the waters off Brest, should 'be more careful in future'.[72] Wyllie's name was not mentioned. His career was not to be tarnished by an official sanction, and he was free to continue his maritime career without a black mark on his record.

STEAMER *HOPE* 1860–1862

With yet again another brush with death behind him, Wyllie now joined the crew of a steamer also, coincidentally, named *Hope*, another of J. Moss & Company's ships. Still working the Mediterranean trade, he served as first mate on the steamer for a year and a half, making journeys to France and the Middle East along with a single transatlantic voyage. It would be this voyage that would lead him to make the most dangerous, and potentially most profitable, decision he would ever make as a mariner.

The *Hope* was a screw steamer built in 1853 by John Laird at Birkenhead, on the banks of the Mersey. It had worked on the African trade out of Liverpool for the first seven years of its career before being purchased by John Moss in 1860. Its captain was Charles Baker, whom Wyllie had served under while first mate aboard the *Tamaulipas*. With increased rank came increased pay: Wyllie's wages were now £8 a month as first mate, up from the £6 he had received while second mate aboard the *Indian Queen* just two years earlier.[73]

The routes that the *Hope* plied were familiar to Wyllie. Its voyages were from Liverpool to French ports, mainly Bordeaux, usually lasting around a month per round trip. On his second voyage as first mate Wyllie would be involved in an event that has been associated with mariners since time immemorial – sailors making trouble while in port. The *Hope* had left Liverpool on 11 February, making a five-day passage to Bordeaux. The steamer was in port for the next few days, unloading cargo and arranging return freight. The usual peace of the monthly trip was disturbed on the night of the 26th when a number of the crew were involved in an altercation in the town. Captain Baker wrote in the ship's log that on that night, between 10 p.m. and 12 midnight:

> A disturbance took place between members of my crew and some of the French subjects of Bordeaux, which resulted in three of them being locked up in prison until 6pm on the 27th.[74]

What made matters worse was that the crew involved were not just humble seamen, but the bo'sun, carpenter, and the first and second engineers – vital for the operation of the steamer. Captain Baker wrote that these men were sent for trial on a charge of 'rebellion against the Police'. The exact nature of the offence was not elaborated upon, but a good guess was that they had been out for the evening, things turned sour, the police were called, and the sailors got into a fracas with the officers. Three of them faced no serious charges, but the captain had to hand over the effects and wages of Charles Harris, the first engineer, to the British consul. In addition Harris was discharged from the *Hope* and left at Bordeaux. His activities in the fight must have been more serious than the others, as the consul went on to record in the steamer's papers that Harris was then 'committed to prison for breach of the peace'. Harris spent several weeks in a French prison, but was picked up by the *Hope* when it made its next trip from Liverpool. His time was served and, although he might have been in the captain's bad books, he resumed his role as first engineer when the *Hope* sailed for Liverpool on 23 July. His conduct had obviously not been serious enough to prohibit him from once again becoming a member of the crew, nor would be enough to stop him working with Wyllie again in the future. Though neither of them knew it on that summer's day in Liverpool, three years later they would once again be in the same crew, Wyllie as master and Harris on the engines, as they sought to escape not the attention of the French police but the fire of Union cannon while running a wartime blockade.

After several more trips to French ports during the autumn and spring of 1860/61, the steamer set off on a special delivery towards the Middle East on 25 July 1861. On board was not the usual merchandise from British mills and factories but 70 thoroughbred horses for the Pasha of Egypt, procured from some of the finest stables in the United Kingdom. They were destined for the pasha's cavalry, local press noting that 'His Highness intends improving the breed of horses at present in general use in the Egyptian Army'. The horses were accompanied by a number of bulldogs, greyhounds and pointers intended for the royal household.[75] Although this was a much more lively cargo than Wyllie was accustomed to, the voyage passed peacefully and the *Hope* made Alexandria on 13 August.[76] The only event of note was a fall that Wyllie suffered on 28 August while in port at Alexandria; it was noted in the ship's log that he had hurt his ankle and foot, and aid was obtained.

After a second voyage to Egypt the *Hope* was back at Liverpool making ready for a much longer journey, one that would take Wyllie across the stormy seas of the North Atlantic in the middle of winter to the great metropolis of New York. On New Year's Day 1862 an advertisement appeared in the *Leeds Mercury* for the imminent despatch of the 'superior first-class steamer *Hope*' to New York. It continued 'This vessel offers an eligible opportunity to shippers of cotton etc.'[77] This was the large amounts of cotton that sat at British ports, recently received from the plantations in the Confederate States of America, having been run through the naval blockade that had been implemented at the start of the American Civil War in April 1861. Although cotton was desperately needed in the mills of England and Scotland, there was also a lucrative market developing in the transport of this contraband cotton to the mills of the north-eastern United States. The mills in Massachusetts were as vital to the economy of the North as those in Lancashire were to that of Britain. The *Liverpool Mercury* of 6 January reported that large amounts of cotton had been purchased in the city during the past few weeks for reshipment to America, and several steamers had been despatched to carry this cargo – the *Hope* was thought to be taking 1,000 bales. Freight rates were noted to be 2d (pence) [2*] per pound plus 5 per cent primage. However, one of the companies offering carriage to New York, the famous Inman Company, offered the usual rates of cargo, stating that they would 'decline availing themselves to the present crisis to raise their freights to their customers, therefore adhere to the customary charges.' [78] This statement indicates that the rates offered were inflated, as a result of the continuing lack of shipments from the cotton-producing states of America, they having seceded from the United States in March 1861 to form the Confederate States of America.

The *Hope* and its crew of 30 set off on from the Mersey on 9 January to brave the stormy winter Atlantic waves. The passage was indeed rough, and when the *Hope* arrived at New York on 4 February it was described as having 'experienced very heavy weather' with the loss of both lifeboats during 'huge pyramidical seas, the ocean boiling with great fury'. On 26 January, it had even appeared that the vessel would be lost: the log noted 'steering binnacle washed away, skylights, bridge binnacle and everything on deck that was movable; all hands lashed to the deck'.[79]

With so much damage sustained, the *Hope* required repairs and would need to spend the next month in port.

Wyllie's first visit to the United States came at a time of immense strain; he was stepping into a city and a country being torn apart by the Civil War. The conflict had yet to reach the end of its first year, having begun with the bombardment of Fort Sumter in Charleston,

---

2* There were 20 shillings in a pound sterling (£1), and 12 pence per shilling, hence 240 pence per £1. (NB the pound referred to in the text is a pound avoirdupois ('lb') – ie mass, not £1.)

Wyllie's first visit to the United States came as 1st mate aboard the steamer Hope *in January 1862 when it carried 1,000 bales of blockade-run Southern cotton to New York. It was Wyllie's first connection with the American Civil War.*

© CSG CIC Glasgow Museums Collection

South Carolina, on 12 April 1861. Since that time forces from the Confederate States of America, having seceded from the Union in the spring, had prevailed in the first major battle at Bull Run (also known as the First Battle of Manassas), Virginia, on 21 July. The war, which many in 1861 had thought would not last the year, would resume fully with the coming of spring 1862. Splashed across the front pages of the New York newspapers were daily reports of the progress of the conflict. While Wyllie and his crew were waiting on the repairs they would have read of a major victory: the battle and ultimate capture by Union forces of the Confederate-held Fort Donelson on the Cumberland river on the border of Kentucky and Tennessee. Partially led by the as yet unknown Major General Ulysses S. Grant, the fort fell on 16 February, and soon news of the first major Union victory of the conflict made it to New York. Just before the *Hope* steamed for Liverpool the news broke of the battle at Hampton Roads between the Union vessel *Monitor* and the Confederate *Virginia*, the first battle between ironclad warships, to be considered one of the most important naval battles of the conflict.

Finally, the *Hope*'s crew would have read of the ongoing reports of the blockade of the Southern ports: British-built steamers, both paddle- and screw-propelled, were being bought in Britain and taken across the Atlantic to attempt to run into Confederate-held ports like Charleston, South Carolina, Wilmington, North Carolina, and Mobile, Alabama. Many of the vessels were crewed by British officers and sailors, and the rewards for successfully passing through this blockade thought to be eye-watering: pay on these vessels could be an order of magnitude higher than the wages of a sailor on a merchantman like the *Hope*. With thoughts of the possibility of making a vast fortune in their minds, the crew made the steamer ready and on 13 March it departed New York for Liverpool.[80] After an uneventful passage it arrived on 1 April, carrying 284 tons of bacon, 95 tons of cheese, ham, pork, rosin (used for 'sizing' cotton, to facilitate its manufacture), tallow and lard.[81]

News of the fall of Fort Donelson, the first great Union victory in the western theatre of the war, broke while Wyllie was in New York. As the war dragged on the supplies brought in through the blockade were essential for the Confederacy's outlook for success.

Courtesy of the Library of Congress

Liverpool at that time was a city gripped by the reports coming out of America. Liverpool was the main English port for cotton imports from the Southern states, so the disruption caused by the war was a major concern to the commercial interests of the city. News of Liverpool-built and -owned ships being used as blockade runners and armed cruisers were included in the papers almost daily. As in New York, Wyllie could read in the papers – here, the *Liverpool Mercury* or the *Daily Post* – of the daring escapes of such vessels and the cargoes they delivered under the shot of Union cannon. It seemed that every day another ship was travelling to run the blockade, with each one needing a full crew of experienced seamen. The reports of success and monetary gain must have been an incredible incentive to sign on to one of these vessels.

Perhaps the most thrilling stories to come out of this early part of the war was the capture and dramatic escape of the Liverpool-based ship *Emily St Pierre*. Wyllie was in the city when the heroes of this event were lauded and paraded through it. The *Emily St Pierre* had been captured by the Union warship *James Adger* on 21 March off the South Carolina coast near Charleston. The Liverpool-owned ship had been trying to run in through the blockade to deliver a cargo of gunny sacks that it had taken on board in Calcutta (Kolkata). The Union's *James Adger* had spotted the *Emily* on the open sea, and after a short chase detained it, following orders that any vessel approaching the port would be considered as trying to run the blockade. The *Emily* was then boarded and the crew was formally charged with trying to make Charleston through the lawful blockade. Per procedure, most of the crew were removed from the ship and taken into custody aboard the *James Adger*, with only *Emily*'s captain, its steward, Matthew Montgomery, and a cook remaining on board to assist with the vessel's trip to the prize court in New York or Boston.

It was then that the story of the *Emily St Pierre* would turn into front page news. The captain, cook and steward overpowered the Union seamen and officers that had been assigned to take the vessel north. Wilson then brought the *Emily St Pierre* back to Liverpool across the vast Atlantic with only the three crew to work the ship, with the Union officers chained below decks. This amazing story concluded with the ship arriving back at the Mersey on 20 April to great fanfare in the local press.[82]

Captain Wilson was greeted as a hero for saving his ship and cargo as well as outwitting his Yankee captors. There was a degree of support for the Confederate cause in Liverpool at that time, and the story of the *Emily St Pierre* was viewed as truly a punch in the eye to the United States. The brokers for the ship were the Liverpool firm of Fraser, Trenholm & Company, then well known for supporting the business of the Confederacy in England. The full story, recounted by Wilson himself, was given during a grand reception in his honour at the rooms of the Liverpool Maritime Mercantile Association on 3 May 1862. Wilson was lauded, presented with tokens of appreciation and generally made to feel a hero. It was reported that the room was bursting, and listed as being in attendance were many local ship owners, captains and officers.[83]

Wyllie was in the city at that time, awaiting the next voyage of the *Hope*. If he himself had not been lucky enough to attend the reception, he could have read a full description of the event in the papers over the following days. Those in the audience must have been drawn to the heroics of Wilson, but there would have also been an air of desire and anticipation: the chance of financial gain from the blockade, as well as this reception for an English hero, would have once again encouraged many to seek their chances on one of the steamers heading out at an ever-increasing rate to Bermuda and Nassau, towards the blockade.

Two more voyages for Wyllie as first mate on the *Hope* soon followed. As he arrived at Liverpool on 4 August he made the fateful decision that would lead him into the greatest dangers he would face while a mariner. No longer would he sail the warm waters of the Mediterranean aboard the *Hope*. He would now seek a more perilous destination, one to the west, and full of lurking warships. He would seek his certificate of competency as a master and then head again to North America – not to the bustling port of New York, where he had experienced the Civil War through newspaper reports, but to the war itself. The lure of the vast fortunes convinced him that his future lay on the bridge of a paddle steamer running the blockade to the Confederate ports.

3

BEGINNINGS OF THE BLOCKADE

> We come now to the great blockade running period of his life, when his name and portrait were as familiarly known in America as those of the most prominent British statesman in this country at the present moment.
>
> – From 'Risen from the Ranks: Captain Wyllie, the Great Scottish Blockade Runner', *The People's Friend*, July 1889

The docks and quays along the Mersey were alive with activity as stevedores, merchants and ship owners went about their daily work. Ships were made ready as customs agents checked the cargoes that would soon sail out of the river, destined for all parts of the globe. Liverpool was the gateway to the British Empire, a huge melting pot of cultures, an important centre for businessmen who dealt in cotton, coal, tea, sugar and countless other commodities. Lancashire, the county in which Liverpool was located at the time, was the powerhouse of the British economy. And no industry was more important than that of cotton. Thousands of men, women and children worked endlessly to turn the raw fibres that came from America into thread, cloth and printed fabric.

The docks of Liverpool were where the cotton came and went. But the American Civil War had brought that industry and the economic growth to a halt, as cotton was now hard to come by. The reason was the blockade established around the ports of the Southern states, which meant fewer and fewer bales of the cotton making it through to the mills of Lancashire. People in towns like Bolton, Preston and Bury began to experience the hardships of what became known as the Cotton Famine.

The blockade of the Southern states had been one of the first acts instituted by the newly elected president, Abraham Lincoln, after his inauguration on 4 March 1861. His election the previous year – as the first Republican to hold the highest office of the land – was the start of a series of events that would lead to the creation of the Confederate States of America and the Civil War. Starting with South Carolina on 20 December 1860, several Southern states declared their secession from the Union, fearing that the newly elected Republican president would seek to limit the spread of slavery to the western territories – and would also, many believed, end slavery completely. There were in fact some members of the Republican Party who sought the complete abolition of slavery, but the platform of the new president and the Republican-controlled Congress was not so extreme. But the fears of such actions motivated politicians across the slave-owning states to seek an exit from the 84-year-old union, and by March 1861 six other states had joined South Carolina in declaring their secession: Mississippi, Florida, Alabama, Georgia, Louisiana and Texas. This number would ultimately rise to 11 by the end of May, those joining being Virginia, Arkansas, Tennessee and North Carolina. It was the biggest crisis in the history of the United States thus far.

The Confederate States of America had been officially born on 8 February 1861 with the adoption of a Provisional Constitution by the states which had at that point seceded. This was a month before Lincoln was due to take the Oath of Office. The states that made up the Confederacy were mainly rural, agricultural-based economies, with cotton being the main revenue crop. It was exported to the mills in the North such as New York and Massachusetts, and to Britain. Cotton could not be grown in the cooler climate of the British Isles, so all cotton had to be sourced from warmer climes, the Southern states of America being the biggest source. It was on this fact that the leaders of the Confederacy based their early strategy to succeed as a new nation. King Cotton would be used as a bargaining chip to persuade Britain and France to recognise the Confederacy and possibly provide aid to it in its conflict with the Union.

Although the Confederacy had a significant asset in its cotton, a major disadvantage was that its industrial might, including the manufacture of weapons, iron mining and shipbuilding, was almost non-existent. Most of the arsenals, mills and naval yards lay in the Northern states, which was to put the Confederacy at a significant disadvantage in the coming battles. The materiel for its armies and navy, as well the materials required to provide the trappings of a new nation, needed to be sourced from outside its own boundaries. This situation being recognised by President Lincoln and his advisors, they developed a policy of isolating the South.

Isolating the breakaway states meant limiting their access to foreign goods. A system was needed to stop items going back and forth, and the accepted and legal form this took was a naval blockade. This meant both a blockade on paper and a physical one. Lincoln declared the blockade of the Southern states on 19 April, a week after the official start of the Civil War when Fort Sumter was attacked. The text, in part, was as follows:

> I, Abraham Lincoln, President of the United States, with a view to the same purposes before mentioned and to the protection of the public peace and

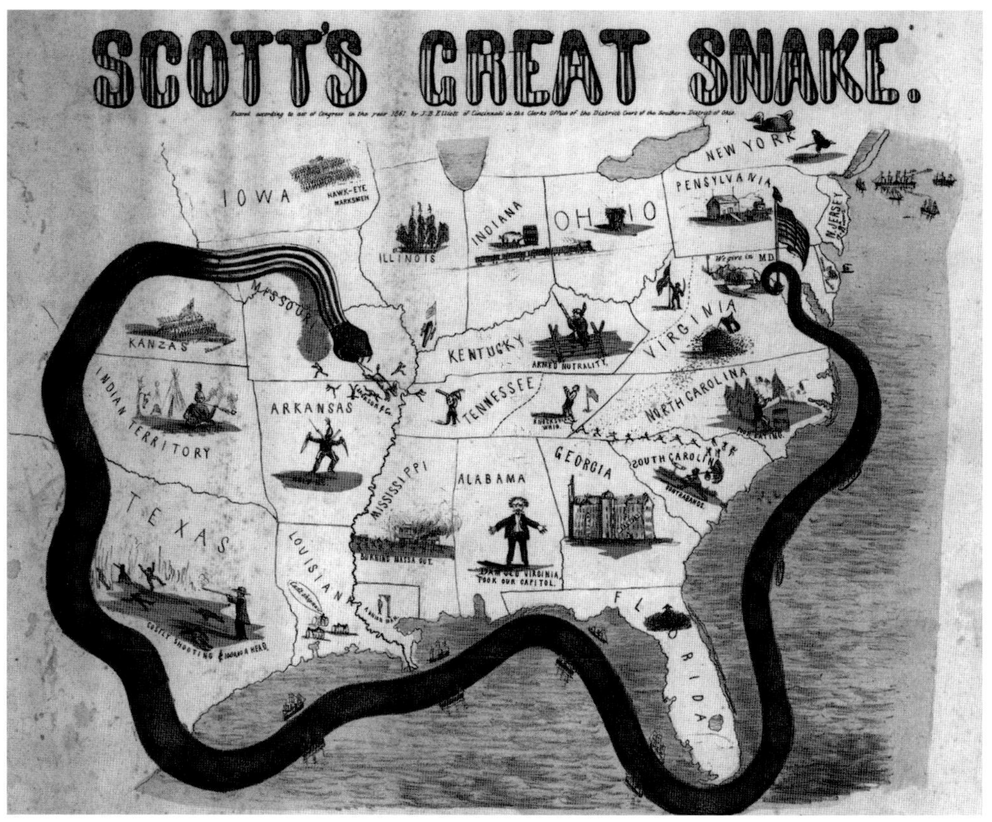

A contemporary illustration of Union General Winfield Scott's Anaconda Plan, the North's strategy of squeezing the Confederate States by blockading its ports and rivers, thus denying the rebels their vital military supplies.

Courtesy of the Library of Congress

the lives and property of quiet and orderly citizens pursuing their lawful occupations until Congress shall have assembled and deliberated on the said unlawful proceedings or until the same shall have ceased, have further deemed it advisable to set on foot a blockade of the ports within the States aforesaid, in pursuance of the laws of the United States and of the law of nations in such case provided. For this purpose a competent force will be posted so as to prevent entrance and exit of vessels from the ports aforesaid. If, therefore, with a view to violate such blockade, a vessel shall approach or shall attempt to leave either of the said ports, she will be duly warned by the commander of one of the blockading vessels, who will endorse on her register the fact and date of such warning, and if the same vessel shall again attempt to

> enter or leave the blockaded port she will be captured and sent to the nearest convenient port for such proceedings against her and her cargo as prize as may be deemed advisable.[84]

For the blockade to be legal it required both a written warning posted in those ports and an active fleet to enforce the decree. From the start the Union Navy had few vessels available to be stationed off the ports of the Southern states, and those that could be called upon were mainly slower, older warships. But so too struggled the states of the new Confederacy: few merchant vessels were owned by the South or operated from its ports; the main ports in America, like Boston and New York, were to be found in the North. Few transatlantic routes provided a direct service to and from the Southern ports of Norfolk, Virginia, Wilmington, North Carolina, or Charleston, South Carolina. New Orleans was of course home to a significant maritime trade and was indeed the port where much of the cotton from the South was exported. But it was farther away for the European traders, and was identified quickly as a target to be taken by the forces of the Union.

From the start the blockade was slow to materialise, the North having too few ships to patrol the high seas as well as maintaining station off the Southern ports, and the Confederacy lacking both ships and suitable ports for their exports. But this would soon change as vessels were identified that could be used in the smaller ports of the South and

While American brothers fight, the great European powers, represented by John Bull and Napoleon III, stand back, claiming neutrality. This contemporary cartoon highlighted the believed complicity of the Europeans, helping the Confederate States through the supply of armed frigates, the operation of blockade runners and use of their Caribbean ports.

Courtesy of the Library of Congress

were fast enough to outrun the Union forces, which month by month were increasing in both number and ability. Many of the South's new vessels were built in British shipyards and carried British crew. The vessels that were ideal for its needs were the side-wheel paddle steamers built for the coastal and cross-channel trades. Built mainly for passenger traffic, they did not have large cargo holds, but they were fast, and crucially had shallow drafts that allowed them to negotiate the South's shoaling coastal waters. They were not designed as ocean-going vessels, so the first hurdle in using them to run the blockade was getting them across the Atlantic.

Once they had managed that, they were stationed at the colonial possessions of Britain and Spain in and around the West Indies. The harbours of Nassau in the Bahamas and St George's in Bermuda were ideal for running to the ports on the Atlantic coast of the Confederacy. Havana, on the northern coast of Cuba, would suit for runs to the ports along the Gulf of Mexico such as New Orleans, Mobile and Galveston. It would, however, be Nassau and St George's that became the main focus for blockade running during the war. They were close to both Wilmington and Charleston (Nassau was 570 nautical miles (nm) to Wilmington, 515 nm to Charleston, with St George's being 674 nm and 772 nm respectively). In the well-protected harbours of Nassau and St George's, cargo could be transhipped from the ocean-going ships from Europe to the blockade runners, to make the shorter runs to Confederate ports. Bermuda, the Bahamas and the West Indian ports were outside the control of the Union forces, and although stern complaints were made by officials from Washington, the ships were able to operate under the protection of the British government.

But these ports did have a problem. Until the start of the Civil War both were small backwaters with few visits from large ocean-going ships. In pre-war days Bermuda was described as:

> comparatively unknown to the world, except as an important British naval station. No startling episode in the great concatenation of events had occurred for many years to disturb the tranquil repose of her many peaceful islands.[85]

The war would soon change these quiet ports into a bustle of ships, sailors, cargo, speculators and spies. From the start of their use as blockade-running ports they became a type of wild west free-for-all. Thomas Taylor, one of the most famous of the blockade-running captains, recalled life in Nassau during the war:

> Money flowed like water, men lived for the day and never thought of the morrow, and in that small place was accumulated a mixture of mankind seldom seen before. Confederate military and naval officers; diplomatists using the blockade as a means of ingress and egress for their beleaguered

> country; newspaper correspondents and advertisers of all kinds, – some rascals no doubt; the very cream of the English Navy, composed of officers on half-pay who had come out lured by the prospects of making some money and gaining an experience in their profession which a war such as this could give them.[86]

Taylor's mention of the prospect of making some money is what attracted thousands of British officers and seamen like himself to the blockade during the conflict.[87]

As mentioned earlier, the profits that could be made from successfully running the blockade were far higher than the usual pay for a mariner, in both the steamers operated by private companies and those run by either the states or the Confederate government. The pay for the crews of the private runners was the higher, as these vessels could carry goods that commanded higher prices – luxury items, liquors, fashions – whereas the government vessels were required to ship mainly items necessary for the war effort. A captain on a private vessel received $5,000 dollars per successful round trip (half paid in advance, half on completion), the first mate $1,250, the chief engineer $2,500 and a seaman $250. These sums would usually be paid in gold.[88] For comparison, Joannes Wyllie's pay as the first mate on the steamer *Hope* in 1862 was £8 a month, equivalent to around $45. So one successful blockade-running voyage, which would usually take around a month, might bring in almost 27 times the usual monthly wage.

There was another advantage to being British on the runners. Although their voyages would be attempting to break a blockade, they were not combatants. Runners carried no weapons of war, and when they were spotted at sea their pursuers would seek to capture the vessels and not sink them. This was an opportunity for the crews of the blockade ships to gain a great payday, because the whole crew of each vessel involved in a capture would, if that vessel was deemed a lawful prize by the courts in New York or Boston, get a share of the prize money realised from the sale at auction of the steamer and its cargo. So it was in no one's interest to sink a runner on the high seas, and if a runner did end up beached or stranded in the mouth of a river outside a port, its cargo might yet be saved by the local forces, and not be captured by the blockade fleet. If a runner was caught, a foreign sailor could plead ignorance of the blockade and would, by convention, be released if no aggressive action had occurred. At least that was the theory; some of the sailors were imprisoned and so needed to appeal to their government to plead for their release by the Union officials.

To a British sailor the blockade of the Southern states must have seemed an opportunity they could not pass up. Easy money if your voyage was successful, with little chance of violent conflict, the main hazard being the stormy seas of the Atlantic. A few successful voyages could bring riches beyond any wage that could be earned on a merchant vessel. Political or ethical considerations regarding the support of the new Confederacy aside, it was a chance of a lifetime, and one that many took up.

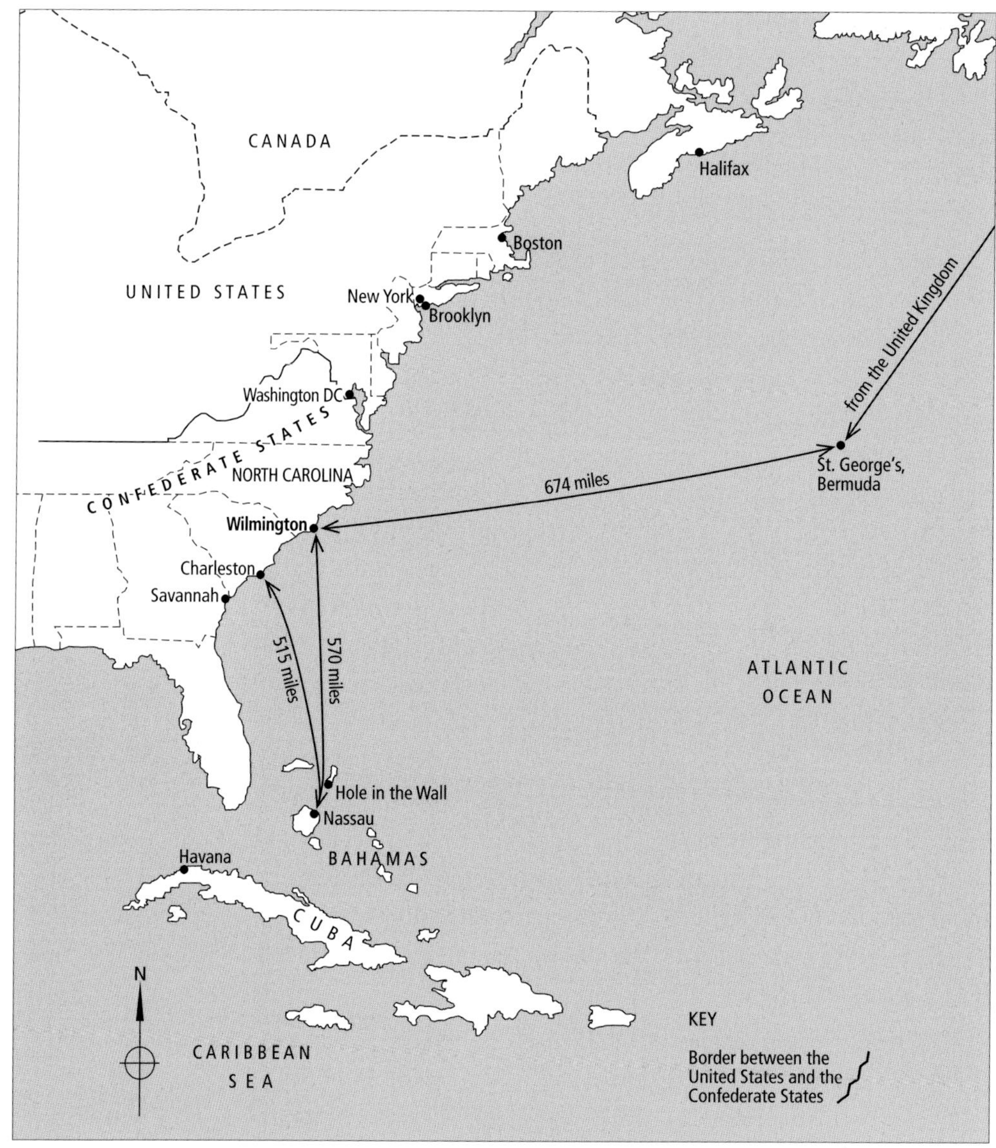

North America and the Caribbean at the time of the Civil War, showing the distances in nautical miles between the blockade ports

LIVERPOOL, AUGUST 1862

By August 1862 the Civil War had been raging for 16 months and was bringing hardship for many, both in America and in the cotton towns of Britain. But it also meant great opportunity for those who wished to engage in running the blockade. It was into this mix of profit and despondency that Joannes Wyllie took his first steps towards becoming a blockade runner. He had called Liverpool home since he had returned from his first voyage in 1853. Since then he had served on a barque, a clipper and several screw steamers. He had journeyed around the globe, and had gained rapid promotion, from apprentice to first mate. He now sat the examination for master, in order to be able to take command of a vessel, and was passed by the Board of Trade in Liverpool on 13 August 1862. Wyllie was now ready to serve as captain.

His first command was on a steamer that had already passed twice through the cordon of Federal gunboats. He signed on as master of the *Bonita*, a Clyde-built screw steamer, 190

By The Lords of the Committee of Privy Council for Trade.

Certificate of Competency as MASTER,

To Joannes Wyllie

Whereas it has been reported to us that you have been found duly qualified to fulfil the duties of Master in the Merchant Service we do hereby in pursuance of the Merchant Shipping Act 1854 grant you this Certificate of Competency.

Given under the Seal of The Board of Trade this Twelfth day of August 1862

By order of the Board

Registered

Officer of the Marine Department.

Entered at the General Register and Record Office of Seamen on the 21st day of August 1862

Wyllie gained his certificate of competency as a master mariner at Liverpool in August 1862. Only weeks later he gained his first command: the steamer Bonita *on its voyage towards the blockade.*

© CSG CIC Glasgow Museums Collection

feet in length, powered by a 100 hp engine, and of 572 gross tons. It had recently returned to Liverpool from a voyage to the Caribbean and was well known to the Federal consul in that city. It had been built on the Clyde in 1860 by Archibald Denny shipbuilders of the famous Denny family in Dumbarton. The name given it at launch was *Economist*, and in early 1862 it had set off from Liverpool, bound for the blockade. After arriving in Nassau, it continued to Charleston, South Carolina. It successfully evaded the blockaders, even though they were gaining in number and power by the month. This was still quite early in the war, and larger, ocean-going vessels like the *Economist* were still able to make successful runs; but their deeper draft and slower speeds meant they would soon be easy prey. It arrived at Charleston on the morning of 13 March, and according to the *Wilmington Journal*, brought '35,000 stand of arms, including 12,000 Enfield rifles, about 60 tons of gunpowder, and immense stores of blankets, shoes, accoutrements for artillery, medicines and other articles, of which our army stands badly in need'.[89] The *Economist* had been chartered by the Confederate government, and its cargo would have been an immense help to the army in the upcoming summer campaigns. It sailed out on 2 April, once again successfully avoiding the Union blockaders, and arrived at Nassau on 6 April, carrying 1,100 bales of cotton.[90] From there the steamer made the transatlantic trip back to Liverpool, bringing a cargo of 838 bales of cotton and 404 barrels of rosin.[91]

The *Economist* was now a known blockade runner, and its return to Liverpool was reported across Britain. The vessel attracted the attention of Federal agents in the city, who suspected it was being prepared for another run. Something needed to be done to throw these agents off the scent. So the owners, Fraser, Trenholm & Company, known Confederate associates, arranged an elaborate ruse to try and confuse the Federals. On 27 August, Fraser, Trenholm arranged a false sale of the *Economist* to what were described in the Register of Shipping as 'Foreigners', changing the ship's name to *Bonita* – and then quickly sold it on to a third party, Melchior Klingender. Klingender was a Liverpudlian businessman working for Fraser, Trenholm as an advertising agent. By selling the ship to another owner and changing the name, Fraser, Trenholm hoped it might be cleared of its past, fooling the Yankees, and be made ready for another trip towards the blockade unnoticed. But the ruse was not a success. Thomas Dudley, United States consul in Liverpool, reported to Secretary of State Seward that the *Bonita*, late the *Economist*, was being made ready for sea and was about to take on board a cargo of iron plates; he had even spoken to members of the crew who had told him the steamer would sail to Nassau and thence to Charleston.[92] These plates could be fixed onto the hulls and decks of Confederate naval ships such as gunboats and ironclads, greatly increasing their defensive abilities. This would be a very valuable and important cargo for the Confederate war effort.

The *Bonita*, with Federal agents tracking it and with an important Confederate cargo on board, became the first ship under the command of Joannes Wyllie. Exactly how he was given this command is not known, but of course even though he was newly rated he did have relevant experience in transatlantic voyages. He had just left his role as first mate on the steamer *Hope*, where he had served the previous two years. This steamer had made a voyage from Liverpool to New York in January 1862 with almost 1,000 bales of cotton; cotton that had been run out of the blockade and transported to England. The *Bonita* was similar to *Hope*, also being a screw steamer, and of roughly the same tonnage, length and breadth.

Wyllie signed on as master on 4 September 1862 for a voyage to 'Nassau then to any other ports in the West Indies, the Atlantic Ocean and back to a final port of discharge in the United Kingdom, the term not to exceed 6 months.' On board was a crew of 35, all British except for one Swedish seaman. The managing owner was listed as Melchior Klingender.[93] With master and crew signed on and cargo loaded, Wyllie gave the order for the boilers to be fed and steam raised. The engine churned, the screw turned and the *Bonita* steamed down the Mersey and out to sea on 7 September, bound for Nassau.[94]

Wyllie recounted this first voyage in the pages of *The People's Friend*. He stated that the cargo, 'three hundred tons of plate iron … which was exceedingly valuable', was shipped at Liverpool.[95] He was under secret orders (presumably given to him by the owner, Melchior Klingender), in case they met any Yankee cruisers, to make for Nassau, Bahamas, in the first instance.[96] He records that all 'was going well, until he sighted the Western Islands', the Azores. This was a common refuelling and landing site for ships making the transatlantic trip. It was also an area that was being actively patrolled by United States naval ships looking for Confederate warships and merchantmen bound for the South. Just previous to the *Bonita* making landfall at the Western Islands, what would become the most famous Confederate warship had also set out on its first voyage; the CSS *Alabama* had sailed from the Mersey on 29 July and made its way towards the Western Islands. There in late August it was fitted out with weaponry before being commissioned into the Confederate Navy in early September. With this powerful warship at large the US Navy was being particularly vigilant.

It was near these islands that Wyllie recounts that the *Bonita* came upon a ship flying a distress signal. Suspecting no subterfuge he acknowledged the signal. A boat was then put off from the mysterious ship and approached the *Bonita*. As it neared, and with the reports of the *Alabama* near the Azores, something 'flashed through his (Wyllie's) mind that all was not right' and he ordered his engineers to be ready to make a run. Wyllie said that the men in the boat were 'as cut-throat a looking set as I had ever seen'. The deputation in the boat announced that the coal bunkers on their ship were empty, but Wyllie suspected the worst and ordered full speed ahead, leaving the boat behind. When the ship noticed that its boat had not been taken aboard the *Bonita*, now moving away at speed, it opened fire. Wyllie later recounted that he had never been witness to a dirtier trick, and that he could not have possibly received a better lesson for the work in which he was engaged.

Wyllie does not name this deceitful ship, nor can it be confirmed that it was a Union warship. What we do know is that the US Navy had ships in the area at the time of the

Bonita's voyage, and so Wyllie's description, and the fact he was on board a known runner, make this account credible.

After this escape, the *Bonita* continued on its voyage across the Atlantic. It made slow progress as it encountered 'contrary winds' which meant that its boilers used more coal than anticipated. When the *Bonita*'s bunkers were close to empty the ship's boats and 'such other things as would burn' were broken up and tossed into the firebox. Sensing the danger of becoming a 'mere hulk on the waters' and easy prey for Yankee raiders, Wyllie steered the *Bonita* for the closer, neutral port of St Thomas in the Danish Virgin Islands (now the US Virgin Islands), arriving there on 3 October.[97] There he was able to restock and repair, and replenish his coal bunkers, and then proceed west-north-west to the Bahamas per his orders.

Wyllie had eluded a human trick in the Western Islands, but on approaching the Bahamas he would soon run into a natural obstacle that could have ended his running career before it had even begun. His orders were to take the *Bonita* towards the island of Eleuthera, on the eastern edge of the Bahamas archipelago. There he was to run along the edge of the island, flying the Union Jack, and await a pilot to come out to the *Bonita* for its approach to Nassau. The pilot would take him through the Ship Channel, approaching Nassau from the south-east. According to Wyllie, this route was known only to local 'fishermen and wreckers.' But when no pilot came, Wyllie was forced to make for the port on his own. He had been instructed not to attempt to use the common entrance, known as the Hole-in-the-Wall, to the north of Eleuthera. This route was monitored, and the *Bonita* might be seen – or, worse, captured – if that way was attempted. So Wyllie resolved to hazard the Ship Channel in order to make it to Nassau in a short time without being noticed. Without a local pilot, this was very risky decision; between the Ship Channel and Nassau lay some 30 miles of shallow reef and rock. Drawing just over 17 feet, the *Bonita* made its way in, west by north-west. Wyllie took the ship at a snail's pace, taking soundings all around the ship. Luckily, the ship made it over half the distance without more than a light graze of the reef. But then around 15 miles from safety the ship struck the reef and stuck fast. The *Bonita* was now a sitting duck. Wyllie recounted that he had, in his own words, a 'bad half hour' in which he could not command his men, and he sulked in his cabin, contemplating his fate. He feared that his first command would fall prey to a 'lubberly Yankee tub.' However, he snapped out of his melancholy as inspiration struck. On consulting his logs he noticed that they had entered the channel at low tide. Soon the water would rise … but would it be enough to free the ship? Several hours passed, during which time, thankfully, no Yankee tub came to capture them, and then finally the hull cleared the reef and they were able to make progress again. Wyllie quickly made for Nassau, even then, ever cautious as they went, scraping and bumping along at several points. The exact date of arrival is not recorded, but it was reported in the *Nassau Guardian* that the *Bonita* had arrived with 'a cargo of brass, iron, quinine, etc.' sometime before 13 October.[98] Wyllie himself recounted that for a day or two he was made a 'little lion of', possibly being teased and scolded by more experienced captains.

NASSAU, OCTOBER 1862

In Wyllie's memoirs he notes that he was due to attempt to run the *Bonita* through the blockade from Nassau. Local officials and Union naval personnel, most notably Rear-Admiral Stephen Du Pont, also believed this was to be the case, noting on 13 November that 'the *Economist* ... with iron plates, will attempt to run in'.[99] However, for some unknown reason the *Bonita* would never again chance its luck by speeding into a Confederate port. Maybe the damage was too great to be repaired in Nassau, and it was felt it might be easy prey. Also, by the autumn of 1862 the Union blockade had been strengthened, with faster, more powerful vessels. Slower vessels found it hard to compete with these new hunters. In addition, larger ships like the *Bonita* could not clear the shallower channels and sandbars into the river mouths that led to Charleston and Wilmington. So the *Bonita* spent over a month in Nassau without attempting a run, and in the end was loaded with cotton for a return trip to Liverpool. This must have proved a massive disappointment to Wyllie, as a successful run to a Confederate port could have meant a large payday. But this disappointment would not last long, as serendipity would award Wyllie an opportunity for a much larger chance at fortune and success.

As the *Bonita* was made ready for its return to England, it took on three passengers bound for Liverpool, carrying with them important business for the State of North Carolina. These men were special commissioners appointed by the Governor of North Carolina, Zebulon Vance. Vance had been elected very recently, in September, and one of his first

Colonel Zebulon Vance (1830–1894) was just 32 years of age when he was elected Governor of North Carolina in 1862. One of his first acts was to send agents to Britain on a mission to purchase goods in aid of the state, and a steamer to bring them in through the blockade.

Courtesy of the Library of Congress

policies was to seek supplies for his state from abroad. The commissioners were to travel to Britain in order to procure supplies, and ships to transport them, to assist with the war effort and the welfare of the citizens of the Tar Heel[3*] state. As these gentlemen boarded the steamer, Wyllie would have welcomed them, and during the ensuing three-week crossing, his path to become a blockade runner would be realised.

The three men were led by John White,[100] a businessman from Warrenton, North Carolina, who had arrived in Nassau from Charleston aboard the blockade runner *Leopard.* White was seeking to sell cotton bonds to interested parties in England and he planned to use the profits to purchase and outfit a fast runner. The second commissioner, Thomas Morrow Crossan, a former officer in the US Navy, was now an officer of the nascent North Carolina State Navy. He had been tasked with identifying a suitable vessel for purchase and taking command of it. The third commissioner was Theodore J. Hughes, a businessman from New Bern, North Carolina,[101] who was being sent to England as a purchasing agent for his state. Wyllie now found himself in a superbly fortuitous situation; on board his ship for the next three weeks or so were some powerful men looking for a fast steamer, a good crew and experienced officers. Wyllie might not have made it to the blockade and its associated promised fortune on his first voyage – but providence had given him a second chance. He did not recount exact details of the voyage, but the three passengers would have been in close quarters with him as captain. During the voyage Wyllie might have been able over, say, a glass or two of port after dinner, to offer advice on the state of shipping at Liverpool and Glasgow, both cities that were home to major shipbuilders who might supply a suitable vessel. Old country ties might also have been renewed, as both White and Wyllie were Scottish – and, indeed, both from Fife: White had been born in 1814 in Kirkcaldy and had emigrated to the United States in 1828.

Wyllie's one recollection of the voyage, from one of his later public lectures on his start as a blockade runner, was that he 'met in with a Pathhead laddie in Mr John Whyte, and he had a good crack with him about old times'.[102] Pathhead was a small village just outside Kirkcaldy, near Wyllie's father's farm. The two families might well have known each other, and it is not hard to imagine that these bonds would have endeared Wyllie to White and the others. From casual reminiscences of the old country to detailed discussions of ship purchases, Wyllie appears to have made a very favourable impression upon these special commissioners.

The *Bonita* made it safely back to Liverpool on 23 December, and was there consigned to Fraser, Trenholm, the company that had sold it to Klingender in August. Its cargo was listed as 800 bales of cotton.[103] Wyllie completed all the necessary paperwork for his cargo and ships documents and stepped off the desk of the *Bonita* for good.

His connections successfully made, Wyllie would next appear in the historical record aboard the vessel that White and Crossan purchased for Governor Vance. He would leave

3* The moniker 'tar heel' had arisen from the tar industry based on the resin from the plethora of pine trees in the state.

John White (1814–1894) was sent by Governor Vance to be the state's purchasing agent in Britain, with power to issue cotton bonds in exchange for materials and, more importantly, a steamer to transport them.

Courtesy of the North Carolina Museum of History

Liverpool behind, the city he had called home for the last ten years, and make his way north to Glasgow, the place where his maritime career started, and thence on to a career on one of the most successful, and famous, blockade runners of the entire Civil War.

WAITING FOR THE CALL, JANUARY–MAY 1863

White and Crossan had quickly set about their work in England after their arrival on the *Bonita*. White approached some firms in London and Manchester, seeking buyers for his cotton bonds from the State of North Carolina. However, it would appear that he struggled to find buyers, meaning that Crossan could not yet purchase a vessel. On 7 March Crossan wrote to Vance from London to explain his situation;

> as soon as Mr White effects his purpose I will get along. I hope swimmingly. I am impatient to get off. Circumstances have detained so far beyond our wishes and expectations, but I feel assured when explained will meet your entire approbation.[104]

Wyllie remained in Liverpool during this time, possibly acting on behalf of White and Crossan. The *Bonita* made no more runs to Nassau, being sold by Klingender to the Royal Netherlands Steamship Company in early 1863,[105] then sailing from Liverpool for Amsterdam under the command of a Captain Lovins on 23 February.[106]

It would appear that Wyllie did not go back to sea at that time.[107] He too could have been waiting, like Crossan, for the bonds to be sold and the steamer purchased. The only known record of his activities in spring 1863 comes from the archives of a masonic lodge in Liverpool, which show that in March he was initiated into Mariners Lodge 249. As he had been a resident of the city while not at sea since 1852, this does not come as a surprise. He may also have visited his father at this time as well. The reverse of the only known photograph of Wyllie is marked 'Taken about 1862'. The photograph came from the studio of David Gordon in Sinclairtown, near Wyllie's father's farm in Fife. So Wyllie might have gone home to see his family, to recount some of his exploits at sea and share some of his future plans.

After months of frustration, White could finally inform Governor Vance in May that his mission was a success, the bonds could be sold, and funds released.[108] In a letter to the governor, written in Glasgow and dated 20 May, White states that Crossan had finally procured a ship.

> After many unavoidable delays and disappointments, I have at last been successful in obtaining a loan of money for the State from Messers. Alexander Collie and Company of London and Manchester, which has enabled Col.

Thomas Morrow Crossan (1819–1865) was an experienced naval officer, having served mainly on sailing warships in the US Navy. Until the time of writing it was believed that he had been in command of the Lord Clyde *as it left Scottish waters.*

Courtesy of the North Carolina Museum of History

> Crossan to purchase a steamer and me a portion of the goods required by the State. The loan or advancement made by them is predicated upon the sale of cotton at 5 pence sterling per pound …
>
> Col. Crossan will take out with him from 110 to 120 tons assorted merchandise, which will leave of what has now been bought I suppose about 150 tons that I expect to ship by a sailing vessel to Bermuda to be there in time for Col. Crossan's second cargo.

Alexander Collie & Company was an English firm, with offices in London and Manchester, which would assist White and other agents of the Confederacy in their purchases of merchandise in Britain for transportation to Bermuda and Nassau, and thence through the blockade. Now that Collies had made funds available for Crossan and White to purchase a ship for Vance on a state account, they would go on to sell interest in four other blockade runners to them.[109]

Wyllie could well have played a vital role as an aide to Crossan and White in their search for a suitable vessel for Governor Vance and North Carolina. Although a former US Naval officer, Crossan did not have any experience in Britain or with British shipping companies. But Wyllie, of course, had contacts with shipping agents in both Liverpool and Glasgow, and would have many connections with shipping masters and sailors who might be interested in serving on a steamer for North Carolina. As Crossan was searching for suitable vessels, it is quite possible that Wyllie was filling an important role as advisor and link to British shipping, allowing Crossan to find the best-suited vessels as well as experienced crews to work them.

While Crossan's search for a vessel is documented in his letters to Governor Vance, Wyllie's whereabouts is a mystery. If he had sealed the deal for employment with White and Crossan during the voyage from Nassau it is it is likely that he spent this time assisting in the search for a suitable steamer, and that ultimately this led to the purchase of the newly built Clyde steamer *Lord Clyde*.

GLASGOW, AND TO THE BLOCKADE, MAY 1863

The paddle steamer *Lord Clyde* sat on the north bank of the Clyde, opposite the town of Greenock. It was a sight to see for those who passed up and down the river. It had been brought out of the water for fouling – that is, for its hull to be cleared of the barnacles and other marine creatures that would slow it as it streaked over the waves. It had been recently purchased from the Dublin and Glasgow Sailing and Steam Packet Company, where for the first six months of its career it had been employed as a mail steamer across the Irish Sea between Glasgow and Dublin. It was steel-hulled and equipped with powerful and reliable engines, and could speed along at 18 knots. Its spacious cabins and saloons were filled with luxurious interiors, and as it had been designed to carry livestock its holds were large and easily accessed. The ultimate in steamer design, it was now being made ready for the ultimate game of cat and mouse in the stormy and heavy seas of the Atlantic and the Caribbean.

The *Lord Clyde* had been built by Caird & Company of Greenock in 1862, and was launched on 3 July. It was named after Glasgow-born Baron Clyde, Colin Campbell, a hero of both the Crimean War and the Sepoy Mutiny in India (the First War of Independence). He had been made a baron in 1858, so was eligible to sit in the House of Lords, and he was one of the celebrities of the day. On the *Lord Clyde*'s maiden voyage in September of 1862 the *Greenock Advertiser* described it thus:

> This superb steamer is 230 feet in length, 23 feet broad, and 15 feet deep. She has two masts and two funnels, and is driven by engines on the good old substantial side-lever principle, of 350 h.p. nominal, is fitted with a pair of tubular boilers fired from both ends, and has patent feathering floats. She also has steam winches, and is fitted on her very roomy fore-deck, with horse boxes, and in the hold with extensive movable accommodation for horses and cattle, most admirably ventilated … it is needless to say that every modern accommodation and luxury that experience could suggest has been adopted in fitting the ship for sea and the comfortable accommodation of passengers of every class, as well as for the conveyance of livestock and general cargo.

The design of the *Lord Clyde* made it perfect for the role of blockade runner. It was fast and was fitted with the latest engine technology that the Clyde engineers could provide. The holds were extensive and could be enlarged if the passenger saloons and accommodations were removed. The steamer's accomplishments, from its high-speed voyages across the Irish Sea to its ability to take various types and sizes of cargo, were regularly reported in Glasgow and Dublin newspapers. The *Greenock Telegraph and Clyde Shipping Gazette* noted its voyage from Dublin to Glasgow in late October 1862 as being the 'fastest on record' while carrying 'a large cargo, and a heavy deck load of cattle'.[110] The same newspaper remarked that 'the *Lord Clyde* [has] great speed, combined with good carrying and weatherly qualities [which] have been everywhere so highly spoken of'.[111]

The shape and role of this new steamer was captured in an oil painting by the famed maritime artist William Clark. Clark, who painted many nautical scenes of ships and the River Clyde from his home in Greenock, portrayed the steamer battling high seas while on a voyage from Glasgow to Dublin, and completed the work in November 1862. It was the first of what would be several artistic interpretations of the fine vessel, and shows the steamer in its civilian livery, untouched by the alterations and trials that would soon come to it as a blockade runner.[112]

The Lord Clyde *was named after Colin Campbell (1792–1863) the Glasgow-born soldier who found fame as a general during the Crimean War and in colonial India. As a result of his achievements he was made Baron Clyde in 1858.*

© CSG CIC Glasgow Museums Collection

Lord Clyde, like many Clyde steamers, was eyed for the task of running the blockade. Even before its maiden voyage, reports of steamers being sold to the Confederacy littered the local press. The *Greenock Telegraph and Clyde Shipping Gazette*, on announcing its arrival after the first voyage from Dublin on 27 September, carried an article immediately below the notification entitled 'ANOTHER CLYDE STEAMER SOLD TO THE CONFEDERACY', reporting that the 'well-known fast-sailing steamer *Ruby* has been lost to Rothesay travellers, by being sold on Tuesday to the Confederate Government.'[113] Throughout the end of 1862 and into the beginning of 1863 more and more steamers were sold for the purpose of running the blockade. By the spring of 1863 the trickle looked to become a flood: on 13 May 1863 the United States Consul in Glasgow reported to the Federal government that:

> within the past three weeks, it is my painful duty to inform you, not less than thirteen of the fastest and best light-draft steamers of the Clyde have been purchased by various parties to run into the blockaded ports on our coast. Some of the purchases have been made, I have reason to believe, by agents of the Confederate Government and for it. Most of them, however, have been made as bold and gambling adventures by private parties allured by the enormous but in most cases, no doubt, falsely reputed profits of the enterprise.'[114]

Listed among the vessels thus identified was the *Lord Clyde.* Four months after his arrival in Britain, Crossan's efforts to secure a vessel finally came to fruition when the successful sale of the *Lord Clyde* was announced in the *Greenock Advertiser* on 23 April 1863 for the sum of £34,000.[115] This was a week before White reported the sale of the North Carolina cotton bonds to Governor Vance. Exact details of the transaction and business dealings between Crossan and the Dublin and Glasgow Steam Packet Company can only be guessed at as the company records are not known to have survived; but what is known is that this was not the first time the company had done business with Confederate interests. In 1861 it had sold the *Herald* (latterly named *Antonica)* to Fraser, Trenholm & Company, and in early 1862 it began running into Charleston. The *Havelock* (renamed *General Beauregard*) was sold in November 1862, and quickly made its way out of the Clyde. Both were well-known passenger steamers, and their purchase and removal from service was widely reported.[116] Both went on to have a highly successful careers as runners, being operated by the Chicora Importing and Exporting Company of Charleston, before their destruction by Union ships within weeks of each other in December 1863.[117] The *Lord Clyde* had been built as a passenger steamer to replace these vessels, but it too was quickly snapped up as a runner.

The *Lord Clyde* had one final duty while serving on its original Irish Sea route: to transport the 3rd (King's Own) Hussar Regiment from Dublin to Glasgow, a task that would be completed on 15 May. The *Scotsman* newspaper reported that the *Lord Clyde* 'after fulfilment of this contract … will be handed over to the Emperor of China, who has lately been speculating so largely in the purchase of British steamers'.[118] The 'Emperor of China' was a well-known British press euphemism for Confederate agents looking to buy fast steamers.

This brisk trade in steamers was good news for the shareholders, and in 1863 the company directors offered their shareholders, in addition to the usual dividend of 6 per cent, 'owing to exceptional circumstances, having realised a considerable profit by the sale of two of the company's vessels, a bonus of £5 per share, both free of income tax.'[119]

The new owner of the *Lord Clyde* was not Thomas Crossan or John White, but a John Key[120] (sometimes spelled Kay), a successful steam engine manufacturer whose works were located in Kirkcaldy. There he built maritime engines, a lucrative trade in Scotland if your products were robust and reliable. However, in 1863 he was not in the business of owning paddle steamers. The mystery is how he came to be associated with the sale of the *Lord Clyde* at all. An answer could be family ties, as it turns out that he was brother-in-law to John White, having married White's sister Sarah in 1845. No records of transactions between White and Key are known to exist, but the family connection would make sense if a Confederate agent wished to mask a sale of a British paddle steamer. As Key was a Scot, his ownership would help maintain the fiction that the *Lord Clyde* was merely a British merchant vessel, being British built, registered and owned. Thus, if the vessel was captured, the argument could be made that it was not a Confederate supply ship but a neutral British merchantman. Shortly after the purchase of the *Lord Clyde*, Key established his own shipyard in Kinghorn, Fife.[121] It can only be speculated that he might have benefited from an injection of funds for his part in the sale of the *Lord Clyde*, thus helping him in setting up his new works.[122]

Key's assistance was deemed so vital that after the war the State of North Carolina offered him a financial reward. This he refused, but his wife was presented with a silver coffee service which was inscribed:

> Presented together with a Coffee and Tea Service to Mrs. John Key, by John White, T.M. Crossan and T J Hughes of North Carolina as a mark of their esteem for the disinterested and valuable services rendered to the State by her husband 1863.[123]

The service was purchased some time before 1967 by Mrs H.W. Palmer, grand-daughter of John White. In a letter to the editor in the 1 November 1967 edition of *The State Down-home in North Carolina*, Mrs Palmer gave a brief history of John White's role in the war and how she came to own the set, by purchasing it from Mrs M.W. Hutchison of London, the great-grand-daughter of John Key.[4*]

Crossan was not mentioned in any of the local Glasgow newspaper reports at the time, but descriptions like 'American Confederate Government', 'agent of the American Government', 'American Account', and 'Transatlantic Account' were all used with regard to Confederate representatives seeking to purchase vessels. These could have alluded to Crossan as well as the other private and government agents in Scotland at the time. Interestingly, one report stated that the famous Confederate agent James Bulloch was in Glasgow seeking new runners, and was followed by an 'Agent of the North'. Bulloch was one of the Confederacy's chief agents in Britain during the war. He had sailed for Liverpool just after the start of the conflict, and worked there with Fraser, Trenholm to further the interests of the Confederate cause. He was responsible for arranging for the purchase of vessels to run the blockade, the sale of cotton run via these vessels, and the construction of armed raiders such as the *Alabama* and the *Florida* for the Confederate Navy. He was a character known to the British press and so any new purported sales of paddle steamers might indeed mention his name. Crossan, on the other hand, was relatively unknown, and his movements might have been confused with those of Bulloch. The report of Bulloch in Glasgow in the *Glasgow Morning Journal* of 23 May stated that he sailed on the *Lord Clyde*, and although this ties in with the time of departure of the vessel, no other records indicate that Bulloch was involved with the sale or repurposing of the *Lord Clyde*.

4* The whereabouts of this set, if indeed it still exists, is not known. There are several silver service sets in the governor's mansion of North Carolina, and it was once thought that one of these might be the one given to Key. But none match the description and engraving as given.

It was at the Customs House at Greenock (left) on 22 May 1863 that Wyllie took official command of the Lord Clyde *and prepared it for its transatlantic voyage.*

Courtesy of McLean Museum and Art Gallery, Inverclyde Council

From the outset it was known that the vessel would be sailing for the blockade. In a report on the final voyage on the Dublin to Glasgow route, the *Dublin Evening Freeman* reported that 'this fine vessel now bids farewell to the Dublin and Glasgow route, as she leaves for the 'Land of the West' in a few days, having been purchased by an agent of the American Government'. The agent was of course Crossan, and although he represented the State of North Carolina, not the Confederate government, the newspaper left no room for doubt that the vessel would soon be a blockade runner. The news made it across the Atlantic as early as 18 May, when the sale was reported in New York. The *Brooklyn Daily Eagle* informed its readers that the *Lord Clyde*, having arrived on the Clyde after its last voyage through the Irish Sea, had been reported (by the *Glasgow Morning Journal*) as being on its way west, and 'is to go into dock here to be examined and cleaned, and thereafter will fit out for a passage across the Atlantic'.[124]

Previous histories of the *Lord Clyde* have placed Crossan in command, but new evidence suggests this is not correct. In White's 20 May letter to Governor Vance, in which he states that a vessel had been purchased, he writes that Crossan will be taking it out. However there are no historical records associating Crossan with the steamer while it was in British waters.

Crossan was certainly an experienced mariner, having graduated from the US Naval Academy as a midshipman in 1836. He had served on several navy vessels, both sailing ships and steamers, completing tours during the Mexican–American war aboard the sloop *Albany*,[125] and when promoted to lieutenant he commanded the steamer *Despatch* during a tour of the Gulf of Mexico.[126] His final assignment before resigning his commission in 1857 was aboard the frigate *Cumberland*. Then at the start of the Civil War, Crossan joined the new North Carolina State Navy and in June 1861 was made master of the *Warren Winslow*, the first ship it purchased. He commanded the steamer for several months, harrying Union cargo ships and capturing four vessels.[127] His command of the *Warren Winslow* ended in November 1861 after it struck a submerged rock in Ocracoke Inlet, east of New Bern, North Carolina.

Crossan's 21 years in the US Navy and his brief role in the North Carolina State Navy made him a very experienced mariner, but having served on only one steamer, and one that at that had been built as early as 1852, might he have sought the assistance of a mariner who was more familiar with modern steamer design and technology? Wyllie was certainly experienced in this field, having been first mate or master on four modern steam-powered vessels. He had also crossed the Atlantic four times in 1862, making him acutely aware of how to deal with the dangers posed by the open waters of the great ocean. He was well prepared for the role that Crossan presented him with on the *Lord Clyde*, and would have been an excellent tutor in modern British steamers for the experienced Crossan.

Contemporary newspapers reports list Wyllie as master, and when the certificate of registry for the *Lord Clyde* was amended on 21 May 1863 it confirmed the transfer of command from John Stephen Byrne to him.[128] In addition the Agreement for a Foreign Going Ship for the *Lord Clyde* makes very interesting reading. It states that the vessel at the time of its sailing was British owned, mastered and crewed. Not a single American is listed in the crew or noted as a passenger. Several of the crew had previously been on vessels with Wyllie when he was based in Liverpool, including the carpenter Charles MacMillan who had served him on the steamers *Hope* and *Bonita*, indicating that Wyllie himself would have been involved in the recruitment of the crew. This would make sense, as although White and Crossan had the funds to purchase a vessel and the nautical skills to command it, as foreign envoys they would have little or no connection to the current maritime employment situation in Liverpool or Glasgow. Retained by Wyllie from the previous crew of the *Lord Clyde* were the first engineer Alexander Roy and second engineer Thomas Miller, both highly important for the forthcoming Atlantic crossing. Wyllie's knowledge thus proved critical in gathering the first crew for North Carolina's new runner.

The first mention in the press presenting Wyllie as master was on 23 May 1863, when it was reported that the vessel had been taken out a few days before into the Gareloch, a sea loch arm of the Firth of Clyde, just to the north of Greenock, to swing (adjust) its compasses.[129] As already noted, Wyllie was a highly experienced British mariner familiar

GREENOCK ADVERTISER.

AND CLYDE COMMERCIAL JOURNAL.

The Lord Clyde.—This fine steamer crossed to Gareloch on Thursday to adjust compasses, and afterwards sailed for Nassau *via* Cardiff. She had on board coals and a few cases containing medicine and surgical instruments. She is commanded by Captain Wylie.

The news that Wyllie was master of the Lord Clyde *was reported a day after he took command.*

Newspaper image © The British Library Board. All rights reserved. With thanks to The British Newspaper Archive (www.britishnewspaperarchive.co.uk)

with the waters of the Clyde and Mersey. Having him in command at this point would seem a sensible move. It could also be noted that by listing Wyllie as master, the true nature of the *Lord Clyde* could once again be masked, as Wyllie was not a recognised Confederate agent or captain. However, as already shown, this was a dead argument as the *Lord Clyde* was known to have been sold to Confederate agents who intended it for the blockade. So would using Wyllie as a cover really have made any difference to Crossan's intentions?

Under Wyllie's command the *Lord Clyde* set off from Greenock on 21 May. It was the day before his 35th birthday, and so there was more than just the commencement of his blockade-running career to celebrate. The destination was given as Nassau via Cardiff. Initially the cargo of the *Lord Clyde* was said to be military in nature, with up to 130,000 lbs of gunpowder on board. But this was a mistaken report, as that cargo had actually been shipped on the *Claymore*, destined for Singapore and Penang. In fact the *Lord Clyde* carried from Greenock a cargo of 43 boxes, 2 casks and 15 kegs, 1,150 yards of cotton goods, chemical products to the value of £20, surgical instruments to the value of £350, and medicines to the value of £500.[130] The mistaken reporting of gunpowder as cargo can be viewed as part of the wider mystery surrounding any vessel bound for the blockade. The uncertainty and clandestine nature of the purchase and sailing of these vessels led to some hyperbole in the press; any steamer that put to sea might be made ready for use for a raider or be carrying contraband cargo. The reports of vessels bound for the blockade from the docks and shipyards fed the daily news in Liverpool and Glasgow, some of it proving to be rather too rich.

Wyllie steered the vessel down the Firth of Clyde and made a dash towards the Irish Sea, hugging the coast, skirting the Mull of Galloway at Scotland's south-western tip, down past the Isle of Man and the Welsh coast at Holyhead. The steamer made great time, travelling the 280 miles in only 26½ hours, arriving at Cardiff docks on the evening of 22 May. The speed was listed in the Glasgow papers as 14.5 knots, but it was noted it could have been higher if necessary and that the steamer had faced a foul tide for most of the journey. The final destination, after coaling in Cardiff, was given as the Celestial Emperor, another title for the Emperor of China. [131]

The sailing was noted in the *Liverpool Mercury* as being that of a 'Suspected *Alabama*,' meaning that the *Lord Clyde* might be taking up a raider role instead of that of an unarmed blockade runner. Such was the hysteria at that time that that any fast, new British ships known to have been purchased by Confederate agents might be seen as heading out to sea armed and ready for a fight with the Union's navy.

When the steamer arrived in Cardiff the *Cardiff Times* listed Wyllie as master, stating 'The *Lord Clyde* is commanded by a Scotchman, who appears well qualified for the position' and it gave the following description of the vessel, leaving no doubt as to its purpose:

> She is a new vessel, fitted up in a manner which has made Clyde-built vessels world-renowned; and it appears to be an axiom at the present moment, that a vessel built on the Clyde has some mysterious connexion or other with the Confederates.[132]

The only listing of cargo when it arrived in Cardiff was 'Sundries, not to be discharged'. This was from the Arrivals listing in the *Cardiff and Merthyr Guardian, Glamorgan, Monmouth, and Brecon Gazette* of 29 May 1863, which listed the vessel as registered in Kirkcaldy.[133] The error would have arisen from the Agreement of Foreign Going Ships, which listed John Key of Kirkcaldy as the owner.

The *Lord Clyde* had to be moored outside Cardiff's tidal dock as its paddle boxes were too wide for the lock gates. There, more cargo was taken on, and best Welsh coal filled the bunkers for the trip across the Atlantic. The official record from the bill of entry office shows that the *Lord Clyde* took with it 343 tons of coal, 2 cases of clothing, 46 bales of blankets, 99 bales of woollens, 9 bales of hosiery, 37 cases shoes, 6 cases cotton and 6 cases woollen shirts.[134] The Cardiff records make no mention of the medicines, chemicals and surgical instruments noted in the Greenock papers. The broker for the cargo was listed as T.J. Hughes, the commissioner from North Carolina who, it would appear, was not in the crew but would go on to take on the role of purser of the *Lord Clyde* once the ship had made it to Nassau.[5*]

Its presence at the docks was noticed by the United States consul in the city, Charles Dexter Cleveland. Cleveland had been appointed by President Lincoln as consul in 1861

5* The purser listed in the crew agreement was Hugh Ronald of Ayrshire. Of note was that this was listed as his first ever voyage and so he was an inexperienced holder of a vital role on board.

Charles Dexter Cleveland (1802–1869) was the first American official who attempted to stop the Lord Clyde. *As the US Consul in Cardiff, he forced a search for contraband while the steamer was in port.*

Courtesy of Archives and Special Collections, Dickinson College, Carlisle, Pennsylvania

after serving as professor of Latin at the University of New York. He was described as a proponent of international peace and the abolition of slavery.[135] On being alerted to the arrival of the *Lord Clyde*, he suspected the paddle steamer was intended to supply the Confederacy, and applied directly to Earl Russell, the British foreign secretary, to have the vessel inspected for contraband of war. As the *Lord Clyde* was awaiting its final cargo to be delivered by the South Wales Railway, the local collector of customs was ordered to board and search the vessel. The search was recorded by Consul Cleveland in a letter published in the *Boston Traveller* dated 15 July:[136]

> I sent you a Cardiff paper with an article on 'Consular Interference.' I have had a great deal of trouble and anxiety as regards the steamer *Lord Clyde*. She came into the east basin, right opposite my office, on Saturday, the 23d, a little after noon. I had my suspicions aroused concerning her, and [???] going alongside I saw she was very sharp, and evidently, a very swift sailer. At the gangway was posted, 'No admission except on business,' I set a man to watch her. On Sunday P.M. I felt uneasy and walked down to the east dock; was surprised not [???] see her there; went on further and found her still in the basin, and alongside of her a large coal barge partly emptied. She had been taking in coal all the previous night. I felt there was no time to be lost. I went home and wrote to the Collector my suspicions. After church, at 8 o'clock, I took a carriage and rode out to his country residence, about three miles. He

received me most kindly, and after reading my letter said he was ready to do what I wanted, I said that the steamer ought to be forbidden taking anything in at night. He said it should be done. Come with me in the carriage to town, and thence to the docks. We went on board; it was quite dark, and we had to go down by a ladder. The Collector, of course, went first. As he got on the deck, a man who was walking guard said, 'You can't come here, Sir.'

'Do you know whom you are speaking to? Speak so again and I will send you to the Police station. Go tell your master, the Captain, that the Collector of Customs wishes to see him.' Accordingly he went, and the Captain soon emerged from the cabin. Said Mr. MILLER, 'I am the Collector of Customs; I understand you have been taking in coal to-night -- and I forbid your taking in any more till 6 o'clock to-morrow morning.'

The next day I wrote to Mr. ADAMS, and the Collector wrote to his authorities. Tuesday came and no reply to either. In the meantime I thought the steamer would sail on Thursday; and on Wednesday I wrote to the Collector, entering my solemn protest against her sailing without being searched. I took the letter to him myself. He would have been glad to do it, had he authority.

Thursday came, and the Collector had received no message.

On Friday night, a little before 10, Mr. MILLER rode up to my house and showed me a telegram just received from the Admiralty at London -- 'Search the suspected packages forthwith.' He asked me to go with him, and try to find two laboring men, of whom I had told him, who came to me privately, (as they had worked on board of the steamer,) and told me where the suspicious bales and cases were. It was near 12 before I found them.

In the meantime, the Collector, with his men, 22 in number, had gone on board, and begun their search. When I got the men down in front of my office, I sent for the Collector from the steamer. He came. The men told him that the packages were in the after hold, under the lower cabin, and that coal was piled up in front. The Collector then went on board, and told the Captain he must go into the suspected place, and examine. So the Captain had a portion of the floor taken up. They opened a number of bales, &c., and found various soldiers' clothing, blankets, &c., but no guns nor ammunition; and as she was going to Nassau, she could not be stopped, and went next morning. Of course, I wrote early, and afterward to Messrs. SEWARD and WELLES[137], all about her. My opinion is that she is to be converted into a light-armed steamer to prey on our commerce. She is very fast.

In his last line, Consul Cleveland expressed a concern that the *Lord Clyde* was to be turned into a raider, as the Liverpool papers had reported. Despite this concern, with no contraband found on board the collector of customs could not hold the ship in port. So after the search, possibly sensing more interference from the local authorities, and taking advantage of a favourable tide, Wyllie quickly took the *Lord Clyde* to sea. So quickly, in fact, that the ship broker John Owen was still on board as the steamer made its way into the Bristol Channel and had to be landed by boat at Ilfracombe on the Cornish coast, fully 39 miles from Cardiff.[138]

The events in Cardiff were widely reported across Britain and America. The *Western Democrat* of Charlotte, North Carolina, noted that the *Lord Clyde* had been searched (it mistakenly asserted that this had been done at Liverpool), and the paper's editor angrily complained, 'Why don't the English authorities search Yankee vessels?'

Consul Cleveland's description of the *Lord Clyde* and its cargo match the official records from both Greenock and Cardiff. He had reason to believe that a ship coming from the Clyde was to be fitted out as a raider, as the local *Cardiff and Merthyr Guardian* had reported the news from Liverpool that a new *Alabama* would soon sail from Glasgow.[139] So when the *Lord Clyde* appeared, he had rushed to try and get it detained and searched. The news of this threat had also reached the Union Navy, with Captain John Winslow of the *Kearsarge* noting in a letter to Secretary of the Navy Gideon Wells:

> Information has just been received that a new *Alabama*, late *Lord Clyde*, had got out of Cardiff under Commander Bulloch. I shall proceed as soon as provided to Madeira, thence to the Western Islands, in hopes of intercepting this new freebooter.

The letter being dated 14 June from Cadiz would have meant that this effort would have been in vain, as by 4 June the *Lord Clyde* had made Fayal (Faial) in the Azores.[140] We know that the *Lord Clyde* had always been intended to be a blockade runner for the State of North Carolina, but with the CSS *Alabama* and other British-built raiders causing havoc on the high seas, any reports of fast, steel-hulled vessels during this time aroused suspicions and fears of vessels converted from merchantmen to armed raiders.

It should be noted that in none of the newspaper reports from Cardiff is anyone other than Wyllie mentioned as master of the *Lord Clyde*. Indeed, although the steamer was thought to be headed to the blockade, no Confederate officers or crew were listed, even in passing. T.J. Hughes, the commissioner from North Carolina, was only mentioned as the shipper of cargo aboard the steamer, and not identified as a Confederate.[141] If Thomas Crossan was on board, his presence went unnoticed.

The *Lord Clyde*, loaded with a cargo for the State of North Carolina, now set out on its career as a blockade runner. But as it slipped the lines, paddles splashing noisily as the steam pressure built up for full speed on course for the Caribbean, it was Joannes Wyllie who was on the deck, orders in hand, compass set, bellowing orders as commander of this speedy greyhound on its way out to its dangerous Atlantic voyage.

BERMUDA JUNE 1863

The *Lord Clyde* made the voyage to Bermuda in just 15 days, arriving at St George's on 14 June. There the official records of inward ships listed the commander of the vessel as J. Wyllie. While the steamer lay in the harbour it was reported as receiving modifications intended to make it ready for its role as blockade runner. Although as a fast steamer it was well suited to outrun the blockading vessels, its appearance as an Irish Sea steamer was not conducive to its new occupation. Physical alterations to camouflage the blockade runners had become necessary as the war progressed and the strength of the blockade fleet increased. In early 1862 the slow and distinctively painted, tall-masted *Bonita* might have evaded the Federal warships, but by the summer of 1863 any vessel, even a sleek paddle steamer like the *Lord Clyde*, required alterations to increase its chance of success. So it was painted light grey to help hide it on the open water, and its topmasts and spars were removed to lower its profile against the horizon. More space in the hold was turned over to bunkers to enable it to steam at high speed for long periods if so required. The *Lord Clyde* spent eight days in harbour at Bermuda, and would have left sooner had it not been delayed by waiting for a suitable Wilmington pilot. The customs manifest for the steamer notes that the cargo from Cardiff had not been unloaded, while an extra 100 bags of coffee, 180 kegs of rum and 69 boxes of brandy were loaded, adding a bit of luxury to the more utilitarian items carried from Britain.

The only known photograph of the Ad-Vance *as a blockade runner. The location and date are noted as Nassau, 1863. The steamer is sitting very high in the water, possibly beached, appearing to be having its hull painted. Flying from the stern pole is a Confederate flag, indicating the steamer's new allegiance.*

© CSG CIC Glasgow Museums Collection

A close-up view of the photograph, tantalisingly fuzzy, shows four men, some of them bearded, and one of whom may be Joannes Wyllie. The man at the top of the paddle box appears to be looking directly at the photographer through field glasses or binoculars.

© CSG CIC Glasgow Museums Collection

The steamer finally left for Nassau on 22 June. Wyllie's name continued to be associated with the command of the vessel, as both US consular reports and *The New York Times* mentioned the Scotsman.[142] Crossan's name was once again noticeably absent from the records.

In reports up until this point the vessel's name is listed as *Lord Clyde*, but that would soon change. As it now found a new role, so would it find a suitable name for its new career; it was rechristened *Ad-Vance*.[6*] The exact meaning and spelling of the name have been debated since the time of the war: *A.D. Vance* was a version said to be in homage to the wife of Governor Vance; her name was Adelaide, and as she was known as Addie the steamer's name was pronounced *Ahh-Dee Vance* in her honour. Another explanation was that *Ad-Vance* was used as the vessel was 'Advancing to Vance'. Contemporary archival reports vary, but Governor Vance himself refers to the steamer as *Ad-Vance* in his correspondence during the war, and James Sprunt, a former crew member who would later go on to write an account of his time on board, stated that it was *Ad-Vance* and not *A.D. Vance.*[143]

The *Ad-Vance* was ready for its first run, and at its helm, according to all contemporary reports and primary sources, was Joannes Wyllie, not Thomas Crossan. From Glasgow to Cardiff to Bermuda, it was Wyllie's name that was associated with the vessel and he who dealt with all issues arising from its voyage, from readying it for sea in Glasgow, to fielding the customs searches in Cardiff, to overseeing the blockade conversions in Bermuda. Stephen Wise, in his book *Lifeline of the Confederacy*, also notes that it was Wyllie who had brought the *Ad-Vance* to Wilmington from Britain. This goes against the view that Crossan became master only when the *Ad-Vance* began its blockade-running career.

The only known account of the first run through the blockade comes from Wyllie himself, taken from *The People's Friend*. Wyllie gives a detailed personal description of the readiness and professionalism of the steamer's crew as it set off on the first run, to cover the 570-nm between Nassau and the coast of North Carolina under the cover of darkness.

6* The ship's name was given in spellings ranging from *Ad-Vance, to A.D. Vance, AD.Vance* and *Advance*. For want of clarity, it will be referred to as *Ad-Vance* unless the title forms part of a contemporary quote or source whose original has been reprinted in this book.

Waiting for them were patrolling Union warships, constantly keeping watch for any vessels that might be seeking to break their blockade. At Nassau they took on a skilled pilot whose job was to guide the steamer through the shallow waters and ever-changing sandbanks along the approaches to the Cape Fear River. The real danger of blockade running was now upon Wyllie and the crew, along with the incentive of the promised rewards – if they were successful. Wyllie's account does not list any names of crew members or officers, but he does indicate that it was he who was in command:

> [F]irst run in with a cargo of bacon and clothes for the Southern army. When the night came on he had got into a fairly good position. Every aperture through which a ray of light could penetrate was carefully screened. Every man took his station, and every heart beat high with hope, excitement, and expectation. The captain and pilot were on the bridge, with the men at the wheel standing quite near. All the firemen in the stock-hole. All the sailors were standing round the bulwarks scanning every point, and the look-out men were on the paddle boxes, one on each. Anxiously they looked for what they did not want to see. From one of the paddle boxes came the distinct whisper, 'A steamer three points on the starboard bow.' 'How standing?' 'Northward.' 'All right, Starboard a little, and steady, steady.' The danger passes. They creep slowly on. Another whisper from the paddle box. 'A vessel right ahead, sir.' 'Stop her' is the word to the engineers; 'and stand ready for a run.' The pilot hints she keeps a careless look out. Says one of the paddle box men, scarcely above his breath, 'she is moving Southward.' 'East ahead,' is the captain's order. A few minutes of almost intolerable suspense and the outer cordon is safely passed. Slowly they glide along till they come within the range of the second line. 'Two vessels on the port side,' from the husky voice of a seaman in the bow. 'Another, a quarter of a point further to port.' 'Another, right ahead and heading down on us.' A whew and a hiss from a lively rocket. 'We are seen. Full speed ahead.' Then the fiddlers play up, and the dance becomes lively. A flash and a roar. A shot passes between their masts. 'Well fired,' shouts the captain. 'Now give it her, stokers and enginemen.' The sky is all scored with pencils of fire. The cannon boom. The hunt is up. The dogs close about the hare. The iron rain continues; but, thank goodness, not a drop has fallen on the engines. The *Advance* has cleared the circle of death, but is still within range of the cruiser's guns. 'Stop her,' or the good ship *Advance* will be run ashore. And 'stop her,' is the word, and 'stopped she is.' The signalman plies his lamps, while the shot hurtle and splash about them. It has only taken about two minutes to make the signal, but to our eager-hearted captain, with all his blood up and all his energies on the strain, it has seemed an hour. Two lights are placed on the beach. The pilot knows his work. 'Pile on the agony, boys' is

> the captain's word to the stokers. 'Give it her, engineers, double full steam if you can.' The *Advance* plunges forward. Thanks to the darkness, her colour, and the absence of every ray of light from her hull, not a shot strikes her. The pace is hot, but in a few minutes they are over the bar, and the blockade had been run. 'Grog-o for all hands, and flowing bumpers!' There is light in every eye, triumph on every brow.

The true issue of who was in command of the *Lord Clyde/Ad-Vance*, however, continues to be murky right up until the moment when it sailed into the Cape Fear River and up to Wilmington at the end of this first successful run of the blockade (see Appendix 1).

WILMINGTON, JUNE 1863

As the sun rose on the horizon, a new day broke over the river. The loud reports of the guns from the previous evening were now long-gone echoes. That night yet another skirmish had occurred in the continuing conflict, but the heated chase had not led to a capture and the prey had escaped. The *Ad-Vance* had made the mouth of the Cape Fear River. It had come over the bar, slowed its engines and allowed the steam to die down. After a night of evading the eager Union fleet, the *Ad-Vance*'s crew and cargo were safely under the watchful eye of the guns of Fort Fisher. Now they were forced to wait out their time in quarantine, like all other vessels, by a sandbar just below the city. (The quarantine system is detailed in Chapter 4, as part of the history of Wilmington.) As soon as the health of the ship and crew could be confirmed, it headed to the wharfs of Wilmington, where its cargo was be unloaded. Wyllie, Crossan and the men of the *Ad-Vance* had succeeded in their long Atlantic voyage and had passed through the hornets' nest, and were now successful runners.

The date was 26 June 1863, and the local press remarked that its cargo was 'clothing for our soldiers'.[144] This description matched both the customs reports from Cardiff and the description of items shipped by White in his letter to Vance on 20 May. Listed as being in command was Colonel Crossan, the first time he had been identified as master of the ship in any news source. Yet his true role was still not quite clear. The *Wilmington Daily Journal* of 29 June[145] included the following news item:

> The iron steamer *Clyde*[146] arrived at our wharfs yesterday afternoon. She is a fine looking vessel, and is said to bring a cargo on State account. Captain T. Crossan comes in command of her, we believe. He comes in her at any rate.

To add importance to the arrival of his new ship, Vance himself hurried from the state capital, Raleigh, by train to Wilmington to see the steamer. After his arrival in the city he went downriver to the quarantine station. Colonel James G. Burr, who at the time was in the 7th Regiment Home Guard, Armory Guards, based at Wilmington, recalled the event:

> In the spring of 1863 the *Advance* made her first successful trip through the blockaders and arrived safely in the harbour of Wilmington, bringing a large amount of much needed supplies. The Governor (Vance) was informed of her arrival and came to Wilmington immediately, and the next day, Sunday, went down on one of the river steamers with a number of his friends to the ship, which was lying at the quarantine station about fifteen or sixteen miles below the city. After spending several hours on board examining the ship and partaking of the hospitalities of its officers, he was determined to take her up to the city without waiting for a permit from the health officers, as it was assumed the Governor's presence on board would be justification for the violation of quarantine regulations. Accordingly steam was raised and she came up to the city and was made fast to the wharf in front of the Custom House. This was objected to by Major Strong, aide-de-camp to General Whiting,[147] as being in violation of quarantine regulations, and he ordered the vessel to return to her quarantine berth. But the Chairman of the Board of Commissions of Navigation was sent for and he gave a permit for the vessel to remain where she was, and for all persons who wished to land do so.
>
> The *Advance* was a first class ship in every respect and had engines of great power and very highly finished, and her speed was good … Her officers were Captain Crossan, commander; Captain Wylie, a Scotchman, who came over with her, sailing master.[148]

Governor's Vance's visit was a significant moment, both for him and for the crew of *Ad-Vance*. As he had only been elected in September the previous year, the arrival of his first blockade runner with supplies for his state would have been both a personal and a political victory: the *Ad-Vance* was owned by the state, and thus its success would be vital for the martial and domestic success of North Carolina during the war. To be able to show off his prize to the people of Wilmington, and to be seen on it, was an important public relations moment for Vance. His initial reaction to the steamer and its cargo is recorded in a letter to White dated 10 July in which Vance states

> Col. Crossan has arrived safely with the steamer and cargo. I am much pleased with the result of your negotiations and approve most cordially of your whole conduct.'[149]

Wilmington during the Civil War. Previously a minor trading centre, the town was pressed into service as a main port for the Confederacy.

Courtesy of New Hanover County Public Library, Wilmington Harbor Collection.

For the officers and crew it was the end of their first voyage and, it would appear from the account, they were to be congratulated and celebrated. Crossan, having completed his task, had returned home a hero. He is listed in overall command at this point, with Wyllie being listed for the first time in American sources as the sailing master and also as a 'Scotchman'.[150] He too would have been received by Governor Vance, congratulated on his safe arrival and introduced to Carolinian politics. No recollections are recorded of this first meeting between the two men, but we might speculate that the governor could have asked about Wyllie's nautical record, Wyllie then entertaining him, in his known comfortable and emotive style, with some of his daring exploits on his previous ships like the *Hope* and *Indian Queen*. Or perhaps Vance might have asked how he came to be master of the *Ad-Vance*, with Joannes responding about the connection made with John White during the voyage of the *Bonita* and tales of family back in their 'old country' of Scotland. Vance, himself only 33 years of age, would see a man of similar age whose knowledge and maritime skills had brought home his prize. In any case, this first meeting was the start of a good relationship that would last for the next 15 months that Wyllie served aboard Vance's new blockade runner.

MASTER, COMMANDER ... BOTH

Now that the *Ad-Vance* had arrived at Wilmington the issue of command appears to have been settled: Crossan was formally named commander and Wyllie sailing master. Whether or not he was in fact the commander, what we can be certain of is that Wyllie was involved in the command of the *Ad-Vance* from its first days of ownership by the State of North Carolina while still on the Clyde until this arrival outside the Custom House at Wilmington. Wyllie is listed as master in all British newspaper reports and primary sources, and Crossan's name is not to be found in any contemporary maritime sources, as either master or captain, until the *Ad-Vance's* passage up the Cape Fear River.

Wyllie's listing as master could have been a subterfuge by the North Carolina commissioners to mask the true purpose of the purchase and use of the *Ad-Vance*. But, as illustrated by the articles in the Glasgow and British newspapers, the purpose of the *Ad-Vance* was to be a blockade runner, like many other fast steamers from the Clyde purchased by American agents in the spring of 1863. So, if Wyllie's listing had indeed been intended to be a cover, it was blown out of the water before he ever set about adjusting the vessel's compasses.

To have a North Carolinian in charge of the state's valuable investment was the prudent and political move for Governor Vance. Crossan fitted the bill perfectly, as a former naval commander and time-served member of the state's navy. But his lack of recent maritime experience, especially on British-built vessels, meant that an experienced British master was a useful addition to Vance's great purchase. Wyllie was the perfect sailing master to Crossan's commander, a relationship that would prove most successful as the *Ad-Vance* now set about its blockade-running career.

With the quayside celebrations and visitations complete at Wilmington, the *Ad-Vance* now made ready for its next run. Cotton bales were tightly packed – as many as the steamer could take – and its bunkers were replenished with coal, and its crew set off on the 670-nm voyage to Bermuda. As the ship steamed away from Wilmington, down the Cape Fear River, Wyllie would once again be hoping to make this run a good one, not knowing at the time that he would in fact become one of the most successful commanders of any blockade runner of the war.

4

ONTO THE BLOCKADE

Captain Wyllie is a warm hearted Scotchman ... big, burly and red faced, full of enthusiasm, full of poetry.

– From the diary of Reverend Moses D. Hoge,
passenger on board the *Ad-Vance*, October 1863

PART I

July 1863 was one of the most desperate months of the entire Civil War, beginning with carnage in the fields and hills around Gettysburg, Pennsylvania. There, General Robert E. Lee's Army of Northern Virginia met the Army of the Potomac led by General Meade, and over the course of three days over 50,000 casualties were sustained. It was the bloodiest battle in American history, and one that both sides had hoped would be a turning point in the war. Just a day later, as Lee's Confederate forces were retreating southwards towards Virginia, the city of Vicksburg, Mississippi, fell to Union forces. This strategic point on the Mississippi river had been under siege for six weeks, and its capture further squeezed the Confederacy, closing off its land routes for trade and external help. Leading the Union forces at Vicksburg was Major General Ulysses S. Grant, destined to become the North's most successful commander. But these victories did not end the war, and although some might sense that the tide was indeed turning there were still years of struggle ahead. Now, even more than before, the Confederacy needed its supplies to be maintained by the fleet of blockade runners making their runs through the Atlantic waves.

While these momentous events were unfolding, Joannes Wyllie and the crew of the *Ad-Vance* remained at the dock in Wilmington, awaiting their chance to steam down the Cape Fear River, past the guns of Fort Fisher and Fort Caswell, and out through the lurking ships of the blockade. The steamer's crew spent the next month loading cargo and awaiting the most opportune time to start their journey. The spring tides just after the new moon were the best time, allowing an easier escape through the shallows under the cover of near-darkness. But the moon was not always favourable, or the loading of cargo might take longer than expected, so it was up to the captain to make the final decision on just when to take the chance.

LEAVING WILMINGTON

On 24 July the steamer was finally ready to sail. It was a week after the new moon, but rather than waiting for the next one, Crossan and Wyllie decided to risk it. The holds were full of cotton bales and some were even stacked on deck. The crew, containing almost all those who had come over from Glasgow, were ready for the run back to Bermuda. One of the new men aboard the steamer was North Carolinian James Maglenn, who took up the position of first engineer. He recalled the process of leaving the Cape Fear River, avoiding the blockade fleet and making for their destination:

> The way we had to get out was this. We would come down the river and go over a little bar to get ready to go out. On account of the danger to the ship we had to do this in the day time, and the fleet outside would see us and know that we were getting ready to go out. Naturally they would be on the watch, and when night came would slip in as close to the fort as they dared and we would have to do mighty close work getting past. It was our speed that carried us through. The *Ad-Vance* would make about twelve knots, which for those days was pretty fast work. All lights were out, of course, and the darker the night the better for us. Every now and then we'd almost bump right into one of the fleet and then it was helm down hard, and we would be off in the darkness before they could hope to get us.
>
> Then presently we'd run into another, and turn again and then maybe, they'd catch our direction and send a rocket the way we were going so as to put the rest of the fleet on its guard, but of course we knew what the rocket meant, too, and as soon as we saw it we would change our course again. 'How long would it take us to get out?' Sometimes all night, never less than two or three hours. Sometimes it would be day when we'd get clear and there would be ships to chase us, but our speed carried us through.[151]

The high speed of the *Ad-Vance* was one of its greatest advantages. Its powerful machinery, its experienced and disciplined crew, and the best coal meant it could outrun almost any Union vessel. This first 670-nm run took just three days, and by the 27th the steamer was reported safely at St George's. As the *Ad-Vance* lay at the dock there, the Bermuda customs officers came along and made note of its cargo: it had brought in 500 bales of cotton along with ten barrels of turpentine, a typical cargo for a blockade runner. The steamer had 42 men in its crew – and interestingly, Joannes Wyllie was still listed as master. Crossan's role being, at least on paper, the commander of the vessel, he is known to have been on the steamer for this voyage, but his involvement continued to be underplayed, at least in the Bermudan official documents.[152]

The arrival at St George's also marked the completion of the sailing agreement for the crew that had joined up in Greenock. All members of the crew, from Wyllie to the carpenter, cook, seamen and firemen, were listed as discharged on 10 August in Bermuda, all paid off and released from their contract. This would not have been a problem for them: the steamer still needed a crew, and there would have been other opportunities awaiting any unemployed mariner at the port. It is not, however, known how many of the crew signed up again immediately for continued service on the steamer, to make their way home to Britain, or signed up in the crew of another ship then at anchor in St George's.[153]

Wyllie's pay for this first successful run, entailing the voyage from Greenock to Bermuda, then the run to Wilmington and back to Bermuda, can be found on two copies of the bills of exchange that he had been given when he was discharged. The copies in question were kept by the officials of the State of North Carolina, and they give the first indication of just how profitable being a blockade runner could be. The first is dated 10 August and signed by both Wyllie and Theodore Hughes, the North Carolinian commissioner who by this time had officially taken up his role as purser of the *Ad-Vance*. Wyllie was paid £176 6s (shillings) in pounds sterling, roughly equivalent to $1,250 at that time – and £16,500 today (see Table 1). The second, dated 12 August, was for £54 3s 4d.

There is no indication on the bills themselves what the payments were for, but it can be inferred that the larger amount was for the longer transatlantic voyage from Greenock to Bermuda.[154] The second amount would appear to be for Wyllie's role during the first two runs through the blockade. In later financial archives of the steamer, the amounts paid to the captain of the vessel for a full round trip were listed in pounds sterling as £208 6s 8d (£104 3s 4d for each leg of the journey) which roughly equates to the $1,000 paid to the captains of the state- or Confederate-owned steamers for a successful trip. First mates on these steamers were known to earn 25 per cent of the captain's wage, so Wyllie's pay of £54 closely matches what a first mate would have received for a successful round trip.[155] This would indicate, no matter what the customs records reported in Bermuda, that Wyllie was now officially the first mate, or sailing master, in charge of the day-to-day operation of the steamer, and being paid as such, while Crossan was the captain and in overall command of the vessel.

The records of Wyllie's pay during this early period totalled £230 9s 4d. How did this compare to his pay before his time as a runner? I have been unable to trace any record of

Table 1 The methodology used to compare monetary values of the 19th century and today

In order for a comparison to be made between the values of the 19th century and those of today a standard comparative formula was applied to all monetary amounts. This was completed by utilising www.measuringworth.com, which offers comparisons between the relative values of pounds sterling for any year from 1270 to the last calendar year (2020 at the time of writing), and the US dollar from 1790.
The monetary conversions that appear throughout this book are based on the **real price** of the **commodity value**, utilising the relative cost of a (fixed over time) bundle of goods and services such as food, shelter, clothing, etc. For example, by using this conversion, £1 in 1863 is calculated as **£94 last year.**
The website also provides several other comparison points for value change over time, so estimates can range quite significantly. For example, whereas £1 in 1863 using **commodity and real price** is **£94 last year**, the **economic share** comparison would make the value **£2,377.**

his pay as master of the *Bonita*, but as first mate on the *Hope* he had earned £8 per month. In comparison, just a year later, in August 1863, he had just been paid £230 for four months' service, or £57 10s 0d per month – a massive, sevenfold, increase.

Although the bills of exchange were signed in Bermuda, both were addressed to John White, then in London continuing his service to the State of North Carolina. On the reverse, in his own hand, Wyllie signed the bills to 'Pay to the Order of Alex. Wyllie, Esq, Joannes Wyllie, Master Steamer *Ad-Vance*'. Wyllie's first payments as a blockade runner were at the earliest opportunity sent to his father back in Scotland, he was quickly placing his new rewards in a safe location, far away from any dangers that his career on the blockade might bring.

THE *AD-VANCE'S* THIRD RUN

With a new crew signed on and cargo loaded for its return to Wilmington, the *Ad-Vance* awaited its chance to leave St George's. A quick turnaround would have been envisioned, but on 4 August the *St George's Bermuda Journal of Commerce* reported that several runners – *Ad-Vance*, *Lady Davis* (a nickname for the *Cornubia*) and *Eugenie* – were all hung up for want of coal.[156] This was a constant issue both in Bermuda and in the Bahamas, and neither had any natural supplies. The best British steam coal, as it was known, came from the collieries of South Wales, much of it exported from Cardiff. It was here that the *Lord Clyde* had taken on a large supply on its way to Bermuda in May. The bulk of the coal used by the runners was brought over from Britain, but from Pennsylvania came a smaller quantity of quality anthracite, which produced little smoke when burned. Both of those forms of fuel were highly valued by the captains of that era, as they would not give away their position on the open sea. From time to time, large heaps of coal lined the quaysides of both Nassau and St George's, and the coal merchants in these towns would make their profits by providing runners with up to 200 tons for each run. Yet another source of income from the blockade. Meanwhile, loading the coal was hard work, done almost completely by hand, and this arduous task was listed as being done by low-paid local black labourers.[157]

As the steamer waited for coal its cargo was loaded, and recorded by the customs officials in Bermuda. Once again the vagueness of the descriptions of items marked merely as boxes or packages of merchandise make it difficult to ascertain exactly what was being carried. The most notable item that was detailed was 400 pigs of lead – lumps of solid metal which could be transformed into rifle bullets. Yet again Wyllie's name appears in official documents as master while the *Ad-Vance* made ready for departure.[158]

With a quantity of coal finally procured, the steamer left on 14 August under a new moon, and three days later the vessel's arrival at the mouth of the Cape Fear River was relayed immediately via telegram to Governor Vance by William Lamb, commander of the garrison at Fort Fisher.[159] The steamer again made its way upriver to the quayside at Wilmington to discharge and prepare for its next run. The city, some 20 miles upstream of the mouth of the Cape Fear River, had been utterly changed by the war due to its vital role as one of the very few ports available to the Confederacy. Before the conflict had begun the city had been a minor port on the Atlantic seaboard, home to a few vessels and barely troubled by transatlantic traffic. Founded in 1739, the small settlement was by the time of North Carolina's secession from the Union in 1861 a modest port with rail connections to the state's interior. It was not as large or urban as the other Atlantic blockade-running port of Charleston, located 152 miles to the south.

The coming of the war to Wilmington had brought with it a huge influx of people, from soldiers, sailors and Confederate officials to merchants and manufacturers looking to make a quick fortune. The city was swamped by these men, who brought with them some additional, unwanted visitors like disease and unrest. For example, the arrival of the steamer *Kate* in late summer 1862 brought not only a heavy cargo of supplies but also the scourge of yellow fever carried by crew members infected by mosquito bites while in the tropical port of Nassau. The population of the city was ravaged, with over 1,500 cases of fever and 700 recorded deaths – 15 per cent of the population. This was why the quarantine system had been instigated. Runners were required to stop for a period at locations like the town of Smithville, just inside the protection of Forts Caswell and Fisher at the river mouth. This was the quarantine that had been violated during the *Ad-Vance*'s first run through the blockade.[160]

John Wilkinson, captain of the famed and highly successful runner *Robert E. Lee*, recounted the state of Wilmington in his memoirs of the war, *Narrative of a Blockade*

Runner. The influx of sailors, merchants and Confederate officials involved in blockade running was described:

> The staid old town of Wilmington was turned 'topsy turvy' during the war. Here resorted the speculators from all parts of the South, to attend the weekly auctions of imported cargoes; and the town was infested with rogues and desperadoes, who made a livelihood by robbery and murder. It was unsafe to venture into the suburbs at night, and even in daylight, there were frequent conflicts in the public streets, between the crews of the steamers in port and the soldiers stationed in the town, in which knives and pistols would be freely used; and not unfrequently a dead body would rise to the surface of the water in one of the docks with marks of violence upon it. The civil authorities were powerless to prevent crime: *inter arma silent leges!*' (*sic*) (For among the time of arms, the laws fall mute). The agents and employees of the different blockade-running companies, lived in magnificent style, paying a king's ransom (in Confederate money) for their household expenses, and nearly monopolizing the supplies in the country market.

The inhabitants of Wilmington not only suffered the behaviour of all these new neighbours but also felt the hardships of any population in wartime. Wilkinson wrote about the shortages of vital foodstuffs and the huge inflation that occurred as the war continued:

> Towards the end of the war, indeed, fresh provisions were almost beyond the reach of every one. Our family servant, newly arrived from the country in Virginia, would sometimes return from market with an empty basket, having flatly refused to pay what he called 'such nonsense prices' for a bit of fresh beef, or a handful of vegetables. A quarter of lamb, at the time of which I now write, sold for \$100, a pound of tea for \$500. Confederate money which in September, 1861, was nearly equal to specie in value, had declined in September 1862 to 225; in the same month, in 1863, to 400, and before September, 1864, to 2000! [161]

Wyllie would have been an eyewitness to these events. Over his years at sea he had been exposed to a myriad of locations from quiet backwaters, to ports under the ravages of sickness, to thriving metropolises, but he would never have experienced the impact of modern warfare on a populace like that of Wilmington's. The details of his time in port are unknown, so where he stayed, what he did when away from the steamer or who he associ-

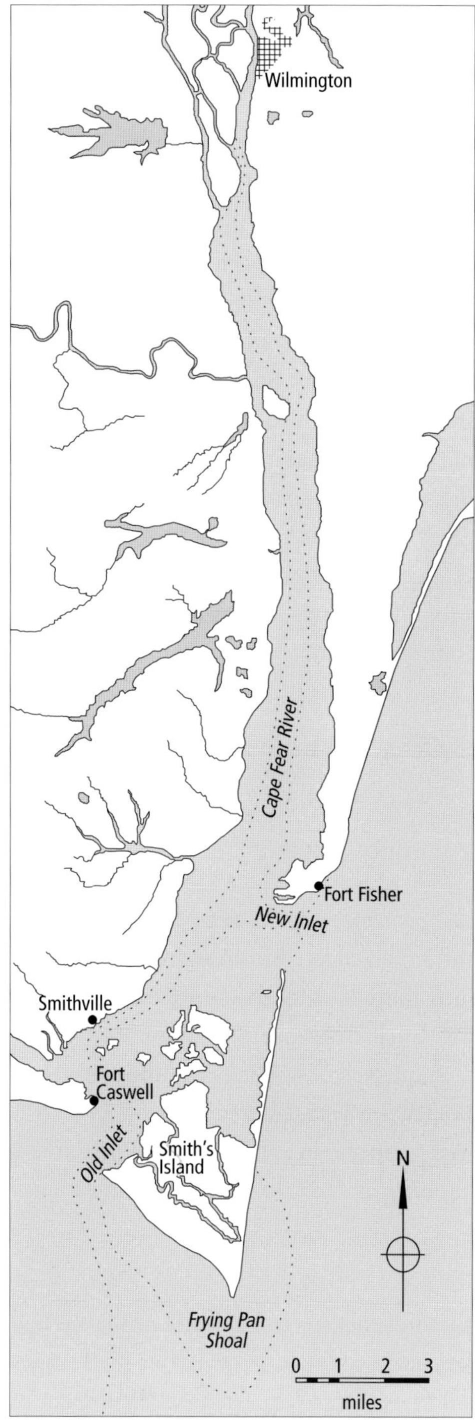

Wilmington, the Cape Fear River and its approaches

ated with can only be speculated. Might he have stayed aboard the steamer, or ventured further afield outside Wilmington? As an employee of North Carolina, might he have received invitations from Governor Vance or other politicians for events or dinners in the state capital of Raleigh? Whatever his activities, his time in port was always short, overseeing cargo loading, awaiting the next new moon and its high tides, and looking for the best chance to make the run.

Stories from the Blockade

Several of the voyages of the *Ad-Vance* were recorded in the diaries and letters of the crew or passengers on board. These included representatives of the State of North Carolina, plus businessmen, clergymen, historians, families and foreign visitors. They give unique insights into the operation of the steamer and crew as well as the writers' own trepidation, excitement and fears experienced while running the blockade.

The first account was written by 19-year-old John Baptist Smith, who held the vital role of signalman on the steamer. Smith had joined the crew after its first arrival in Wilmington, and his role was to signal the Confederate forces on shore to identify his steamer to them as a friend. He would then read the shore-based signals, which could convey information such as the status of the guns at Forts Caswell and Fisher, or the best times to run the blockade or the condition of the river. Although just a young man, Smith had already made a huge impact on the progress of the conflict. He had abandoned his studies at Hampden-Sydney College on 15 April 1861, three days after the bombardment of Fort Sumter, and volunteered for a newly formed North Carolina regiment. He quickly attained the rank of sergeant and became involved in signalling, both on the battlefield and at sea. He devised a new form of signalling, one that did not depend on the established system of codes that used flags during the day and torches at night; the torches were hard to make out on both the shore and aboard a ship due to wind and waves. The growing importance of night-time operation meant that a more reliable system would be a great advantage, and Smith proposed a solution whereby the operator would sit between two lanterns, one white and the other red, then opened and shut sliding doors on them to send coded signals. His proposal was examined by a special board and was ultimately adopted for use by blockade runners. It was this innovation that gained Smith a place on Vance's new steamer as signals officer.[162]

Smith's account was published in 1896 under the title *The Saucy Blockade Runner*; it described a run from Bermuda to Wilmington during the summer of 1863 in which the steamer survived a daylight sprint past the blockading fleet. He starts with a description of crew and his interactions with Wyllie, who he identified as the sailing master:

> On the afternoon of the second day out, as usual, all hands were called up and told off by the First Officer to their respective boats. It was the purpose of our Captain, Thomas Crossan, if about to be captured, to scuttle the ship, and by means of the ship's boats to endeavor to make our way ashore.
>
> What a motley sight our crew presented! With the exception of our Sailing Master, our officers were Southerners, but the crew was composed of men of every nationality, adventurers attracted to this most dangerous service by the tempting offer of enormous bounties and wages paid in gold or silver.
>
> On account of my youthfulness I was much petted by the officers, especially by the Sailing Master, who was a bluff, typical Scotchman. Heaven bless him! Though by no means of exemplary habits himself, he watched over and guarded me against the temptations to which I was exposed as carefully as a father could have done. He always assigned me to his boat; but Kit Morse, our Wilmington pilot, counted the most skilful pilot and surfman on our coast, would always whisper to me: 'Never mind, Smith, if ever we do have to take to the small boats, you just step in my boat, take a seat by Kit Morse, and if any boat can live through the surf, I will land you safe on North Carolina grit.' This always placed me in a quandary, in which adherence to orders and personal safety struggled for the mastery.

Smith's description of the crew points to the full change of officers when the *Ad-Vance* made St George's after its first outward run in July. This matches the crew agreement for the *Lord Clyde*, which had stated that all crew were to be discharged. This leaves open the number of hands (i.e. crew members other than officers) that were retained, but the description of the international nature of the crew might show that many sailors or firemen may have retained their place. Wyllie's interaction with Smith harks back to his previous role as teacher, looking after the younger crewmates with a special eye, making sure they were well attended to. The unsavoury habits exhibited by the Scot are not elaborated upon, but Smith seemed fond of the sailing master by any account.

As the ship was deep-laden, their intention was to enter Cape Fear River on the floodtide at around 3 a.m., but things did not go to plan.

> It was the intention of our Captain to make the coast of North Carolina at some point about twenty-five miles above Fort Fisher at New Inlet to the Cape Fear River, then to steam down the coast and run in about 3 a. m., which would be flood tide on the bar (our ship being so deeply laden we could not get over the bar except at high water). Owing to our having run off our course to dodge steamers, we made Hatteras light-house about 1 a. m., and although we steamed down the coast under full head of steam, daylight found us some twenty-five miles above Fort Fisher, and brought to view the Union blockading fleet of five vessels, stretching in a line abreast of Masonboro Sound, and standing off about three miles at sea. The closest scrutiny with the aid of our glasses failed to show any sign of life on their decks. But we knew they always kept up full head of steam. The Captain called Mr. Morse, the pilot, Mr. Morrison, the Chief Engineer, and myself to him and said: 'We have either to run off the coast with chance of a long chase from those fellows out there,' pointing to the Federal vessels, 'and try to get in to-night, or under cover of the fog and smoke from the surf and salt works hanging over the coast line, try to slip by them.' Then, after a minute's pause, said, with a sparkle in his calm blue eyes, and with compressed lips, 'I am going to take the risk of running by them. Mr. Morrison, be ready to give her all steam possible. Smith, stand by to signal Colonel Lamb to man his guns to protect us. Pilot, take charge of the ship; put her in if possible; if not, beach her.'
>
> An extra hand was sent to the wheel, and as I, with my signal flag in hand, took my position on the starboard side of the quarter deck, to the right of the pilot, he said: 'Smith, old boy, we are in for it.' We steamed on at a moderate speed, hugging the shore line as close as possible to keep under cover of mingled fog and smoke, which stretched like a veil along the coast.

Scanning intently the line of blockaders, I began to flatter myself we were unobserved until we were off Masenboro (*sic*), and abreast of the line of blockaders, when up went a signal from the flag ship of the squadron, and in a moment each vessel, having slipped her cable, was in motion under full steam. One steamed in shore to our rear, three came bearing obliquely on our port beam, and one, the '*Connecticut*,' the fleetest of the squadron, steamed to head us off, and we saw that we were in a trap that had been set for us. 'Full speed ahead the pilot,' signalled the engineer, and the bonny ship bounded forward like a racer. 'Up with the colors,' spoke the Captain, and the Southern Cross fluttered in the morning breeze from our flag staff astern.

Intense excitement prevailed among the sailors and firemen off duty as they gathered on the forward deck, of which, from our position, we had full view. Among them our chief cook, 'Frenchie,' who was wont to boast a cap carried off his head by a Russian bullet at Sebastopol.[163]

'Smith,' said the Pilot, 'twenty miles to Fort Fisher.' A puff of smoke, and a cannon ball from the *Connecticut* skipped the crest of the waves to the forward but short of our ship. I recognized it as a gentle hint to round to and surrender. The motley crowd on the deck, supposing it to be the extent of the *Connecticut*'s ability to coerce, gave vent to their feelings in a suppressed cheer. Alas for the hopes! the last spark of which was soon quenched. The *Connecticut*, our course not being changed, sent the next shot whistling between our smoke stacks, across the three mile strip of land into the Cape Fear River, as I afterwards learned. 'Oh, good God,' said Frenchie as he darted for shelter, towards the forecastle, but was intercepted by a shot across our bows.

The firing from the fleet had now become general, and amid the whistle of shot and bursting of shell all about us the Pilot said with a smile: 'Smith, look at Frenchie dodging about like a partridge in a coop.' Just then the signal station highest up the beach hove in sight, and my time for action had arrived which required me to become oblivious to the terrors menacing destruction and death, and by waves of my signal flag spell out, letter by letter, this message to Col. Lamb, commandant at Fort Fisher: 'Col. Lamb: Have guns manned to protect us. Signed Crossan, Captain *Ad-Vance*.'

No one can imagine how glad I was at the close of my message to catch the shore operator's reply of 'O. K.' My official responsibility being now ended, the peril that environed us burst upon me with full force. Fifteen miles to Fort Fisher! For fifteen miles to be subjected to such an ordeal or that of being dashed to pieces in that fearful surf which mingled its ominous warning with the reverberating roar of the pitiless cannon. I tried to read my destiny in the imperturbable countenance of my companion, a wave of whose hand could consign me to a Northern prison, or perchance to a watery grave. As well seek to penetrate the secrets of the Sphinx as the thoughts of Kit Morse. Yet I knew he loved me, thought of my safety even with this great responsibility resting upon him, for once, as the fragments of shell were falling all about us, he pushed me under the lee of the Sailing Master's cabin, saying: 'Smith, that may keep a piece from striking you.' How slow we seemed to be running! People ashore likened our speed to that of a bird seeking safety by flight. Minutes to us seemed hours, yet slowly, so slowly as scarcely to be perceptible, we were gradually forging ahead of all except the *Connecticut*, which was running in a straight line for the inlet, to cut us off, while we had to follow the curves of the shore. On sped the chase! In the press for speed the *Connecticut* fired only from her starboard guns.

We had now reached the last curve of the shore which projected out seaward, and would have to be turned before we could enter the inlet. This the Pilot traced with his finger and said calmly: 'Smith, that will bring us in a hundred yards of the *Connecticut*. I wonder why Lamb doesn't fire.'

Bang! went a gun from the shore battery, and a Whitworth shell bored through the hull of the rear vessel, being in point blank range. Suddenly the vessels to the rear gave up the chase and steamed seaward. Not so with that dreaded *Connecticut* which seemed right across our bows, with our ship as a shield, to protect her from the guns of the fort.

How fast we were approaching her! Every motion of her gun crew became plainly visible, even that of the gunner, as he pulled the lanyard and sent that fearful missile of destruction aimed at our water line, but buried in a wave twenty feet short.

'That got us,' said the brave pilot to me. Then, with a quick wave of his hand and a cheery voice of command, 'over, hard over.' The wheel rolled under the willing hands of the brave steersman; and with the speed of a chased stag, and the grace of a swan, the bonnie craft rounded the point, entered the inlet. The guns of Fort Fisher belched flames of fire, and we were safe.

'Safe! thank God!' burst from a hundred lips! Even a cheer went up from the deck of the intrepid *Connecticut* as she headed out to sea. A tribute (as we afterwards learned from a New York paper) from her brave crew to the daring act of the 'Saucy Blockade Runner,' as they designated us.

> Col. Lamb signalled off to know the extent of our damages. I replied: 'None visible.' He at once pulled off, and as he greeted me with a hearty shake of the hand, he said: 'Smith, I knew you to be a truthful boy, but could not believe it possible for any vessel to be subjected to such a fire as that and not be badly damaged.' Upon careful inspection, the only damage to our good ship was found to be a dent made by a fragment of shell striking one of our smoke stacks.'[164]

They had survived what was considered one of the most dangerous, and indeed foolhardy, acts of blockade running. It made a big impression on Wyllie, and he would often mention it when he recalled his time on the *Ad-Vance*. His memories of the event were written down in the *People's Friend* article of 1889. Most of his details match those of Smith, although, as is common with recollections made later in life, some details are different, including the names of the Union vessels that had chased the *Ad-Vance*. Might Wyllie have combined the stories of several runs into one single, more thrilling, depiction?[7*] Both accounts were written down long after the fact, so might the intervening decades have led to embellishments or omissions? Despite the discrepancies, Wyllie's accounts are as compelling as Smith's. Here is another one from Anton's pen:

> Captain Wyllie often ran in without ever being noticed. He did, however, what was only done by one other vessel during the whole time of the blockade – he made the 'run in' in broad daylight. It was a foolhardy escapade, only to be justified by the circumstances in which he found himself. Having left Bermuda with a full cargo he encountered stormy weather. This greatly extended the time occupied in the run across. More coals had been burnt than he could well spare. The weather was dirty, and he had had no observation of the sun since clearing Bermuda. When they neared the American coast they did not know where they were. It was night; they threw over a kedge anchor, and determined to wait for the day. The next day was a Saturday. Just when it dawned – and there is little dawn in that region – good gracious! – what was their dismay to find they were in the middle of a veritable nest of hornets. Five steamers – all birds of prey – lay right about them. 'East ahead,' was the word. They hoped the watches might be careless and drowsy, and they would get beyond range without being seen – but they were mistaken. The stern fellow was wide awake – 'the moon and he.' A loud report broke the stillness of the morning. 'Full speed – we are in for a long

7* In total the *Ad-Vance* made six runs from Bermuda into Wilmington through the blockade. Several of these were accompanied by either stormy weather or a chase by Union warships. Wyllie's own account of the daylight run might have referred to the runs of August 1863, October 1863 or January 1864, or might have contained mixed details from some or all of them.

> chase.' His pursuers dropped off from the chase till only one remained, which could not be shaken off. All the crew and stewards were helping the firemen; but the speed of both vessels seemed equal. Every time the Yankee fired his bow-chasers, the recoil gave him so many yards to gain. The pursuing Yank was the *Quaker City*. The title was surely a misnomer in the circumstances. The *Quaker* could not be shaken off. Deliverance only came with the night. When it fell the *Advance* 'bouted ship, and the *Quaker* went roaring and blowing right onward to Nassau. The chase had lasted for 200 miles. These miles had to be retraced. When Sabbath morning broke they were within ten miles of the New Inlet and close in-shore. They kept in this path, keeping as near to the breakers as they were able. The coals are nearly done, and to stop out another night is impossible. The soldiers on shore who were watching him thought ship and crew were doomed. The cruisers grow in appearance larger and larger. The *Advance* is detected. A gun is fired, and signal flags are set flying from every peak. There was no other way out of the scrape than to put on full speed and make a run for it right through the flock (*sic*) of lions. The *Advance* darted forward like a hunted deer. The safety valves were dangerously loaded. She leapt nearly out of the water as she tore along. As she came on, the cruisers one by one, and in very coolest manner, as if they had been at practice, turned quietly round and poured into her broadside after broadside. For the most part the discharges passed over our heads, howling and screeching and ploughing up the sand on the beach. It was like passing through the very gates of hell. On the fort the Confederate soldiers were standing eagerly by their guns. Every ship, after firing her broadside, went steaming on and loading all the time, to get if possible another chance of destroying the adventurous greyhound. In the excitement they ran within range of the guns of the forts. The artillerymen could not be restrained, and at the risk of sinking the *Advance* they opened a hot fire on the cruisers. In this discharge one shell from the forts hit the cruiser *Niphon*, and killed three of her marines. At this point, between the fires, the noise of the firing and the bursting of shells wholly baffles description. Still dashing forward the *Advance* crossed the bar and was safe, having come through the tempest comparatively scathless. The Confederate soldiers gave three ringing cheers. But the Yankees were not to be outdone in their admiration of genuine pluck. At a signal the lads of the stars and the stripes sent up three hearty cheers in honour of the good ship *Advance* and her intrepid captain.[165]

By what was only their third run, Wyllie and crew had experienced all of the dangers the blockade could throw at them. As the steamer made its way up the Cape Fear River towards Wilmington, the crew were now fully aware of just how alert they would need to be on their next voyage. They would have just over a month to ruminate on these events before they once again set their sights towards the Atlantic.

The next run of the *Ad-Vance* took place in September and featured the first account by a passenger making his way towards Europe on the steamer. It came from what might be considered a rather curious source, a Prussian army officer named Captain Justus Scheibert. The 32-year-old had been sent to America to observe the war, make detailed notes with a focus on the fortifications being erected by both sides and then report back to his high command. He had initially been ordered to observe the Union forces, but due to his sympathies with the Southern cause he was sent on to the Confederacy. He was one of several officers sent by the European powers to investigate how the conflict might have implications on the theory of modern warfare.

In early 1863 Scheibert had travelled through the blockade as a passenger aboard the *Flora* on its voyage from Nassau to Charleston. Over the next seven months he had observed the progress of the war and had been welcomed by the highest echelons of the Confederate army, including Generals Lee, Longstreet and Beauregard. He had been present at the Battle of Gettysburg, and after he had come aboard in mid-September, ready to conclude his assignment by returning to Europe, he would have been able to describe in detail the carnage of those three days in July to the crew, then making ready for their fourth run.

Scheibert wrote in detail about his trip on the *Ad-Vance*, and although it did not mention Wyllie by name, his account gives a good description of just what a run entailed, and how passengers who were not used to the rolling decks and splashing waves of oceanic travel would fare. He first noted that his presence was not exactly warmly welcomed:

> I ran aboard quickly, and the embarrassed captain confessed that he would have liked to leave without passengers, since they were an unpleasant additional burden … since the commander was determined to resist with force of arms any boarding of the vessel.

The two officers mentioned would appear to have been Wyllie as captain and Crossan as commander. If Wyllie was unhappy about Scheibert, he must have been equally concerned by the 12 other passengers on board, all of whom would share the excitements and dangers of a run during the coming few days. One of them was the well-known historian Colonel John H. Wheeler of North Carolina who, despite the war, was setting off on a research trip to England.

Scheibert recounted in detail the story of the run, from his description of the vessel as the 'fastest steamer borne by the waves' to how the Cape Fear pilot held them at Smithville near the mouth of the river as the water over the bar was too low, which meant waiting for up to a week for the higher tides. This week was spent in jollity and frivolity, as 'poetry, literature, and humour … enlivened the ship of evenings' while the days brought hours of sailing and fishing using the *Ad-Vance's* well-equipped boats. During that time, Scheibert recalled observing 17 runners leave and 8 enter.

Finally, the tide was right, the pilot indicated his approval, and the steamer made for the bar, then open water.

> The run began. The wheels splashed water around wildly, and the vessel was flying along. Then the keel scraped bottom. The ship ran aground three times, and then it rumbled up to the pilot light, sliding gently on the sand, and floated off in the ocean, buoyant as a swan. Our hearts beat loud. But not all obstacles had been overcome, for before us the fox lurked for his prey, and a raging storm began to whip its waves straight into our faces. The method by which the narrow channels in the sandbanks were passed was highly ingenious. Lights on the islands, unseen by the enemy, gave us alignments to those points where the pilot had to order a change of course. Our white lantern on the stern was exchanged for a red one when we ran aground, and the friendly light immediately gave us a signal as to how we could get afloat. The lights finally came to an end, and the sea and the fleet lay before us.
>
> Dark night, cover us with thy protecting mantle and conceal us from all eyes! But a Supreme Being keeps watch above and will not let us perish without plan or purpose! The moon has sunk below the horizon an hour before this time, but its gentle light is still hovering over the heavens, which gratefully reflect its glow! The ship is as silent as a tomb, and all eyes are prying through the darkness, anxiously searching. 'Look there! Is that a cloud? A shadow? A ship?' It resolves itself into vague, nebulous forms on the horizon, for the storm is roaring madly. Thank heavens, we are safe!

The *Ad-Vance* had cleared the blockade, and the immediate danger of the guns of the Union warships was now behind it. Now came the long run in open water towards Bermuda. Scheibert recalled:

> We moved over the billowing sea like a pale shadow. The passengers were amazed at the indigo blue waters of the Gulf Stream and at the raging of the elements, and they were surprised at the speed of the voyage and the shining of the sea at night. But soon the specter of seasickness lay over the ship, bringing down everyone from commander to passengers. We would lie in the fresh air between the bales of cotton and read very good books from the ship's library.

The last sentence is of note. The steamer appears to have contained a library made available to the passengers. No other mention is recorded in any source of such a library, but it might have been retained from the steamer's days on the Dublin–Glasgow run. We know that Wyllie had once started and maintained a library himself, and he may have had a hand in this one as well.

The final drama recounted by Scheibert was the worry in both Crossan and Wyllie with regard to the coal bunkers of the *Ad-Vance*. The distance from Wilmington to Bermuda was considerable and the consumption and remaining of coal was a constant worry. The threat of capture had diminished as they left the Union fleet behind, but the danger of being left bereft, with only sails to move the steamer, was now of concern. The chief engineer reported that the coal was almost gone, and all available firewood was being eyed. Any miscalculation of their course or a foul wind would force a longer journey – and the break-up of the steamer's boats and other expendable parts in order to keep the fires going. Thankfully these worries proved needless as providence was on their side: the winds were fair and the steamer's course was true, and in just over three days the *Ad-Vance* arrived in St George's harbour with Scheibert recalling:

> 'Land must appear on the starboard side!' the commander called out gleefully. He was right. Soon 'Bermuda, the Queen,' greeted us in the calm, emerald-green water.[166]

The passengers disembarked, either for lodgings in the town or for the larger sailing ships bound for Liverpool. The crew of the *Ad-Vance* then began unloading the cargo, which was reported by the *Evening Star* of Washington DC as being a full load: 530 bales of cotton.

The *Ad-Vance* had now completed four successful trips through the blockade. Only one close call with Union warships had been noted, that being during the dangerous daylight sprint. The luck of the steamer seemed good. Next came yet another clash with the blockaders, and again it saw the *Ad-Vance* sprint towards the mouth of the Cape Fear River in the light of day.

AD-VANCE CHASED AGAIN

The *Ad-Vance* spent the next ten days in port at St George's, and was ready for its departure by 6 October. By this time these trips from and back to Bermuda must have become somewhat routine to Wyllie, Crossan and the crew. The initial excitement of the first run might have begun to fade and the tasks on board become more mundane: cargo loaded, cargo unloaded, with brief flashes of adventure and danger between.

In St George's the next load of cargo was moving from wharf onto deck, into the hold, all supervised and recorded by the Bermudan customs officials. The manifest for this run once again reveals little in terms of detail: not much can be made of items listed as '146 packages general merchandise'. The destination was listed as Nassau, which itself was of note, as most steamers looking to run the blockade would give Nassau, or the Canadian port of Halifax, as their proposed destination – those being neutral, British, ports – to provide some sort of cover for the steamer and crew in case of capture.

Another intriguing item in the details of the voyage is that Thomas M. Crossan was now officially listed as master on the customs record. This change raises an interesting point. There is no doubt he was commander of the vessel on this voyage, but Wyllie's name would once again be used as part of the subterfuge of blockade running, this time on two bills of lading for the *Ad-Vance*. Bills of lading are a detailed list of a ship's cargo given as a receipt by the master of a ship to the company or individual consigning the goods to be carried. Again, the exact nature of the cargo is ambiguous, but the master is listed as Wyllie and the destination as Wilmington and not Nassau. So one set of records showed the true cargo and destination, whereas the other led a false trail: one had Wyllie as master, and the other Crossan. [167]

So the document with the official information regarding the voyage was identified with Wyllie, and the cover document was assigned to Crossan. This would appear to continue the subterfuge that had begun in Glasgow, that the steamer was a British merchant vessel commanded by a Scot whose purpose while transiting between ports in the Caribbean was completely above board. Or at least this is the argument that could be successfully made if the *Ad-Vance* were ever to be captured by a Union vessel. The bills of lading could be produced, so that Wyllie could accept the responsibility and hopefully face little or no retribution or punishment, with Crossan claiming ignorance and innocence.

With cargo loaded and all documents submitted, the steamer set off for Wilmington. As on the previous trip there were a number of passengers on board, two of whom wrote diaries of their voyage. The steamer was once again bombarded by numerous blockaders, this time only just making safety under the guns at Fort Fisher. The frantic details of this voyage come from the Reverend Moses D. Hoge and James H. Burton, and their accounts make this the best documented of any of the *Ad-Vance's* trips.

The Reverend Hoge was a Presbyterian minister and Confederate chaplain from Richmond, Virginia. He was returning home after a trip to England, having run out through the blockade earlier in the year in order to procure bibles and other religious publications for the soldiers and civilians of the Confederacy. His time in England was well publicised in newspapers with opinions of his task mixed. Some reports praised his piety and willingness to spread the word of God during a time of conflict, while others demonised his presence in England as a representative of the slave owners of the Confederacy, going as far as to refer to him as a 'Bible Beggar'. James H. Burton was the superintendent of the Confederate armouries

Reverend Moses Drury Hoge (1818–1899) – a Virginian Presbyterian and Confederate chaplain – was a passenger aboard the Ad-Vance *in October 1863. The diary he kept is one of the most detailed accounts of a blockade run, full of the electric drama of the chase.*

Courtesy of the Virginia Museum of History and Culture (2002.569.3)

in Macon, Georgia. He too was returning from a trip to England; however it was not books so often used to promote peace that he had been seeking, but means of war, having been tasked with searching for the latest machinery, tools and material required for a new armoury.[168]

The voyage began on 8 October with both passengers noting the serene scenes as the steamer passed out of the sheltered waters around Bermuda. Hoge listed the officers, and in doing so gave the first detailed description of Joannes Wyllie as a blockade runner.

> **Bermuda, Wednesday, October 8, 1863**. – At 12 o'clock went on board the *Ad-Vance* (*Lord Clyde*). My fellow passengers are Rev. Mr Terry, Mrs. Pender, Messrs. Burton, Walker and Regnault. Got off at 10 o'clock; beautiful view of Bermuda as we rapidly sped along. The *Clyde* a fine and fast vessel. Officers, Colonel Crossan, Captain Wylie (the English Captain) … Wylie is a warm-hearted Scotchman, though he looks English every inch, big, burly, and red faced, full of enthusiasm – full of poetry.[169]

Hoge and his fellow passengers were obviously immediately impressed by Wyllie. It appears that his experiences as teacher and orator would have come to the fore; one might easily imagine him telling tales of his time on the barque *Hope* or clipper *Indian Queen* to the group to pass the time. The description of him looking 'English every inch' is not explained further; maybe Hoge had been expecting more of a rough-around-the-edges Scot draped in tartan rather than the college-educated Wyllie.

A description of the ship was then offered, with passenger accommodation being singled out by both Hoge and Burton as rather spartan in nature. Burton noted that

> [I] slept in my clothes last night and also each night during the voyage. All my friends doing the same, and sleeping on the sofas of the Saloon.

Hoge went into slightly more detail:

> We have taken no state rooms on the Clyde, although there are a great number of unoccupied ones, but our little company of passengers all stay in the saloon at night. The fare is rather rough, but that is nothing when we have a good ship homeward bound.

The steamer's original design had not included commodious accommodation for longer journeys, and so the reactions by both of these passengers were to be expected. The vessel did still retain some of its former glory in terms of décor, but this would have surely have started to be co-opted to suit its new role: latterly it had lost almost all passenger comforts as more and more space had been turned over to store valuable cargo.

With the passengers ensconced aboard, the voyage began in earnest. The night of 8 October passed without incident, as did the whole of the following day. The activity of note was that the passengers were instructed by the crew to make preparations in anticipation of the run. Burton recalled that passengers and crew were divided into five groups, each of which would, in the event of needing to abandon the *Ad-Vance*, make for one of the five boats it carried. Burton was to be in the boat with 'Capt. Wiley, Comdg. the ship' while Reverend Hoge was to be in Crossan's boat. Burton notes that Wyllie was in command, which indicates that he thought the Scot was in charge of the steamer, at least on the operational side.[170]

That night the steamer was approaching its destination, and at that point is where the excitement, if it can be called that, of the run started. Hoge wrote that as the steamer approached the North Carolina coast both Crossan and Wyllie realised they had miscalculated their course:

> Although the Captain and Colonel made an observation at 12 M., they failed to detect the fact that the current of the Gulf Stream *had swept us far to the north of our course.* At about 9 o'clock at night we saw a light and the dim outline of the land. At first it was thought to be the signal light near Fort Fisher, and Mr. Smith wanted to make signals, but after long inspection, discovered that it was a light-house. We then changed our course southward and ran along shore all night in doubt as to where we were. Colonel C. once thought we might be south of the entrance to Wilmington and running towards Charleston. This shows how completely at sea we were! When it grew light enough to see the coast

more plainly, our officers recognized certain localities on Masonboro Sound, the salt works, etc., and we ascertained we had just made the land north of Cape Lookout, 80 miles from the point we expected to strike. Colonel Crossan prepared to run up near enough to see which blockaders were within view and I supposed he would then stand out to sea and lie off until night and then run in at his leisure, but to my astonishment, although it was about 8 o'clock in the morning, the sun shining brilliantly and the sea level as a floor and three blockaders guarding the entrance, he steamed straight on toward Fort Fisher. The blockaders seemed confused for a few moments by the audacity of the movement, but presently they came about and all three struck for the shore, intending to cut us off. They came on very speedily, but finding that we were running so swiftly they opened upon us with shrapnel, shell and solid shot.

It was a scene of intense excitement. We could see people on the shore, watching the result. We doubted not with utmost interest – the shells were ploughing up the water and tearing up the sand on the shore, bursting over and around us, yet not one struck us. It was almost a miracle. Two or three of their shells struck the sand just at the edge of the water and directly opposite to us. The wonder was how the balls could get there without passing through us. Colonel C. certainly made a hazardous experiment. Had the mist near the coast not veiled us somewhat from the view of the enemy as we approached, and had he [the enemy] seen us in time to make chase ten minutes sooner, he would have headed us off and driven us ashore, or had one of his shot penetrated our boilers, we would have been blown to fragments. Had we compelled to take to our boats, we would have still been in great danger, for we would have been under fire perhaps an hour, when the smooth sea made it as easy to fire accurately from the deck as from the walls of a fort.

Burton, too, recounted the chase and attack by the blockaders. As he was a military man, his description was focused more on the exact nature of the chase, going into great detail on the amount of cannon shot that was focused on the steamer:

The result of all which, with the help of a kind Providence, was that we eventually got safely inside of the inlet, and the Yankees ceased firing, much to our satisfaction. The practice from the Fort was very good, and it is said by the Officers in charge, who afterwards came on board, that one of the large ships was struck twice. Our vessel was under fire during a run of about two miles, or about a quarter of an hour, and about 25 or 30 shots & shell were fired at us, some of large dimensions. The Fort fired about 12 shot & shell, some of the 7½ inch calibre.[171]

Burton then went on to describe how the steamer, in its rush to make the safety of Cape Fear, made for a shallow part of the inlet:

> The tide was ebbing, and in consequence of there not being sufficient water to float us over the 'Rips' just inside the inlet we grounded, and there lay hard and fast, much to the disgust of all the passengers, who were most anxious to proceed at once to their respective homes.

The steamer was hard aground there, and in danger of being a sitting duck if the Yankees could somehow avoid the guns of Fort Fisher. Burton described the lengths that Crossan, Wyllie and Colonel Lamb of the garrison went to in order to secure the vessel from harm:

> During the day, Col. Lamb, Comd't. of Fort Fisher, and several of his officers came on board of us and brought late papers. The afternoon tide failed to float us, so we were compelled to stay on board until tomorrow, when some arrangement will be made by which the vessel can be lightened and the p assengers sent up to Wilmington. Fearing that the disappointed Yankees might make an attempt during the night to take our ship by armed boat crews, Capt. Crossan requested Col. Lamb to send a guard of 12 men on board from Fort Fisher. They came at dusk, and the Saloon on deck was assigned to them as temporary quarters.

Fort Fisher guarded the New Inlet of the Cape Fear River. Its guns and walls were welcome sounds and sights to any blockade runner, as it meant their voyage was almost at an end. It was under the shelter of these guns that Rev. Hoge experienced the grounding of the Ad-Vance *on the conclusion of the run from Bermuda.*

Illustrated London News

But it was not only the soldiers of the garrison that would keep watch. Burton and Hoge, along with other passengers, were armed and made ready to take up defensive duties:

> There were a case of rifles and some ammunition on board belonging to the ship. The passengers were armed with these, and the Rev'd Moses D. Hoge was duly elected the Capt. of the Auxiliary Guard. Each took his rifle & sword bayonet with him when he retired below for the night and placed them handy by his side in case of an emergency.

Fortunately, the night of the 10th came off peacefully with no need for the rifles or any commands from 'Captain Hoge'. As the 11th was a Sunday and the passengers were still aboard, the reverend decided to hold a service in the saloon. Crossan had ordered a steamer down from Wilmington to take off his 'Auxiliary Guard' as well as to start lightening the *Ad-Vance*, allowing it to get free of the sandbar and head upriver to where it would fully unload. The steamer finally arrived at the wharf in Wilmington on the 15th, when a telegram was sent to Governor Vance to advise him of the successful run. It mentioned some of the cargo in detail, which included some vital items for the war effort and for the populace of North Carolina in general: 'twenty four (24) packages medicines – one hundred (100) bales lagging, 113 coils rope, 100 packs cotton card, 17 bales blanket'.[172]

Soon after this run Major Thomas D. Hogg, commissary and ordnance officer, filed a report with the treasurer of North Carolina and with the ordnance department, reporting the amount of stores that had been brought through the blockade. Whereas previous reports in newspapers and even personal telegrams to the governor seem to have either omitted militarily useful cargo or indicated none, Hogg's accounting shows just how the *Ad-Vance's* operation had contributed to the battlefield. Dated 23 October, it listed everything the steamer had brought in through the blockade:

Cargo		*with a value of*
500,000 Musket Caps		$12,500
250,000 Shot Gun caps		$6,250
10,656 Musket tubes		$5,860
1,380 Files		$5,520
370 sheet iron		$33,300
1,000 pounds Borax		$12,000
560 pounds Emery		$3,360
1,123 pounds Steel		$8,984
	Total value	***$91,100***

Cargo of the Ad-Vance*'s run into Wilmington, 23 October 1863*

The cargo largely consisted of raw materials rather than ready-to-use muskets, cannon, pistols and shot. It would then be up to the blacksmiths and gunsmiths in North Carolina or other states of the Confederacy to turn these materials into weapons. It is unclear whether this listing is of the cargo on the arrival of the steamer on 12 October or if it was the grand total carried until that point, which would account for the three inward journeys of the *Ad-Vance*. Using a relative value calculator on the basis of real price, $91,000 in 1863 would today be worth around $1,800,000 (see Table 1). From the high value placed on the cargo it is clear that just five months into its ownership the State of North Carolina was seeing impressive returns from its steamer.[173]

One persistent story of another passenger making her way out of Wilmington to Europe was that of Anna MacNeill Whistler, mother and most famous subject of the painter James Abbott McNeill Whistler. The story goes that Anna Whistler, who had been born in Wilmington, left on the *Ad-Vance* though the blockade to Bermuda and then on to England. Though it is exciting to think that such a famous passenger made the journey aboard the *Ad-Vance*, the story does not correlate with the facts. She did indeed travel during the war from her home in Richmond, Virginia, to London, where her son was living in the autumn of 1863. But this journey took her via New York and not Wilmington. Noted Whistler historians Dan Sunderland and Georgia Toutziari, in the research for their book *Whistler's Mother: Portrait of an Extraordinary Life*, ascertained that the story of Anna on the *Ad-Vance* had been promoted in the 1930s by a North Carolina journalist by the name of Ben Dixon MacNeill (no relation to Anna) who wrote about the story of William Laurie Hill, a tar heel and author, who had claimed that he and his wife had travelled with Anna on the steamer. No other contemporary documents made mention of Whistler on the steamer. The research by Sunderland and Toutziari details that Anna made the trip from New York to Bermuda and then to Southampton. The *Ad-Vance* carried many passengers from Wilmington, but not this famous mother.[174]

The steamer and its crew had now made five successful runs through the blockade. Some runs had gone smoothly with no drama, while some had been in the daylight – the rarest and most dangerous attempts. Wyllie continued in his role as captain/sailing master, proving a trusted and respected officer, but changes were afoot for the crew and steamer as the direction of the war motivated Governor Vance to alter his policies towards blockade running.

PART II: CHANGES ABOARD THE *AD-VANCE*

Daily life aboard the *Ad-Vance* would have been a mixture of long periods of dull monotony interspersed with short, intense moments of action. The officers and crew faced the usual nautical trials of storms and navigational hazards, coupled with the ever-present threat of discovery and capture. In his official role as sailing master Wyllie oversaw the operation of the steamer. The officers and engineers would report to him on the status of their departments, and he would advise Captain Crossan as to the best course to follow. There may have been long bouts of inactivity, but the life of an officer on such a vessel would nevertheless have been taxing and stressful. It might have been such frantic situations that led to a change of command of the steamer just a few months into its career on the blockade. After a year away from home, crossing the Atlantic twice, and making his five successful runs aboard the *Ad-Vance*, Colonel Thomas Crossan made the decision to resign his command. The exact reason was not recorded in correspondence to Governor Vance, but it was known that by this time Crossan was in poor health. He returned to command the vessel in January 1864 for one last time before retiring from state service. He died aged just 46 in October 1865, shortly after the conclusion of the Civil War.[175]

Taking over from Crossan was John Julius Guthrie, a highly experienced naval officer, native North Carolinian and veteran of several maritime conflicts. He had been born in 1814 in Washington, North Carolina. Originally appointed as a cadet to the United States Military Academy in 1833, he left to join the Naval Academy in 1834 due to his preference for a life at sea. He saw action during the Mexican–American War as well as service in the Far East. He had achieved the rank of lieutenant by the start of the Civil War, but on hearing that North Carolina had seceded he resigned his commission. He was then made a lieutenant in the Confederate States Navy, taking command of the converted Mississippi river steamer *Red Rover* at New Orleans. In February 1863 he was assigned command of the CSS *Chattahoochee*, a steam warship designed for river and coastal defence. After a short period in command, Guthrie left after an accident caused a boiler explosion while the steamer was at anchor, resulting in the death of 16 crewmen.[176]

The second Confederate to command the Ad-Vance *was John Julius Guthrie (1815–1877). His career was mainly spent aboard sailing vessels and floating batteries, and he had little experience of fast, ocean-going steamers. He took over command from Thomas M. Crossan in October 1863, but disputes over pay led to his removal on 29 February 1864.*

Photo by the North Carolina Museum of History

This accident seems to have had no ill effect on his navy career, as on 18 October he received a letter from Governor Vance ordering him to take command of the *Ad-Vance* and sail to Bermuda as soon as possible.[177] Guthrie was known to be a well-spoken, intelligent man, his character and demeanour described in a biography written after his death:

> The tincture of classical learning which he had acquired in his youth gave him a foundation on which he laboriously built until his accomplishments as a linguist were remarkable. Among his intimate friends, with whom he felt he could talk with freedom, he frequently embellished his conversation with elegant allusions borrowed from the ancient classics, and his learning was as solid as it was unostentatious.[178]

Although we have no documented proof, this description would appear to indicate that Guthrie and Wyllie would have had quite a bit in common, both having had a classical education and both being adept at oration. Without confirmation through diaries or official documents, however, it cannot be judged just how well they got on as colleagues, but one would think a healthy respect on both a professional and a personal level could have developed between the two men. Wyllie's role, listed as sailing master, continued as before, and his long experience would have greatly assisted Guthrie, whose recent commands consisted of 'brown water' vessels: rivercraft unsuited to open water.

When Guthrie took command, the outlook for successful blockade running seemed bleak. Governor Vance himself expressed this feeling in a letter to John White, then still in England on state business, on the day that he instructed Guthrie to make for Wilmington. In his closing sentence of the letter regarding the state and supply of materials, Vance stated 'In the meantime do for the best. I do not think the '*Advance*' will make but one or two more trips.'[179] Vance's pessimism stemmed from a worry that Union forces would soon mount an all-out campaign to take Fort Fisher and then move towards Wilmington, thus cutting off the main port for his state.[8*]

This apprehension aside, the *Ad-Vance* continued to operate successfully. The steamer left for Bermuda on 23 October and arrived safely three days later, bringing with it 540 bales of cotton, the largest load to date. Another two voyages then passed without any incidents recorded by either Wyllie or Guthrie.

8* The capture of Fort Fisher would in fact not take place until 15 January 1865, after the second grand assault by Union naval and land forces. This led to the capture of Wilmington and the closure of the city as a blockade-running port. But the worry over the possible loss of the fort and the port of Wilmington was one that concerned Governor Vance and Confederate officials alike.

THE IMPACT OF THE *AD-VANCE* AND THE RETURN OF CROSSAN

The full impact of the *Ad-Vance* after eight supply runs to the State of North Carolina was significant. After its fourth run inwards from Bermuda the *Western Democrat* reported that it had arrived safely on 9 November, bringing 18,000 pairs of shoes and 17,500 blankets.[180] This added to the immense number of items already delivered, as reported by Governor Vance in his address to the General Assembly of North Carolina on 23 November:

> The enterprise of running the blockade and importing army supplies from abroad, has been proven a most *complete success* ... large quantities of clothing, leather and shoes, lubricating oils, factory findings, sheet iron and tin, arms and ammunition, medicines, dyestuffs, blankets, cotton bagging and rope; spirits, coffee &c., have been safely brought in, besides considerable freight for the Confederacy.

Vance added that the steamer had carried 2,010 bales of cotton to Liverpool, the proceeds from which had been deposited to the credit of the state. He finished his report by announcing: 'I can safely say that the North Carolina troops will be comfortably clothed until January 1865.'[181] Even with his concerns about the continued business of blockade running, it is clear that Vance was obviously happy with the operation of the *Ad-Vance*.

The eighth run of the *Ad-Vance* started from Wilmington around 19 November, and it arrived at Nassau four days later, on the 23rd. It was the first time the steamer had visited the Bahamas since its initial run in June. It would also be last run to take place before the New Year, and it once again found Colonel Crossan at the helm. No official records between those dates indicate the reason for Guthrie's absence, but he might have been in Eufaula, Alabama: a letter from Lieutenant McLaughlin of the Confederate States Navy, commander of the *Chattahoochee*, mentions that Guthrie was spending some time there in order to purchase a house for his family to live in as the war continued.[182]

Another, more significant, change was the sale of half of the interest in the steamer to the firm of Power, Low & Company of Wilmington. The firm was involved in the transatlantic trade by supplying the blockade runners, but had not operated its own runners. Its purchase of a stake in the *Ad-Vance* meant that the company now had its own transport for the goods it was bringing in from Britain. With the growing dangers of blockade running becoming evident through increased numbers of captures or sinkings, Governor Vance made the decision to diversify the fleet and maximise the inward imports for the state. By selling half-ownership of the *Ad-Vance*, he was able to use the funds to buy shares in four other steamers, all owned by the firm of Alexander Collie and Company of London, which in 1862 had been appointed as agent for the state's affairs. Collies operated in England, selling the North Carolinian cotton, and working with John White to purchase the required supplies as outlined by Vance.[183]

The first run of the *Ad-Vance* under dual ownership would not take place for some time as it would spend the entire month of December at anchor at Nassau. So long in fact that Governor Vance felt it necessary to apologise to his new partners, stating in a letter dated 6 January: 'I regret exceedingly the long delay of the *Advance* both on your account and my own.'[184]

When the steamer did ultimately get under way the course that Crossan set wasn't a return to Wilmington but a trip to Bermuda. The reason was that a cargo for the return trip was not available at Nassau, so the steamer was forced into making this extra journey. From Nassau the steamer headed north-east with only a small amount of cargo in its holds: 10 barrels of whiskey, 10 cases of brandy and five cases of hardware, none of which was to be landed in Bermuda.[185]

Vance's letter to his new partners also mentioned the state of the steamer and some proposed alterations that he suggested would improve its operation. These included cutting away the upper works in order to lighten the vessel and allow more cotton bales to be carried. Also noted was 'a vast accumulation of dirt and rubbish in her hold and coal bunker' which he suggested should be removed. This letter is one of the earliest communications between the two owners, who over the next nine months would exchange frequent letters and telegrams. The sale of half of the steamer meant that all costs of operation would be shared equally, requiring detailed accounts: the most comprehensive records for the steamer's operation come from this post-sale era. The balance sheets from the period, known as disbursements, list in great detail each and every cost associated with the vessel – items such as crew payments, coal purchased, laundry and foodstuffs for each journey. These records, which were made during every visit of the steamer to Bermuda or the Bahamas, offer a unique insight into the day-to-day operations of the steamer.

THE FIRST RUN OF 1864

New Year 1864 marked the start of the fourth year of the Civil War, which still seemed deadlocked. The Union had made gains and so the Confederacy was struggling to maintain its armies on the front line as well as keeping up the hopes of its civilians on the home front. Blockade running was still a big business, ranging from the privately run ships which provided the finer things to steamers like the *Ad-Vance*, contracted to supply the regiments in the field as well as the civilians reliant on the State's endeavours. Even with the increased vigilance and size of the Union fleet, the runners still held the advantage: the number of successful runs into Wilmington in December 1863 was 15, while 3 steamers had been either destroyed or captured. January saw another 15 runners making the safety of Cape

Fear, with another 4 captured or sunk. Over those two months this was a success rate of 80 per cent.[186]

The *Ad-Vance* was amongst those successful January arrivals. After the long lay-up in Bermuda it finally left the packed harbour of St George's on 11 January, bound for Wilmington. Making ready for the approach to the Carolina coast was Signal Officer John Baptist Smith. He once again chronicled his experiences on the steamer as it ran the blockade. Later in life he recounted this experience in a letter entitled 'The Stranded Blockade Runner'.[187] This trip once again returned the steamer to the dangers of the trade – but this time it would not be the cannons of the Union fleet so much as the fierce forces of Mother Nature that would put the ship and crew in mortal danger.

As the Carolina coast was approached the young Smith was preparing the signal lanterns in anticipation of the run, but his vital role was delayed first by the weather, which forced the steamer back out to sea, and then by the ships of the blockade fleet. Smith recounted the actions of the crew as he prepared to set his lights:

> The first night she was prevented by a dense fog and drizzling rain which obscured all lights and landmarks. The second night she was sighted and chased off to sea by the blockading fleet of federal vessels. The next day (Sunday) we lay off the coast of South Carolina some distance at sea, keeping a sharp lookout for Federal cruisers none of which made their appearance, much to our joy. The day was spent by our ship's crew in restful enjoyment of the beautiful weather and tranquil waters.

This tranquillity was soon broken. Crossan grew anxious, and his reading of the changing weather gave him pause as to the next course to set. He spoke to the officers: 'Gentlemen, I don't like the looks of the barometer.' Then he asked the chief engineer about the state of the coal on board, the reply being that due to their already protracted run there was only enough coal left for 24 hours. A critical choice now needed to be made: they must either head back to Bermuda or make the dash to Cape Fear. Crossan chose to run the risk of the storm, and signalled a course northwards to the coast. Their luck held as they approached Cape Fear and were ahead of the storm, but then a calamity occurred:

> After several hours of steaming, the coast was sighted by the pilot and we were congratulating ourselves in the belief that we were past all danger when all at once the ship struck a sand bar with such violence as to throw us off our balance. The engines were quickly reversed, but 'full speed astern' failed to budge her.

Now they were stranded, unable to escape both the human and the natural dangers that were bearing down on them. The spirits of the crew sunk with the realisation that they were out of range of the home fort's guns, meaning that if any Union ship happened upon them they would be a sitting duck. As the steamer sat there, Smith recalled the mindsets of the officers.

> 'Twas a most anxious watch, that which was kept all night by the ship's complement of officers, for the impending danger banished all thoughts of sleep. Closely and anxiously was the horizon to the seaward scanned at the first dawn of the morning, when, greatly to our surprise and joy, not a Federal vessel was in sight. Anticipating the storm, they had sought shelter in a friendly port.

The storm was yet to hit and as dawn broke steps were taken to try and extricate the steamer from the sandbar. First a signal was sent to Fort Caswell to relay the message to Wilmington that help was required to lighten the ship, and as a result river steamers were sent out at speed to remove cargo. As this help arrived the crew quickly set about offloading boxes and crates. There was still no sign of the Union fleet and the feeling was that their efforts might just succeed. But then, just as the engines were being made ready to release them from the bar, the captain's experience told him that they would once again be in harm's way.

> About 4:00 P.M. the bulk of the ship's cargo was safely discharged, and the impossibility of extricating the ship was apparent. Just as the last steamer was about ready to leave, the captain of our ship had all hands called up and addressed them as follows: 'Shipmates, from my experience at sea I am satisfied we are on the verge of a great storm, and feel it my duty to you to say it is very doubtful about the ship, in her helpless condition, being able to live through the night, but I am determined to stand by her and would like for as many of you to stay with me as will do so voluntarily; but it must be entirely of your free will. And those of you who do not care to take the risk are at liberty to go ashore on that boat,' pointing to the steamer alongside our ship.

Many of the crew chose to board the river steamers and make for safety, but the officers, several of the seamen and a few firemen remained on board the *Ad-Vance* to try and ride out the storm and save their runner. Smith signalled his willingness to remain with the ship, but Crossan confronted him: 'Jump aboard the boat, my lad, and go ashore.' Smith replied,

'Captain, I alone can communicate with the shore and I think I ought to stay with you.' Once more Crossan implored the young man to save himself: 'My lad, 'twill be impossible for any help to reach us from the shore. You have a father and a mother to live for; jump aboard the boat before it is too late.' But Smith wouldn't have it, and he, Wyllie and their fellow crew readied the steamer for the coming tempest.

> No mortal pen can picture the awful sublimity of a storm such as that which was soon to burst upon us. The sea had become one vast mirrored surface, not a breath of air rippling its placid serenity. With notes of warning, the sea birds had taken their departure, save the 'Mother Carey's chickens,' birds of ill omen, which gleefully flitted around our vessel as if in anticipation of the terrible fate that awaited us. A cloud the size of a man's hand now loomed up in the offing. Strange weird sounds, groans of the mighty deep came to our ears. A great wave, the skirmish line of the dreaded foe, bore down upon us in one unbroken swell, struck our ship on her starboard quarter and forced her stern squarely to the sea from her former position, with broadside exposed to the breakers.
>
> 'Thank God for that!' exclaimed the captain. 'Now, my lad, if we can keep her stern to the storm there is a chance for our lives. Stand by all hands to hoist sail!' …
>
> The suspense was dreadful! The little cloud grew greater and greater and approached faster and faster, gathering strength and velocity as it came, until the sea and clouds mingled in dense, struggling, writhing masses, and with the speed of a whirlwind and the road of a tornado the allied forces of wind, water and darkness burst upon us, howling and shrieking through the ship's rigging like demons gloating over their helpless prey.

Faced with the full force of nature's power, the remaining crew used their wits and skills to maintain the steamer's orientation during the pounding. The wind continued to howl:

> In the battle for existence, every man became a hero. In spite of the combined powers of wind and waves, a few yards of canvas had to be carried to prevent the ship from swinging broadside to the breakers. Never did the officers respond with greater alacrity to the commands of a captain than did that brave crew of the *ADVANCE* to the orders of their intrepid commander. All rank was forgotten; all hands hauled away together on the ropes; all hope was centered upon the ability of a few yards of canvas to hold together, and so the

> ship was kept sharp stern in position to cut asunder the fearful waves dashing in mad succession upon us, at times lifting the vessel upon their crests and then dropping her upon the sands as if determined to break her keel in two.
>
> In spite of all, the staunch craft, though wrenched and twisted by the violence of the waves and knocked against the land, held together, and after a night of mingled hopes and fears daylight found her lying safe and sound in the placid waters of the Cape Fear River.

The *Ad-Vance* was now safe from the Union ships, as it was now too close to the forts for them to approach. Yet the waves and tides could still sink the runner if the captain and crew were not vigilant. It remained at the mouth of the Cape Fear River until the 24th as lighters shuttled back and forth, taking off more cargo and coal in order to lighten it further; eventually it broke free of the shoal. When all was said and done, this was another successful trip as it had brought in 10,000 pairs of shoes, 12,000 blankets and 8,000 cotton carding combs.[188]

The long lay-up on the sands did not come without cost. The constant battering by the tide and waves had caused a significant amount of damage to the boiler and the engine. Immediate repairs were required, and Power, Low & Company employed Thomas E. Roberts of Wilmington for the work, which cost $7,721. Roberts had sent the owners an invoice on 1 February outlining the repairs, which included new boiler iron, plates, fire bricks and brass fixings. The steamer's continued operation was now in doubt due to the overworking of its machinery and the damage caused by its several beachings. Although some repairs could be completed in Wilmington, these were only patching up the main problems. A full overhaul could not be completed, as there were no suitable shipyards or dock available – nor any experienced engineers.[189]

The trials and near-destruction of the *Ad-Vance* was reported widely in North Carolina in the days after its arrival in the estuary. All reports mentioned that it had stuck fast on the sands and it was hoped to be freed soon, but some feared the worst. A full report of its activities came from a Union naval report by Commander J.M. Frailey of the *Quaker City*. Although he could not positively identify the name of the steamer, he reported that an English runner had beached and that he was unable to attempt capture as the storm had forced him to leave his anchorage and seek shelter.[190]

News of the near-disaster even made it to Europe. The *Liverpool Daily Post* of 18 February 1864, citing an article from the *Richmond Whig*, listed the vessel as having been ashore but with its cargo now safe and well. Two days later the *Glasgow Saturday Post* decided to inform its readers of the loss of the 'Old *Lord Clyde*'. In noting that crew and cargo had been saved, the paper mentioned the history of the steamer including the purchase price paid by White and Crossan. But most interestingly it too stated that it was Captain Wyllie who had been in command when the steamer left the Clyde the previous year.[191]

THE CREW OF THE *AD-VANCE*

Command of the state steamer would again change hands as it sat at the wharf in Wilmington. It had arrived on 21 January, and a week later Governor Vance again summoned John Julius Guthrie, writing 'You will once proceed at once to Wilmington to take the command of the steamer *Ad-Vance*'.[9*] Crossan's departure from the helm was not noted in Vance's letter, but it might have been due to his aforementioned ill health. A new purser joined the crew to replace Theodore Hughes who, although ordered by Vance to continue his role, refused the command, citing 'the character of the ship has now changed', which he claimed had resulted from the change of ownership. In his place, Vance appointed Dr Thomas Boykin, a native North Carolinian who, after moving to Nebraska in 1856, had at the start of the war made a speedy return to his home state, where he was to serve as a regimental surgeon. In Vance's letter to Boykin the governor listed exactly what cargo he expected the new purser to load: 'First, cotton cards and machinery and wire for making them. Secondly, shoes and leather. Third blankets, then card cloth for factories. Cloth, readymade clothing, etc.'[192]

Wyllie was now almost a year into his service on board the steamer. His role and personality had been noted by several of the passengers and crew. His official rank aboard was sometimes referred to as 'sailing master' or as '1st Mate', while Crossan and Guthrie held command for the State of North Carolina. I have been unable to trace any form of crew list relating to the period after the steamer's departure from Scotland in May 1863, so the relevant official titles on the Atlantic crossing are impossible to record. The first recorded crew list dates from February 1864, just after Guthrie's re-appointment as commander; it survived in his own personal papers, now held by the State Archive of North Carolina.[193]

The '*Officers and Crew List of the AD.Vance*' is a three-page handwritten document. It is the inward list relating to the steamer's arrival at either St George's on 9 February or Wilmington on the 16th. It is not known who compiled or wrote the list; the candidates include Guthrie, the ship's steward George Hunt, the purser Thomas Boykin, and a customs official in St George's. But one thing is known for certain: Wyllie's was not the hand that penned it. Like many documents before and after this one, his name was spelled incorrectly, as Johanes Wilie. All crew had their rank and 'nativity' (i.e. place of birth) listed, with Wyllie's given as first officer and Scotland. The fact that the nativity was listed offers another useful point of reference, as the diverse and international makeup of the crew can thus be confirmed.

There were 56 crew members, 21 of whom were American: 12 of these from North Carolina, 4 from Virginia, 2 from Maryland, 1 each from New York and Rhode Island, and 1 possibly from Pennsylvania. 34 were European: 14 Irish, 9 English, 4 Scottish, 3 French, and 2 each from Sweden and Portugal. Finally, there was 1 Canadian (a British subject at the time). On the face of it this was quite a cosmopolitan crew. The use of the word 'nativity' does, however, bring up a notable question, as this term refers directly to

9* Note that Governor Vance uses the wording *Ad-Vance* himself when referring to the steamer.

the place of birth and not necessarily nationality. Joannes Wyllie was clearly a Scot and Guthrie a North Carolinian, but examining the list in more depth identifies up at least two discrepancies. Second officer William C. Jones' nativity was listed as Scotland, which would make him one of the foreigners. But in fact he had been living in New Bern, North Carolina, from at least 1860. So although he was not a native-born Carolinian, could he be considered a Southerner? Similarly the first engineer, James Maglenn, listed as Irish, was also a resident of North Carolina in 1860, having been born in Ireland and emigrated to America in 1852. More of the men listed as Irish or Scots or Swedes might have indeed been 'new' Carolinians, and listing their original birth country might allow them, if the steamer was captured, to escape punishment. As this crew list appears to have been part of the ship's papers, it would be an official document that could be produced and cited to back up any claims of being a citizen of a neutral nation (see Appendix 2).

Whether 'new' Carolinians or old Scots, the promise of high pay and the hope of fortunes to be made on the blockade were a temptation to many sailors, mates and engineers from Europe. Even with the issue of nativity taken into account, almost 66 per cent of the crew were listed as foreign. In this the *Ad-Vance* was not an aberration: most of the runners that had come over from Britain had substantial, if not majority, crews of European sailors and officers. Thousands of mariners came from the British Isles, with an estimate for the Scottish contribution alone given at up to 3,000 men by Dr Eric J. Graham in his book *Clyde Built*.[194]

With its crew of 56 the *Ad-Vance* left Wilmington on 6 February, and its voyage, like the previous ones with Guthrie in command, came off with no incident recorded. The steamer arrived at St George's three days later with 689 bales of cotton, surpassing its previous record of 540.[195] For the first time the cotton was listed as not just a single number of bales, but as being distributed amongst three consignees.

Looking at the Books

The steamer spent just four days in St George's, making a very quick turnaround for its next voyage. During this short period there would be a flurry of ship's business, as recorded in the first disbursement by Francis William Jones (F.W.J.) Hurst, the managing clerk and agent in Bermuda for the shipping company of Edward Lawrence & Company of Liverpool. Power, Low & Company had entered into a partnership with that company in order to transport its cargoes from Bermuda.[196]

Hurst's list is the first detailed examination of the operations of the *Ad-Vance*, coming almost a full year after its purchase in Glasgow. He records its total operating costs as £3,695 6s 4d, half of which would be covered by the state and half by Power, Low & Company.[197] It is a fantastic window into the day-to-day operations of a blockade runner. By far the largest outlay is wages for captain, pilot and crew, which came to a total £2,412 4s 10d. This included cash for cotton seized and the bounty paid for the successful trip inwards as well as for the upcoming voyage. The wages given to Guthrie (listed as both $500 and £104 3s 4d) and to Wilmington pilot C.C. Morse (£520 16s 8d) were listed, but the rest of the crew's wages were lumped into one line at $4,282; this would have included Wyllie's pay. If he was still receiving 25 per cent of the captain's pay, that amounted to $125. Only one other crew member is mentioned by name: John Stewart, a Scottish seaman, whose pay had been left out of the otherwise complete list compiled by the purser. It is rare to find the detailed payments to ordinary seamen, so Stewart's inclusion offers a useful insight into the remuneration received by the wider crew: his pay and bounty for the previous voyage was listed at £8 19s 2d – for just three days of work. Comparing this to the wages Wyllie had received per *month* on his previous ships, it is easy to see why the blockade was viewed by many sailors as a bonanza.

As well as the payments to the crew, the disbursement lists more mundane items, all of which were vital to ship operations. Every penny needed to be accounted for, so items such as the ship's washing (£3 4s 7d), and cash for a new marine glass (£3), and stationery (10s) are all listed. The cook, a Frenchman named Venerman, had his supplies restocked with groceries (£180 17s 2d) and wines, spirits and dried fruit (£136 0s 2d). Finally, fuel for the next run was procured: 262.5 tons of coal were ordered at a cost of £721 17s 6d, representing the second largest outlay for the steamer.[198]

With all the bills paid, and provisions and coal loaded, the *Ad-Vance* left St George's on 13 February 1864. Guthrie and Wyllie would be racing to make Wilmington while the nights were still dark, the new moon having been on the 7th. The events of this voyage would be once again be documented by a passenger, and were widely reported in newspapers across North Carolina. Appearing first in the Raleigh *Semi-Weekly Standard* on 23 February, the article described both the outward and inward journeys through the blockade to Bermuda. Cryptically the author signed themself only as W, so the newspaper's readers were left wondering just who this mystery passenger was. The name was never revealed in later reprints in other newspapers, nor does a passenger list exist from this journey, so their identity may never be positively confirmed.[10*]

Their account opens with the words: 'a short history of the trip may be acceptable to the public generally, and to the people of North Carolina especially'. The writer would appear to have been a supporter of Vance's plan for the steamer, and the article expounds its value as well as admiring the professionalism of the crew and officers. The outward run started at the cotton-filled docks of Wilmington and then went out to sea, which W described as 'running the block':

> The *Ad-Vance* left her wharf at Wilmington on Saturday morning, 6th inst., at 8 o'clock. About 10 o'clock she got aground on the Lower Slough, where she

10*One possibility is this account was written by Frank Inge Wilson, a North Carolina newspaper editor and colleague of W.W. Holden, editor of the *Weekly Standard*. Wilson is known to have been a passenger on the *Ad-Vance* for one or more journeys, as he recounted these in a letter to Captain Guthrie on 6 April 1864.

> remained until 4 o'clock, P.M., waiting for the tide. By night she had succeeded in running the 'home blockade;' by which, I mean she had passed out of reach of the military and naval authorities, some of whom came on board for some purpose or another at almost every fort, station etc.

Once again the shallow waters and shifting sands of the mouth of Cape Fear had grounded the *Ad-Vance*. This instance of incarceration did not, however, place the steamer in any immediate danger, and the crew had needed only to wait for the rising of the tide. The detail about military authorities coming aboard could indicate that these personnel were alerting Guthrie, Wyllie and the officers both as to the current state of their guns atop the battlements of Fort Caswell and Fisher and their up-to-date intelligence of the lurking Union warships. Next, W described the run, which came off with no real drama of note:

> And now commenced what is generally termed 'running the block.' The anxiety of all on board, and especially of the officers, may well be imagined. The sea is calm, and it is very pleasant on deck. Our lights are out, and we glide almost noiselessly along. Every eye is straining out upon the dark bosom of the ocean, and every ear is listening out attentively for the voice of the watch at the masthead. More steam is crowded on, and away we dart. But one blockader is seen and that is too far off to occasion the least apprehension, even if we are discovered. Presently two lights are seen far to our right, but whether on shore or on vessels we neither know nor care. By midnight we consider ourselves out of danger, and all 'turn in' except those necessary for working and watching the vessel.
>
> The weather remained mild and balmy. We passed several sails each day, to one of which we showed the Confederate flag, but obtained no response. On Tuesday evening, we were near Bermuda, but as we could not go in at night, we tacked about until morning, when a pilot came on board and carried us in.
>
> The *Ad-Vance* carried out 670 bales of cotton, which were soon rolled out upon the wharf. On Thursday night the cotton was discovered to be on fire, supposed to have been the work of an incendiary. Comparatively a small quantity was consumed – perhaps 40–50 bales, burned and injured.
>
> My impressions of Bermuda were favourable. It certainly presents a romantic appearance. But as I only design an account of our trip I will not now speak more of the island.

The risk of fire was constant due to the nature of the two primary cargoes of the steamer: tinder-dry cotton loaded side by side with barrels of highly flammable turpentine. This fire was, however, minor: Thomas Carter, agent of the state, later reported that only 25 bales had been burnt. But conflagration seemed to be shadowing the *Ad-Vance*, as in addition to the fire after its arrival in Bermuda it had left behind a much worse calamity in Wilmington. Just two days after the steamer headed downriver a fire broke out on the wharf in which 1,025 bales were destroyed at an estimated loss of $700,000.

The stay at Bermuda was a short one; the steamer was ready for its return leg just four days after arrival. This would prove a much more interesting voyage, as W recounted:

> By Saturday evening we had taken in our return cargo, and just before night we steamed away. We found the ocean rougher than on our outward trip, but we still made good progress until Monday Night, when it blew a furious gale. It was well for the writer that he was a 'land lubber,' and did not know when to get scared. The vessel was eased to about 4 knots an hour (*sic*), but even at this speed the deck was flooded continually with the briny waters. The cold was also intense. Truly was the *metal* (*sic*) of both ship and crew tested; and just as truly was it proven *pure.*
>
> With the coming of the day the storm abated some, though the wind still blew strongly, and the waves frequently broke [on] the deck. It became a matter of doubt whether we could make the distance, so as to run through the blockading fleet during the few dark hours after the moon down that night – or rather the next morning. It was important to do so, as the dark hours were growing fearfully fewer every night. But we succeeded.
>
> And now behold us without a light on board, the wind, though much abated, still blowing cold and strong, darting along at a speed nearly 20 miles per hour. Every man at his post – every one looking for what he hopes not to find – a blockader. But we did find not only one, but seven. We felt them upon our right and our left. It were contrary to the human mind not to feel a deep anxiety at such a time; but I do not believe there was a quailing spirit on board. All felt the utmost confidence in the vessel and her officers, and that confidence gave them courage.
>
> And now we are nearly out of reach of the huge monsters lying behind us, not one of which has perceived us. All feel relieved – congratulations are passing – we feel that we are delivered from peril. But hark! 'We are aground!' was passed from mouth to mouth. It was too true. There we were, too far from our own forts to be protected by them, and with but an hour of friendly

darkness in which to get afloat. Like Joshua, we would then have stopped the sun in his course, not to prolong the light but the darkness; but we had not his faith and did not try to exercise his power. On the contrary we went to work and threw a quantity of lead overboard. Still we were aground. The boats had previously been made ready for lowering, and every one was fixing his little package of valuables to take with him. But to give up our gallant ship! That touches every heart. Only at the last moment would it be done; but the moments were flying fast. Soon the sun and the blockaders would be upon us with their lights – the former with his warm beams – the later with their hot flashes. How long we were aground, the writer will not presume to say, but he is honest enough to confess, (as he believes all on board would confess,) that to him it *seemed a long time.* Still there were increased exertions to get off. There was no excitement – no blustering hurry –but commands were quietly given and promptly obeyed. A few moments before day the joyful cry of 'we are afloat!' was rung from stem to stern through the noble steamer. The relief we all experienced, we leave to the imagination of the reader.

We were soon under the friendly guns of Fort Caswell, and that evening came to our wharf at Wilmington, again successfully running the 'home blockade.' The return cargo of the *Ad-Vance* consisted mostly of blankets and shoes for our State troops, with merchandize for several firms and individuals. The trip was made, counting from the time when we crossed the bar, in ten days and a half.

To speak of all the officers and crew and passengers, the jokes told, the wit and humor evolved, and the cordiality of all, would consume too much of my time and occupy too much of your space; but I must be permitted to say that in my opinion the service has no more skilful officer and no more perfect gentleman than Capt. Guthrie, a native son of North Carolina, of whom she is justly proud. He is kind but firm, mild, but decided. The officers under him are worthy of him, but to name one I must name all, and I have already sufficiently trespassed upon your columns.[199]

Once again the steamer's draught, known to be deeper than that of some of the other runners making for Wilmington, had caused the bother. The professionalism of the officers and crew was on display, as they were able to free the vessel by quick thinking and hard graft, with the loss of only a small amount of cargo. Although W made no mention of any crew by name other than Guthrie, his description of 'wit and humor' with regard to the officers and crew would surely refer to Joannes Wyllie and his poetic nature, something previously noted in the accounts of the Rev. Moses Hoge and John Baptist Smith.

AN UNHAPPY GUTHRIE AND HIS ULTIMATE REMOVAL

The *Ad-Vance* finally made it to Wilmington by 25 February.[11*] Although the steamer had just completed its eleventh successful run, trouble was brewing between the owners and its captain. Guthrie had completed two successful trips through the blockade but was unhappy about his pay. He was receiving the monthly pay of a captain in the old US Navy, as it was termed in the Confederacy, as well as $1,000 per round trip, these being the same terms under which Crossan had been engaged. Although this was a substantial amount, Guthrie was unhappy that he was to be paid his monthly rate in Confederate currency, bills that day after day were losing value through devaluation due to the waning fortunes of the Confederacy. Guthrie had wished to be paid in 'coin': gold would not face the same pressures from the American conflict. But Governor Vance had instructed the steamer's purser that pay was to be in Confederate money, information that was then relayed to the state's partners of Power, Low & Company.[200]

In addition to the disagreement regarding pay, there was also the matter of the suspected smuggling of extra cotton bales and other contraband cargo on board the steamer. By agreement the captain and crew were allowed 24 bales that when sold would supplement their wages. But anything above this, or any other potentially lucrative freight, was forbidden by the owners. Vance had informed both Guthrie and Power, Low & Company that the carrying of extra freight was strictly forbidden without his consent, writing in a letter to his co-owners, 'I have ordered him not to let a pound of freight for private parties go on board without my written consent or yours and hope you will assist in executing the order.'[201]

This issue was significant for Vance and his co-owners: it was a state-owned steamer, and its cargoes were for the benefit of North Carolina and its people. Any extra cargo carried by officers or crew could attract scandal to the project. But news leaked out of such activities, and just a week after Guthrie's return from Bermuda it became a public issue, the *Western Democrat* reporting on 16 February that:

> We have heard say (with how much truth we cannot tell) that the steamer has been partly used for the benefit of certain individuals, transporting their family supplies, &c.; and further, that very little of the fine wines and liquors imported goes down the throats of sick soldiers.[202]

The issue came to a head when Vance sent a letter to Guthrie on 26 February 1864, expressing his disapproval of the operations of the steamer under Guthrie, and stating:

> I have to repeat my former order concerning the shipment of cotton on

11* This is reported in the *Wilmington Journal*. The delay is not reported, nor is it in correspondence, but the steamer might have been at the quarantine stations near Smithville at the mouth of the river.

> private account – Messers Power, Low & Co, are authorized to make all arrangement which it is hoped will be satisfactory to officers and crew. All cotton not appearing on the manifest will be seized and it is c----y [certainly?] hoped the Officers will set an example to their subordinates of promptly and carefully shipping orders.
>
> I learn that you were dissatisfied with your pay. I can not afford to give you the same as is paid by blockade r----s [illegible, *runners*?] to their captains who now ---- [illegible] work for their pay, yet I will pay you what Capt. Crossan worked for …
>
> In conclusion, Capt, permit me to express my regrets at this unexpected rupture of our official relations and wish you a prosperous, and successful voyage.[203]

The end to the letter would suggest that Vance still held Guthrie in enough confidence to retain him. Yet just three days later, as the steamer was once again ready to run the blockade, Guthrie was removed from command and Joannes Wyllie put in his place. Vance wrote again to Boykin to inform him of the change:

> Captain Guthrie, after full consultation with Mr Power and myself (when I trust to give him your ideas correctly) concluded to turn over the command to Capt. Wyllie. Capt. Guthrie's action about the matter and some other little things on the ship were to me rather strange.[204]

The combination of Guthrie's demands and the unsatisfactory operation of the steamer while he was in command seem to have been the main reasons for the change. The decision, as shown in this letter, had been taken with the agreement of both Vance and Power, Low & Company.

So command of the prize steamer, invaluable to both the State of North Carolina and to the other Confederate troops clothed or booted by the cargoes it supplied, was transferred to the Scottish first officer: the fortunes of the state would lie in the hands of this tried, tested and experienced, but 'foreign' captain. After almost a year on board, and now being the last of the original crew who had brought it over from Glasgow, Wyllie finally took command officially. The next seven months would prove even more hazardous to the steamer and to Wyllie than those that had passed, with transatlantic voyages, ill health and chases by the ever-strengthening Union blockade fleet all on the cards for the newly promoted captain.

5

WYLLIE TAKES COMMAND

Capt. Wyllie has done well for the ship, a better commander cannot be had for her.

– Joseph Flanner, agent for North Carolina in London and former purser of steamer *Ad-Vance.*

PART I

The extra 24 hours of a leap year might be used for recreation and peaceful reflection, or might be full of excitement and conflict. Leap year day 1864 was the latter for Joannes Wyllie and the *Ad-Vance*. On 29 February there occurred a flurry of news and correspondence relating to the future of the steamer. The order having gone out from Vance to Guthrie that his time in command was at an end, the new arrangements for the steamer were being hurriedly confirmed by the captain, the officers, the governor and his fellow owners.

Wyllie must have known before that day that he was to be the new captain, but it was now that he received a letter from Guthrie which formally passed command to him. The letter was curt and straight to the point. Guthrie wrote:

> With the consent of his Excellency of Z Vance, Governor of the State of N.C., I have the honor to invest you with the command of the N.C. S S. *Advance.*
>
> His Excellency directs in written instructions received today, that the *Advance* shall sail direct, with as little delay as possible, for the port of St George's, Bermuda. From which place after landing her present cargo and reboard another for the State, she will return again to this place. Please therefore consider

> these orders repeated to you in the most urgent manner from which there is no other authority except his own that will justify you ignoring.
>
> In conclusion, Capt, permit me to express my regrets at this unexpected rupture of our official relations and wish you a prosperous, and successful voyage.[205]

By this farewell to Wyllie, Guthrie makes it clear that this was a sudden break and the removal of his command had not been anticipated. No ill feelings appear to have arisen from the old captain towards the new, and Guthrie's wish for continued success must have stemmed from knowing the importance of the steamer for the State of North Carolina.

The news of Wyllie's promotion quickly made the rounds, starting with the crew of the steamer and then spreading to the citizens of Wilmington where the steamer had sat for two weeks awaiting its next turn. Thomas Boykin wrote to Governor Vance on the 29th with regard to the status of the vessel, its readiness for sailing and the most pressing issue – the change of command:

> Captain Guthrie, after full consultation with Mr Power and myself (when I trust to give him your ideas correctly) concluded to turn over the command to Capt. Wyllie. Capt. Guthrie's action about the matter and some other little things on the ship were to me rather strange, about which I will talk with you more at length when I see you.
>
> After his resignation, our only alternative per your instructions were to give the str [steamer] to Capt. Wyllie. I do sincerely hope he may be successful and that all may turn out to your entire satisfaction …
>
> You can say when the opportunity offers, in reply to this sentiment, that under the circumstances that we had no other alternative and did what we thought was for the best.'[206]

There was obvious regret in Boykin's tone regarding Guthrie's situation, yet the actions that provoked the change could not be ignored. Guthrie's removal left the owners with a single option for a new commander, but handing over the wheel to a non-North Carolinian might have provoked some misgivings: despite Wyllie's experience, both before the war and as an employee of the State, his appointment came with some trepidation. Reactions from crew to the appointment then followed, as Boykin wrote that 'The crew are all delighted with the change though I know there is some outside feeling in town about the idea of a "furriner" having charge of the gallant old craft.' Boykin underlined the colloquialism to drive home his point. He then went on to note that in response to this sentiment Vance could say 'when the opportunity offers, in reply to this sentiment, that under the circumstances that we had no other alternative and did what we thought was for the best.'[207] The trepidation in Boykin's letter regarding the appointment was unwarranted, though, as there was no better person to take command: Wyllie, through his actions and experience, was the most experienced mariner on the *Ad-Vance*, having brought it across the Atlantic, and he had been a loyal member of the crew ever since. The underlying worry with regard to a 'furriner' in command must have been expressed by those unfamiliar with the man, his merit and his reputation.

In the same letter Boykin informed Vance that the steamer was fully loaded with 820 bales of cotton and that the Wilmington pilot was satisfied with the draft. This was by far the largest load the *Ad-Vance* had ever carried, the increase having been made possible by the alterations to the steamer made at Wilmington. Almost all items of comfort and decoration had been stripped out, completing the final transformation from luxurious passenger ferry to sleek, high-capacity runner. The deckhouses had been either cleared of ornamentation or removed completely. The extra capacity meant that the previous record for the steamer of 689 bales was far exceeded. Indeed, Power, Low & Company wrote to Vance on 1 March to say that the steamer could have carried another 100 bales, but that the draft would once again be a concern: it had on both of its last two runs into the Cape Fear inlet become stuck upon a sandbar and dangerously close to either capture or foundering. So despite the capacity for even more cargo, the decision was taken to err on the side of caution.

Many of the items removed from the steamer had found their way to auction in the city – yet another way to turn a profit from the steamer. In the 2 March edition of the *Wilmington Daily Journal* an advertisement by Wilkes Morris, Auctioneer, listed the 'desirable articles removed from the cabin and deck' that could be purchased one week hence from the warehouse of Power, Low & Company. Highlights included gilt ornaments, lamps, carpeting, brass handrails, doors, shutters, cabin partitions, velvet cushions and velvet armchairs. The lists also included washstands with marble basins – just about everything *and* the kitchen sink.[208]

These internal alterations were accompanied by work carried out on the machinery. Vance was informed in the letter of the 29th from Power, Low & Company that 'She would have been ready some days ago, but her machinery had to be put in order which will only be finished to-night.' The *Ad-Vance* had now been operating for almost a year without any major repairs or a refit. The machinery was starting to show signs of strain, and repair facilities were not available in Wilmington, St George's or Nassau. This problem, along with the concerns expressed by Vance in January regarding the cleanliness of the steamer, indicates that the *Ad-Vance* was deteriorating structurally and that its ability to carry out its role was now becoming greatly impaired.

Nevertheless, out went the steamer from Wilmington on 1 March with its new commander, laden with its largest cargo yet, headed for Smithville at the mouth of the Cape Fear inlet, there to await the best time to make its dash. The new moon would not arrive until 7 March, compelling Wyllie to stay at anchor there for a week. Once the nights fell dark Wyllie, in consultation from the pilot, C.C. Morse, made the decision to run. They had the latest intelligence from the observers at the Confederate forts regarding where the blockade fleet was at its strongest and when other runners had last attempted their runs. Confusion could be as strong an ally as the darkness, so changing the pattern of which of the two channels to attempt would keep the Union captains guessing which of them to guard. Finally, the decision of which course to take, based on the knowledge of the tides, shifting sandbars and other mid-river hazards, was of course left to the pilot, on whose shoulders this part of the voyage rested.

The pilots who guided runners in and out of the Cape Fear inlet were among the most important members of the crew, and this was reflected in both their status and their pay. As in other ports around the world, then and now, they were highly skilled navigators with encyclopaedic knowledge of their local waters and their dangers. They were employed by all ships, in peacetime and in war, to negotiate the passage from the open sea into port and back. The main focus of their skill was their knowledge of the channels in the river that were deep enough for the vessel they were in charge of. The Cape Fear River had two such channels, or inlets. The main ship channel, also known as the Old Inlet, was to the south and had been used as the primary route since the founding of Wilmington in colonial days. It ranged in depth from 10 to 15 feet, and its shifting sandbars tested the most knowledgeable pilot. The second channel, the New Inlet, had been created by an extra-fierce hurricane in 1761. The storm had cut a path through the Federal Point peninsula, opening up this second route from the sea to the river. It was located to the east of the main channel and, although shallower than the Old Inlet, was navigable by medium-sized vessels. Both were guarded by substantial forts that would offer cover with their long-range guns once the incoming steamer had made it close to the river mouth.[209]

The *Ad-Vance's* pilot when Wyllie took command was Christopher Columbus Morse (known as C.C. or Kit). He had been born in 1829 on the banks of Cape Fear in Smithville, and from his childhood had been linked to the sea. His father was a boatbuilder, and by the 1850s Morse was employed in Florida as a lighthouse keeper. Before the start of the war he had moved back to Smithville and become one of the handful of Cape Fear pilots.

His association with blockade running began on the *Kate*, a New York-built steamer which made 20 successful runs to Wilmington and Charleston during 1862. This success lasted until a fateful day in November of that year when after a successful run inwards the *Kate* struck an obstruction in the river and sank. Morse then went on to pilot another highly successful runner, the *Cornubia*, for much of 1863, which was making regular trips from Bermuda. The importance of a good pilot can be illustrated by the remuneration

Christopher Columbus 'Kit' Morse (1829–1903) was an experienced Cape Fear River pilot who served aboard several blockade runners, including the Ad-Vance.

Internet Archive www.archive.org

Morse received for a run on *Cornubia*: in May 1863 he was paid $3,000 for a trip, an amount three times the rate that the captain of the *Ad-Vance* was receiving.[210]

Morse continued to serve on the *Cornubia* until November 1863. His luck then ran out again, as on the run in it was seized by two Union warships, the *Niphon* and *James Adger*. After a prolonged chase they forced the *Cornubia's* captain to beach it some 11 miles north of the New Inlet. Morse, along with most of the crew and passengers, abandoned ship and were saved, and the steamer was captured and taken to Boston as a prize. Although both of his steamers had been lost, Morse's skills were still highly prized and he soon found employment again, this time on the *Ad-Vance*.[211]

Morse was highly regarded by captain and owner alike. When the change of command brought Wyllie to the helm, Power, Low & Company noted that Morse would be a steady and stable hand for the new commander, writing to Vance on 1 March that:

> Morse has gone out again on the ship on the same terms … we did not wish to make pay a question with him; we wanted him as he knows how to handle the ship and Wylie being on his first voyage on command, we thought it best – Morse said the crew appear pleased with the change made.[212]

Morse's assistance was an obvious positive for the steamer and its success, but it is curious that the writer of this note seems to have believed that Morse knew the ship as well as, or better than, Wyllie. Morse, given his last attempt with the *Cornubia* in November the previous

The final destination. This wartime illustration of Nassau harbour shows a jubilant runner, flags unfurled, on completion of its dangerous journey. On the right is an example of a large merchantman which brought supplies and contraband from Britain.

Illustrated London News

year, could not have been on board the *Ad-Vance* for more than four runs whereas Wyllie had by that time made 11 runs on it as captain and sailing master. Maybe Morse's nativity, as a natural-born North Carolinian, would have offered the ship's owners a further bit of peace of mind that the state's steamer was in good hands. The change of command is once again noted, with the crew echoing the sentiments already expressed by the owners and purser.

Wyllie was ready to take his steamer out through the darkness, with Morse navigating through the shallows and the surging tides. Out on the edge of the wide Atlantic sat the men in the Union warships, spyglasses to eyes, ears to the waves. Would Wyllie's first run as captain be his last? Once they had slipped out of the river on the night of 8 March, with no cannon shot heard, no flares sent skyward to mark their position, Morse's job was done. Wyllie took the wheel as the *Ad-Vance* sped across the waves. They were safe, and made the 570-nm trip south to the Bahamas, finishing with a smooth entrance into Nassau harbour in just 46 hours.

Wyllie was under orders that once the cotton was discharged he was to make for Bermuda, as again no inward cargo was available at Nassau. Three days of unloading left the steamer ready for the trip north. While in port Wyllie took the time to write to Power, Low & Company reporting the success of his first run and giving instructions for the signal light codes for the return. It is the first document written by Wyllie as captain, and in it he lamented the fact that he could not make a quick return:

> Cargo turned out accordingly to manifest. Start for Bermuda on Monday next. Made the passage in 46 hours. Saw one cruiser between the Hole in the Wall and Nassau, did not see us. Had our cargo been here I could have made a fast trip.[213]

The bustling docks of Nassau during the war. The quiet port had been transformed into a hub of commerce by the conflict, with blockade runners arriving almost daily, their cotton cargo quickly unloaded and transferred for ships bound for Liverpool.

Illustrated London News

The deteriorating state of the steamer's machinery was once again noted after its arrival in Nassau. Writing to Power, Low & Company, Thomas Taylor, the Nassau agent of the firm of E. Lawrence and Company, stated he would place an order for replacement boiler tubes to be sent from England. The final order was for 800 six-foot lengths at a cost of £540, suggesting that the entire boiler was to be re-tubed rather than just the damaged ones replaced. Boiler tubes naturally corroded over time, becoming less efficient at heating and potentially damaged or dangerous, and this could severely limit a steamer's efficiency. After a full year of use without maintenance the *Ad-Vance's* tubes must have been in a precarious state of repair – even, perhaps, on the verge of bursting, which would have been calamitous for the steamer during a high-speed run. The health of the steamer was an obvious concern, and one that would continue until repairs could be made.

Once again the disbursements for the *Ad-Vance* survive for its week-long stay in St George's. Wyllie's pay – listed, as all the items were, in pounds sterling – was 'To Cash paid Captain Wyllie' – was £208 6s 8d, accounting for payment for both legs of a trip through the blockade and back. The largest single item was payment of the bounties to the crew, but buried within the account are some smaller items, interesting in that they indicate the state of the steamer and its ongoing operational ability. Two of these, a 'sheet of boiler iron' and 'sets of Engine keys', both relate to the machinery of the steamer. Boiler iron would indicate a small sheet for a minor repair, while the engine keys were specially fitted wedges which ensured that the engine's connection to the crankshaft remained tight: constant use and vibration caused them to wear, resulting in the mechanism becoming slack and inefficient. Clearly, no set could be found in St George's, as also listed in the disbursement was a payment for 'Carriage hire for Hamilton in search of Engine Keys', for the 12-mile drive to that port made in the hope of their acquisition. Also purchased were a new Confederate flag for £4 2s 6d, a new kedge anchor, and new hawsers (heavy rope for use with anchors or in dock). In total, this visit to Bermuda cost £3,113 19s 3d, of which the State of North Carolina was liable for £1,556 19s 7d.

WITNESS TO WYLLIE'S FIRST VOYAGE

This trip from Wilmington to Nassau, on to Bermuda and then back again through the blockade was documented by passenger Frank Inge Wilson, a Carolinian writer and newspaper editor. Active in politics, Wilson had been known as an old guard Democrat and supporter of the Union. This changed after the election of Abraham Lincoln in November 1860 when Wilson became more favourable to the calls for secession and the establishment of the Confederacy. During the 1850s he founded several newspapers in the State, each with limited success, and on 26 November 1860 he proposed another paper, to be entitled the *Ad Valorem Banner*, to be published in Raleigh beginning in early 1861. Describing the Banner as 'a good Family paper', half of its pages would be filled with poetry, biographical stories and tales, with the rest dedicated to the news of the day. There certainly would be a large amount of news, as his announcement of the inauguration of his new publication came just three weeks after Lincoln's election, thus beginning calls from politicians in South Carolina to secede from the Union.[214]

Wilson's travel to Nassau in early 1864 appeared to have been motivated by health concerns, in the belief that the Caribbean island would be better than Raleigh for his constitution. His account was recorded in a letter he sent to Captain Guthrie on 4 April after the completion of his voyage and his subsequent return to the state capital. It would appear that Wilson and Guthrie were acquaintances, as the text is informal and he writes to the captain as if they had known each other for some time. Wilson noted that this voyage had not been his first on the *Ad-Vance*:

> My associations were not so pleasant as on the trip with you, but I made myself as contended as I could. I had an understanding with Capt. Wyllie

> before we left Wilmington, and he was kind to me throughout the voyage; but I often thought of you.

Wilson does not go into any further details as to what his understanding was with Wyllie, but it would appear that he was not as fond of the Scot as he was of Guthrie, who he described as 'calm, dignified, and urbane, both as an officer and as a man'.

Although Wilson's account of his voyage is relatively short it gives a fascinating insight into the makeup of the crew and the conditions they faced on the open waters of the Atlantic during a run into Wilmington. Though his journey was intended to benefit his health, he found his first destination to be less than adequate for his betterment. He describes the unhealthy conditions that at the time were to be found in Nassau, and states that Bermuda was much pleasanter for him and the crew.

> We lay there (in Nassau) several days under a burning sun. It is needless to say I did not like Nassau. Many of the crew were sick. I was quite sick one day. From Nassau to Bermuda we had a delightful trip, and made it in 70 ½ hours. The change of climate was indeed pleasant and invigorating.

Wilson's dislike for Nassau was so great that further on in his letter he compares it to the upcoming gubernatorial election in North Carolina. He notes that he had 'eschewed politics', preferring storms at seas to the political ones then raging at home in regard to the direction of the war and Governor Vance's policies. Wilson was considered a supporter of, or at least sympathetic to, Vance's opponent in the upcoming contest, W.W. Holden. He concluded that 'Politics may go to Nassau for me – that is just about as bad a place as I could consign anything to.' Whatever Wilson really thought was the worse of the two – a disease-ridden, baking hot island or the red-hot interplay of the political bearpit – he left Guthrie to guess.

The distance between Nassau and Bermuda is just over 1,050 nautical miles and Wilson had listed a journey time of 70½ hours, meaning the *Ad-Vance* averaged a speedy 15 knots during the voyage: Wyllie had evidently wished his first voyage to be completed as swiftly as possible. The steamer docked at St George's on 19 March and loaded cargo and supplies during the following week. The return home to Wilmington began on 26 March and lasted five days. Wilson once again described this trip, and after noting the cargo he described how the *Ad-Vance* would once again barely escape the clutches of a Union warship:

> Our cargo was blankets, cards, sugar, lead, rope, etc. On Saturday evening, 26th, we left St Georges in a strong gale, and had a very stormy passage all

> the way. Indeed it was at times terrific. On Tuesday night it blew a hurricane. The storm we had on the previous passage was child's play to it. On Thursday morning we were 40 or 50 miles off the bar. We cast out a small anchor and stopped, but a big blockader came after us. We cut the hawser and let the anchor go, and we went too, and were soon out of sight, when we lay to. Again the blockader appeared, and again we left him out of sight. We then lay quietly until night, and came in without the slightest difficulty.

So the new hawser and anchor, purchased just days before at St George's, had to be jettisoned in order for the *Ad-Vance* to make its swift escape. After these hectic events Wilson goes on to relate his feelings about the crew to Guthrie, describing his treatment by the officers, including Wyllie, and highlighting possible disquiet amongst some of the crew, noting:

> For myself I have nothing to complain of from officers or crew, but five N. Carolinians left us at St Georges, viz: Mr Carrow, Leadsman, Mr. Jones, Boatswain, Gilligan and the two Sholars.[215]

Although the official correspondence at the time between the vessel's owners noted that the crew had approved of the change in command, Wilson's letter seems to suggest that this feeling was not echoed by all members, with perhaps some of those of North Carolinian background being more averse to Wyllie than the two previous American captains.

As the steamer arrived safely past the blockade it faced one final hurdle; quarantine. The local officials had become especially vigilant since the outbreak of yellow fever at Wilmington in the late summer of 1862, brought in by the blockade runner *Kate*. These health-imposed ostracisms would last days or even weeks until the authorities were secure in their knowledge that no harmful malady accompanied the vessel. Wilson recalled in his booklet *Sketches of Nassau* that a quarantine stay, anchored off Smithville in the mouth of the Cape Fear, was even less preferable to the threat of the fever in Nassau and that it brought to the crew 'ennui, malaria, miasma and musquitos while lying at quarantine for some weeks below Wilmington'. He stated that he once sat through a quarantine, presumably on his previous trip on the *Ad-Vance* while under the command of Guthrie, and that he 'would prefer taking his chances with Yellow Fever in Nassau.'[12*]

Wilson noted that his feelings of distaste were not just for the quarantine itself but also for some members of the crew of the blockade runners. Quarantine certainly meant that

12* This run would appear to have been the return journey from Bermuda in November 1863, with the *Ad-Vance* arriving at Wilmington on 9 November. Wilson does not state that his time in quarantine was after a trip from Nassau or St George's, but any such arrival from these ports was subject to inspection and quarantine.

runs were prolonged or delayed, and with that the loss of potential income from a quick turnaround, which must have caused serious frustration and ill-humour. In addition, being cooped up on a steamer and anchored in the humid swamps of the river was no picnic. He added in his booklet a more dramatic description of these times, written by a member of the *Ad-Vance*'s crew. He noted that 'A poetical companion on board thus vented his troubles. He told me he intended to write more, but "broke daw".' Might this 'poetical companion' have been Joannes Wyllie? He was known for his wit and his skill with language: Moses Hoge had described him as a man full of poetry.

Wilson reproduced the entire poem, entitled 'Lying at Quarantine', which vividly gives picture to the events that had to be endured:

Lying at Quarantine! – lying, lying,
Lying at Quarantine, almost dying,
For home and its comforts sighing, sighing,
Under a burning sun frying, frying,
Obeying a mandate there's no denying.
And seeing nothing that's fit to be seen
Out in the stream of the broad Cape Fear,
Miasma, uprising from far and from near,
The scenery monotonous, disreal and drear
Musquitos assailing with trumpet and spear,
Assaulting in front, on flank, and in rear
And this is called lying in Quarantine
The vessel is dead as the dirty old log
That lies half concealed in yon filthy bog;
While insects swarm round like flees (sic) on a dog
And nothing seems lively save yonder old frog
And his cheeriness is only that of the hog,
To which grief and sadness are both incog.,
The long legged, google-eyed, nasty spaleen
But day after day and night after night
With life scarce sufficient musquitos to fight,
But painfully sensitive to their bite,
Existence known only by its blight,
We suffer the torments of Quarantine.[216]

The identity of the author cannot be known for certain, but use of the words 'yon', a Scots word meaning in the distance, and 'spalpeen', Irish for pest or rascal, might indicate a crew member of Celtic origin. Wyllie would have known many such occasions at quarantine during his time aboard the steamer – not counting his first arrival, of course, when Governor Vance had broken the rules to bring the vessel up to Wilmington before the health of the crew had been confirmed.

As a final point Wilson pondered on the future of the steamer. He told Guthrie that factors both human and mechanical might impair the steamer's career on the blockade:

> It is uncertain when the *Ad-Vance* will go out again. The Confederate government requires that she shall carry out and bring in half the cargo for it, it paying freight. This the Gov. and owners refuse, and negotiations are going on. It is said the machinery also needs repairs.[217]

The cargo requirement made by the Confederate government refers to the then recently passed bill that allowed the South's President Davis and the Confederate Congress in Richmond, Virginia, to regulate all foreign commerce. It gave the president complete control over the export of cotton and other raw materials, and forbade the import of luxury items that were not deemed necessary for the current war effort. The law went into effect of 1 March, just as the *Ad-Vance* was heading down the river bound for Nassau. Davis and his cabinet devised a comprehensive plan to control blockade running to benefit the Confederacy. Then, just four days later, a second bill was passed, which insisted that half of both outward and inward space on runners be taken up by government cargo. This of course had huge implications not only for the private firms but also for Governor Vance and his North Carolina steamer.[218]

While the *Ad-Vance* was being prepared for its next run Vance appealed to Congress and the president for the steamer to be exempted from these new laws. When it had been fully owned by the State of North Carolina, the Confederate government had not sought to interfere with its operation. But now that the steamer was only half publicly owned it fell foul of the new regulations. On 13 April, just a day before Wyllie took out the *Ad-Vance* for his third run as captain, Vance received a telegram from Christopher Memminger, secretary of the treasury of the Confederacy, in which it was made clear the government would not exempt the *Ad-Vance:*

> The question raised in her case has been fully considered, and it has been decided that the authority [is] to make regulations in relation to the exports of cotton so as to render it available for public defense, impose the restrictions that the regulations should be uniform, therefore the requirements that one

> half the cargo of every outward bound vessel should be for account of the Confederate States cannot be relinquished as an exception in your favour.[219]

Vance was forced to give in, as the other states with interests in blockade runners, South Carolina and Virginia, had chosen to follow the new laws. He did, however, threaten to remove his steamers from the operations, but this protest failed to move the politicians in Richmond. The steamer would now be forced to carry half its cargo, as dictated by Davis.

The mechanical factor that Wilson mentioned follows on from the other reports that the steamer was in need of repair and on its last legs. What use would half a cargo for the Confederacy be if the vessel itself could not be maintained? It was an issue that came to a head on the next run, with Wyllie making a much longer journey than one to St George's or Nassau: he would push the steamer once again to make the transatlantic run, to seek the urgent repairs that would prolong its career on the blockade.

A THOROUGH OVERHAUL – THE *AD-VANCE* LEAVES THE BLOCKADE

It was now a critical time for the steamer and its captain. The hull, cylinders, boilers and paddles of the gallant craft had been strained, bent and in some places broken during its time on the blockade runs. The steamer was not even two years old, but the exertions required of a runner had aged this young greyhound before its time. In order for it to maintain its role in delivering the vital supplies to North Carolina it needed urgent attention. As the repairs could not be completed in Wilmington, Nassau or St George's, the *Ad-Vance* was such a highly valued asset that its owners and captain decided on a long and dangerous venture to seek such repairs: the only solution would be an Atlantic voyage, with its high seas, stormy weather and Union warships on the prowl. It would be a costly venture, but one that Governor Vance, his partners and Captain Wyllie would now need to complete if the steamer were to continue to fulfil its role for the state.

The plans were made by Wyllie, the officers and the engineers, then sent to Vance and Power, Low & Company for approval. The proposal was that they would make for Halifax, Nova Scotia, it being on the Atlantic seaboard of British Canada and with a long-established shipbuilding industry, home to the multiple docks, workshops and engineers that could carry out the necessary repairs. It was also one of the regular stops made by blockade runners on their long journeys across the Atlantic, and was even sometimes the destination of runners leaving Wilmington or Charleston.

The parties were in agreement that the proposals seemed fair and proper, and the *Ad-Vance* set off from Wilmington on 14 April, first making for Nassau. It was only stormy weather that hampered the voyage; no encounters with the Union blockade were reported. Wyllie was ready for the next leg to Halifax after a brief stay in the warm waters of the

Bahamas, but before they set off he wrote to Vance on 21 April, assuring him that the plans were sound and that he would endeavour to make the trip as quick as possible:

> I start this afternoon for Halifax. She has run so long and that too far from home where there are workshops with every requisite for repairs that she now wants a thorough overhauling. I shall jealously watch over her interests while there and hope soon to bring her back to you to give as good as new. I have seen your letter to the Purser in reference to the return cargo from Bermuda. It shall be punctually attended to. There are no news here worth writing you about. A dozen steamers are laid up here on account of the new law lately passed in the Confederacy. If I see anything worth bringing you from Halifax I shall do so with much pleasure.[220]

Worth noting is Wyllie's observation of the state of the vessel. This was not just to be a small repair job, but a 'thorough overhauling' that would prepare the steamer for an extended lease on life. Wyllie's mention of a number of steamers laid up at Nassau indicates the effects of the new Confederate laws compromising the successful operation of the blockade runners.

Though this was not a run through the blockade, Wyllie would still earn a considerable amount for this vital mission. In payment for this run from Wilmington to Canada he received £208 6s 8d, the same as he had received in Bermuda the previous month for the last completed run.[221]

The *Ad-Vance* made for Halifax in ballast, carrying no cargo of note. The disbursements noted that it took on 435 tons of coal – double the usual load – for the long journey. Wyllie, aware of his time on the *Bonita* when they had run out of fuel, was determined to avoid that situation again. The arrival of the steamer in Halifax came after a journey of five days during which, according to reports in the *Washington Evening Star*, it had been chased by Union gunboats some getting to within a mile. Even with its rundown machinery the *Ad-Vance* was still able to muster enough speed to outrun almost any Union warship on the open sea.

Its welcome on arrival into the Canadian port can be described as nothing short of a celebratory parade. It was a well-known vessel, with reports of its achievements circulated from the day it had left Glasgow. Its reputation had preceded it and although it was by no means the first runner to visit Halifax during the war, the *Ad-Vance's* appearance led to a reception akin to that of a returning hero. The *Halifax Citizen* reported:

> The iron steamer *A.D. Vance*, formerly the *Lord Clyde*, a successful blockade runner, arrived here on Tuesday evening, after a fine run of 112 hours from Nassau. As she passed up the harbour, bearing an immense Confederate flag

> she was cheered from wharf to wharf by the laborers and others about the docks and warehouses.[222]

The 'immense Confederate flag' might indeed have been the new one noted in the disbursements as having been purchased in Bermuda.

The hero's welcome that greeted the steamer was to be short-lived, though, as a change of plan was quickly devised on finding that repairs in Halifax were impossible. The exact problems were stated in a letter to Governor Vance from Joseph Flanner, the former purser of the *Ad-Vance*, who by this time was in London as a state agent, having taken over from John White. He reported that the *Ad-Vance*, 'being unable to procure necessary repairs at Halifax' had then been taken on the much longer journey to Liverpool, where the facilities required for the overhaul were known to exist. The longer journey was indeed risky with the machinery in the condition that Wyllie had found so wanting, but now there was no other choice. Flanner sent advance word to his contacts in North Carolina to the effect that 'orders have been given at Liverpool for her repairs to be given in readiness and to have her despatched as soon as possible after arrival.'[223]

Liverpool was one of the powerhouses of British maritime industry; it had substantial docks and engineering works that could easily cope with any repairs or replacements that would be required. Like Glasgow, Liverpool had been abuzz with runner-related activities since the beginning of the war, from the conversion of passenger steamers, to the construction of purpose-built blockade runners, to the supply of other vessels on the transit routes to the Caribbean ports. Its dry docks now accommodated some of these vessels, back at their birthplace in order to be renewed and refreshed. Although the *Ad-Vance* had never visited Liverpool before, the city was familiar to Wyllie, who had made the city his home for his ten years ashore; his knowledge of the city and his connections there would be of great assistance on this mission. Finally, Liverpool was home to companies that had existing relationships with the steamer's owners and were sympathetic to the cause. Companies like Fraser, Trenholm and Edward Lawrence & Company were based there, and would be able to assist with the negotiations needed to facilitate speedy repairs.

Wyllie had experienced one transatlantic voyage with the *Ad-Vance*, but that was when the steamer had been in excellent condition, hull recently fouled and the vessel generally made ready for such a long trip. Now this return trip would have been of much more concern to the captain, as his ship was in his opinion close to ruin. Nevertheless over two weeks in May the *Ad-Vance* sliced through the waves of the North Atlantic and made it back to British waters on the 17th. The Liverpool customs bills of entry recorded its arrival, carrying a crew of 57 and bringing the minimal cargo of six bales of cotton and one barrel of turpentine which had been consigned by E. Lawrence and Company.

On its arrival the *Ad-Vance* made for Sandon Dock, one of the many tidal docks located along the river front. Sandon offered safe harbour and contained six graving (dry) docks.

It was located to the north of the city centre and just a few blocks away from Boundary Street, the address Wyllie had called home while in Liverpool. Boundary Street was a typical sailors' road, full of pubs, flats to rent, lodging houses and other establishments that a mariner might frequent when not at sea.

Soon after the steamer had arrived safe and sound Flanner sent word to Governor Vance:

> Steamer '*Advance*' arrived safely on the 16th and is being thoroughly repaired and arranged in a satisfactory manner. She will be homeward bound again about the 23rd: Capt Wyllie and all have done well for the ship, and it is quite a good thing that he brought her to Liverpool for repairs – everything for the best as far as regards despatch economy and durability.[224]

Almost immediately the *Ad-Vance's* presence in Liverpool was noted, and reported widely across the whole of the British Isles. Since the start of the war several high-profile Confederate ships had been built in the city, notably the CSS *Alabama* and CSS *Florida* (also known as the *Oreto*), as well as numerous steamers for the blockade. The details of their construction, fitting out and sailings were headline news in both Britain and North America. So the arrival of a runner returned from the conflict was bound to spark interest. Just a day after its arrival the *Manchester Courier* was first to report the steamer's return, under the headline 'ARRIVAL OF A BLOCKADE RUNNER AT LIVERPOOL':

> *A.D. Vance*, a celebrated and most successful blockade runner arrived … for the purpose of being repaired, no port in British America offering the requisite facilities, and a visit to any Federal port being of course out of the question.[225]

Soon afterwards other papers picked up the story, and news of the arrival spread across the country from Dundee, London and Lancaster to the previous home ports of the steamer, Dublin, Greenock and Glasgow. If Wyllie and the steamer's owners had hoped for a quiet trip with the steamer lying anonymously in the docks, just another paddle steamer amongst the hundreds of other vessels then at Liverpool, then this plan was blown out of the water just 24 hours after it had docked.

In dry dock, the full extent of over a year's nonstop exertions and the damage that this had caused was fully exposed. The task of repair would be considerable – and expensive. The repairs began immediately, and the extent of the work can be seen in the disbursements for the steamer at Liverpool. By far the largest payment was to the firm of Fawcett, Preston and Company, listed as £1,728 7s 3d for what is referred to as simply 'repairs to the steamer'.

The company, known locally as Fossetts, was famed for producing maritime steam engines and boilers of the highest quality at its Phoenix Foundry. Since the beginning of the Civil War it had been involved with the fitting out of several well-known Confederate warships, including the engines for the CSS *Florida*, the guns for the CSS *Alabama*, and the engines and machinery for several blockade runners. At the very time that the order for machinery was put in for the *Ad-Vance*, Fossetts was involved with the fitting out of the recently built runner *Let Her Rip*, which coincidently lay alongside Wyllie's steamer in Sandon Dock.[226]

Fossetts had been employed to install extensive new machinery, including a significant amount of new brass and iron pipework, totalling £968, ordered from the firm of Wilson and Rose. Repairs to the engine room and the purchase of a new capstan were completed by the firm of J. Shepherd. Then a payment of £887 was made to the shipwright firm of William Harley for repairs to the hull, paddles, and decking. This might have been a considerable task after the several beachings of the *Ad-Vance* on the sandbars of Cape Fear, which would have caused significant damage or at the very least stressed the steel plates of the steamer's hull. A new coat of grey paint was completed by 'Carroll' for £205. The grand total for all this work came to the large sum of £4,255 18s 4d.[227]

The steamer had been bought almost brand new by White and Crossan for £34,000 just 14 months earlier, and the cost of repairs in Liverpool equated to 12 per cent of that price. This hefty investment illustrates its owners' belief in the viability of the continued success of the steamer. Though the repairs were expensive they were a shrewd investment compared to the price of a new steamer: on 26 May 1864, in the very week of Wyllie's arrival on the *Ad-Vance*, the *Liverpool Mercury* reported the launch of the blockade runner *Colonel Lamb*, built by Jones, Quiggin and Company and purchased by Fraser, Trenholm for £50,000.

Sandon Dock during this time was a hive of blockade-runner work. After its launch the *Colonel Lamb* was moved there to sit next to the *Ad-Vance*, missing the *Let Her Rip* by only a matter of days, as it had left for Nassau on 16 May. A description of the work on the *Ad-Vance* can be found in a letter in the mails carried aboard the steamer. Dated 11 June, it was written by one Charlie to an unidentified acquaintance. From his description of the steamer and the work Charlie appears to have been a member of the crew.[228] He wrote:

> We have had the boat in the dry dock and painted her bottom and expect to come out on Monday evening. They all say we will be ready for sea in 10 days more, but I allow her 14 days yet.[229]

That the steamer was to come out of dry dock just two days later, on 13 June, suggests it had already been there for some time, possibly since its arrival at the Mersey 25 days earlier; the extensive repairs and installation of new machinery indicate that a considerable time in dry dock would have been required. Charlie's estimate for the time needed to complete the work was not far off, as his 14-day timeline is close to the actual departure of the steamer on 28 June.

In the Liverpool disbursement listing one item stands out: a watch purchased for £50 (worth close to £4,800 today: see Table 1) from a local maker by the name of Harrison and listed as 'watch presented to Captain.' This was a gold pocket watch given to Captain Wyllie as a mark of respect and appreciation on behalf of the steamer's owners. It had been ordered by Joseph Flanner, who had written to Vance of his intention to do so on 11 June, stating 'I have advised Mr Lawrence & Co to have a gold watch with picture of the ship engraved on it presented to Capt. Wyllie. I know it will meet the approbation of all the owners.'[230] It was a tangible recognition of Wyllie's success and his dedication to the *Ad-Vance* by the owners, his crew and the people of North Carolina. It was a gift that Wyllie would hold especially dear and boast about when given the chance.

Wyllie would pick up some other valuable items in Liverpool. On 10 June 1864 he paid a visit to the shop of Dr Daniel Hendry, Chemist and Druggist, located on Great Howard Street, near the docks. Like his steamer, Wyllie was suffering from ill health and in desperate need of help. Dr Hendry prescribed three medicines: Tincture Chinae Composite, ferric tincture, and *nucis vomicae*. The first was an anti-malarial, made from the bark of a tree in the *Chincona* genus, from which quinine was extracted. This might indicate Wyllie was suffering the effects of malaria which he could have caught at one of the Caribbean ports he visited regularly, or even at one of the tropical ports he had called on early in his

Joseph Hutson Flanner (1830–1885) served as both an agent for North Carolina in England and as the purser aboard the Ad-Vance. *He knew Wyllie personally, and it was on his recommendation that a custom gold chronometer was presented to the Scot in recognition of his valued service.*

Courtesy of the North Carolina Museum of History

maritime career – malaria is known to stay within the body and affect the sufferer for years. The second was an iron supplement used to combat chronic anaemia, a symptom known to arise from diseases like malaria. The last, *nucis vomicae*, was a strychnine preparation used at the time in small amounts as a stimulant, a sort of a pick-me-up, and he could use it to help ensure he would stay alert during the long, monotonous night watches: tiredness and lethargy were not conditions conducive to successful captaincy of a runner. (In larger amounts strychnine was of course fatal, a fact known personally to Wyllie from his experience of the sad death of Doctor Bond at Moulmein on his visit aboard the *Indian Queen* back in 1857.) All of these were to be taken in a spoonful of water, three times a day. Dr Hendry's shop was just a short distance from Boundary Street as well, and Wyllie might have made visits there when he had lived in the city.

With his new gold watch in his pocket and the medicines procured, Wyllie walked back from Dr Hendry's shop to Sandon Dock, where the *Ad-Vance* was to be refloated and its new machinery tested. The visit to Liverpool had given the *Ad-Vance* a new lease on life, ready to once again outrun any Union warships, its powerful boilers providing the high-pressure steam to turn the paddles. On the 28th he ordered the crew to cast off, and the *Ad-Vance* made its way down the Mersey and out into the Irish Sea. A quick stop was made at Queenstown (today, Cobh, pron. 'cove') on the south coast of Ireland, in order for the bunkers be topped up with the finest steam coal, ready for the 2,700 nautical mile voyage. The steamer's fame meant that yet again its movements were reported, the *Southern Reporter and Cork Commercial Courier* telling its readers:

> A steamship called *Advance*, which put into Queenstown on Wednesday evening in order to coal, has excited some interest from the suspicion that she is intended for a hazardous enterprise. Nautical men shake their heads while they say 'She is going to Nassau, *moryah*, but she may go farther and fare worse.'[231]

Although the destination was listed incorrectly, the ship's role as a runner, hinted at by the phrase 'go farther and fare worse' would have been well known to anyone in Ireland who was following the daily reports of the of operations of the blockade and the events of the Civil War.

Joseph Flanner, who was making his way back to North Carolina, joined the ship at Queenstown. He once again wrote to Governor Vance, informing him of the state of his steamer and his confidence in Joannes Wyllie as captain:

> '*Advance*' left Liverpool yesterday morning and arrived here this evening. She is now in thorough repair, much improved for her intended business and will

no doubt give entire satisfaction to all her owners. Capt. Wyllie has done well for the ship, a better commander cannot be had for her, and I trust that no influence will be brought to bear and conflict with him.'[232]

The *Ad-Vance* was ready to continue its success as a runner. Wyllie once again proved his worth as captain with an incident-free transatlantic journey behind him, another one in front, and a successful repair mission for his ship. The story of the steamer would continue for many more voyages – at least that was what all involved had hoped. But events in the coming months would scupper those hopes as the *Ad-Vance's* luck would finally run out.

PART II: THE FINAL DAYS OF RUNNING, AND THE CAPTURE OF THE *AD-VANCE*

As Wyllie and the crew made for Bermuda their prospects still seemed good. While they had been in England 21 runners made successful trips runs into Wilmington during the month of May and 17 during June. The capture of Fort Fisher, long feared by Governor Vance, had not materialised. The blockade fleet off the coast had scored some victories: the destruction of *Georgiana McCaw* off the Old Inlet and the capture of several steamers, including *Thistle*, *Siren*, and *Pevensey*, in the month of June.[233] However, the bulk of the vessels attempting to run the blockade still made it through. So much so that Oliver S. Glisson, captain of the Union steamer *Santiago de Cuba* and commander of the first division of the North Atlantic Blockading Squadron, wrote to his superior, Squadron Commander Rear-Admiral Samuel Philips Lee, to report that 'Everything has been done that officers and man could, and yet it is impossible to stop these blockade runners.'[234]

After 16 days at sea the *Ad-Vance* made Bermuda on 14 July, but it had brought no cargo from Liverpool as the space had been needed for the coal she required for the long voyage. At Bermuda the crew bided their time, awaiting the new moon on 2 August. The Bermuda customs manifesto listed its outward cargo as various generic packages, bales, and casks as well as 25 boxes of bacon, 42 bales of cloth and a colourful assortment of cloth dyeing materials, 100 bales logwood (for producing a purple dye), 10 barrels of copperas (ferrous sulphate, for a green dye), and 20 kegs of blue stone (for blue). Although the crew would have their usual reservations about the success of their upcoming trip, they were not to know that this would have been their last visit to Bermuda on the *Ad-Vance*.[235]

After an uneventful run, the newly repaired and refitted *Ad-Vance* steamed into the Cape Fear inlet on the night of 30 July 1864, where it was celebrated in the local newspapers, the *Weekly Confederate* of Raleigh telling its readers on 3 August that: 'The '*Ad-Vance*' steamer is safely in, with more of Governor Vance's blessings for the soldiers and their families.' The continued success of Vance's runner had now acquired a political aspect as well as the crucial military one. After just two years as in office Vance was facing a re-election campaign, and his opponent for the role of governor had rallied against the state's direct involvement in the blockade trade. The *Weekly Confederate*'s mention of Vance's 'blessings' may betray the paper's editorial stance on the upcoming poll.

The *Daily Carolina Watchman* of 2 August reported:

> The steamer *Ad-Vance* arrived in Wilmington on Saturday, freighted with a rich cargo on State account for the benefit of the soldiers and their families.
>
> Let it be remembered that were W.W. Holden governor he would do away with the running of the blockade and leave our brave soldiers to go ragged and half naked, and their wives and little ones starve and perish.

William Woods Holden, Vance's opponent, was a newspaper editor in Raleigh; he was a fierce critic of the Confederate government, and he was the leader of the peace movement in North Carolina. The *Daily Carolina Watchman*, obviously not under the editorial control of Holden, attacked his politics while once again praising Vance. In the event the election was a landslide with Vance taking 80 per cent of the vote, the electors of North Carolina overwhelmingly approving of his policies; blockade running was a major plank in his platform.

The crew and officers prepared for a return trip by making sure that the usual cargo of cotton bales was loaded swiftly. As the steamer had been away for several months there was no problem with supplying a full load to the *Ad-Vance* in a short time. With the steamer now in rude good health, it was expected to make its run out again in as little time as possible. In order to catch the last of the dark nights the outward cargo was loaded in just five days; by 6 August the bill of health and the clearance permissions had been signed by Wyllie and the steamer was ready to head downriver. The cargo was 688 bales of cotton, and the bill of health recorded 17 passengers on board, including John White who was returning to England with his family to continue his work on behalf of the State of North Carolina.[236]

His 15-year-old daughter, Mary, kept a diary of their exciting voyage to Europe. Her diary contains the most detailed account ever written of the operations of the *Ad-Vance*, the makeup of the crew and the experiences of a passenger aboard the steamer. She charted the events of the following month where the *Ad-Vance* would make no less than eight attempts to leave the river, on each occasion being thwarted by one of various misfortunes.[237]

Mary's account began on 5 August when she left Raleigh en route to Wilmington. Conditions on the home front by that time were dire, the war taking its toll on the civilian populace. In addition to this her family had suffered a recent loss, which was what had motivated John White to bring his whole family with him. Mary records the start of her journey:

> I left home for England with Father, Mother, Bro. Andrew, Hugh, Kate and Sue. Father had to go to buy supplies for the N.C. soldiers, and things were so awful here and Mother and he suffered so much being separated and our baby sister Lizzie died while he was away, so he promised Mother he would never leave her again ... It all seems very strange, but we are going with Father and I hope everything will be all right.

Her first impressions of the vessel were mixed:

> We left … Saturday morning for the S.S. *Ad-Vance*, which was lying in the Cape Fear River, near Wilmington.
>
> …
>
> The *Ad-Vance* is a very fine steamer, 235 ft. in length, 22 in width, a very fast ship and successful blockade runner. It was fitted up splendidly, for passengers, before it was put to its present use and was named the *Lord Clyde*. The saloon was removed and cotton bales put in instead and the accommodations for ladies are very poor.

Sense of adventure aside, Mary's journey would be rough and ready, as comfort was at a premium. However, Mary seemed not to mind physical discomfort.

Her account continued:

> We expected to run the blockade that night, but there was some mistake in the ship's papers and before they could be corrected we were too late for the tide and had to cast anchor and lie there all night.

They made it as far as Smithville, at the mouth of the Cape Fear River, but they were unable to get 'across the Rip in consequence of the short tide. She will try it again tonight and every night till she succeeds.'

Mary and family went ashore to Smithville, where they spent the night, returning to the steamer the next day. Mary wrote about the second attempt; they

> started again the next morning about 8:00 for our ship .... We passed Forts Fisher and Caswell and all went well for a time but finally went aground ... Not far behind us is the *Mary Celestia* from Bermuda, in quarantine. It is

The only known photograph of Joannes Wyllie, dated 1862 and taken at the studio of David Gordon in Sinclairtown, Fife, less than a mile from the Wyllie family farm. The date coincides with that of Wyllie attaining the rank of captain, and may have been taken immediately before his involvement in the blockade.

© CSG CIC Glasgow Museums Collection

The painting of the Ad-Vance *forms the centrepiece of the 'Blockade Runners: Glasgow's Role in the American Civil War' exhibition at the Riverside Museum, Glasgow, Scotland. Its display in 2015 prompted the research into the long-forgotten Joannes Wyllie.*

© CSG CIC Glasgow Museums Collection

One of the most poignant events aboard ship was a burial at sea. Wyllie witnessed one on only his second voyage. It had such a profound effect on him that he always included it in his lectures about his time at sea. This solemn moment is captured in the evocative painting, The Burial at Sea *by Frank Brangwyn, held in the collection of Glasgow Museums.*

Courtesy of David Brangwyn.

Wyllie joined the crew of the clipper Indian Queen *in the summer of 1856 after four years aboard the barque* Hope. *The* Indian Queen *would take Wyllie into European war zones as well as on the longest voyage he would ever undertake as a mariner.*

D.M. Little – Pictures Collection, State Library of Victoria

Wyllie's first command was the screw steamer Bonita, *which he sailed from Liverpool to Nassau with the intention of running the blockade in September 1862. It is shown here under its previous name,* Economist, *during its single successful run into Charleston in spring 1862.*

Courtesy of the Museums' Department Collections at Historic Charleston Foundation, Charleston, South Carolina

'She is an extremely fine specimen of the perfection to which naval architecture is now brought.'

This painting by famous Scottish maritime artist William Clark (1803–1883) shows the Lord Clyde *battling the choppy waters of the Irish Sea during its early career as a passenger ferry on the Dublin–Glasgow route.*

Courtesy of the Charleston Museum, Object from the Southern Maritime Collection, State of South Carolina

The "Ad. Vance"
500 tons. Ran the blockade of Wilmington N.C. ten times and returned to Liverpool to repair machinery.
Sailed again for Bermuda and put into Cork June 30th 1864. Coaled and proceeded July 2nd.
A notorious Runner, captured September 10th 1864 on her way to Halifax from Wilmington, by the
U.S.S. "Santiago de Cuba." The Captain of the warship got $3,700.00 as his share of the
prize money.

This unique watercolour sketch of the Ad-Vance *is believed to have been completed during the war as a reference for the identification of blockade runners. It is a rare example of a likeness of the steamer made during the conflict. The note at the bottom appears to have been added later when the final fate of the steamer was known.*

Courtesy of the St. George's Historical Society, Bermuda

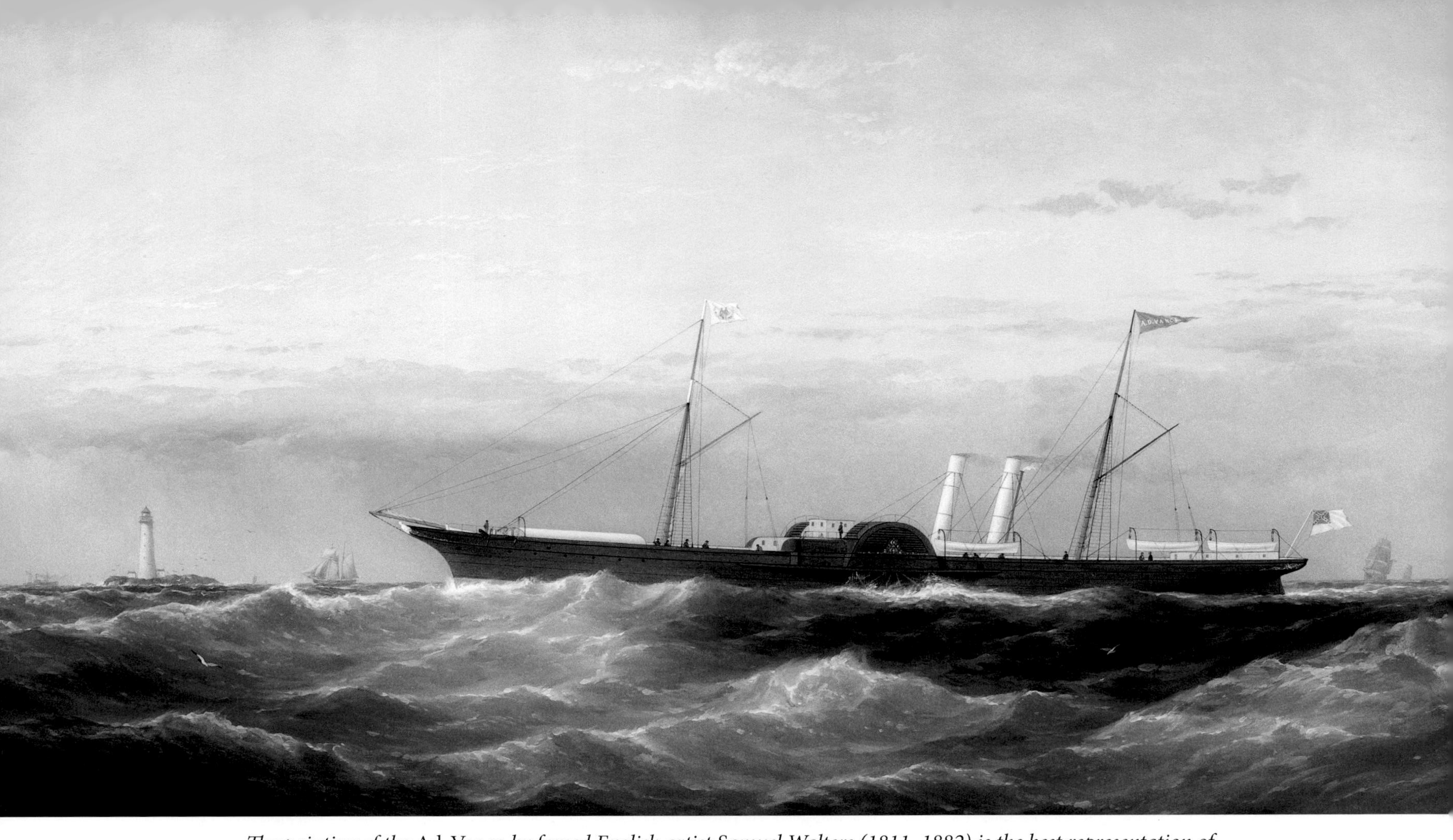

The painting of the Ad-Vance *by famed English artist Samuel Walters (1811–1882) is the best representation of the steamer as a blockade runner. It is believed to have been painted in 1864 during the vessel's visit to Liverpool.*

© CSG CIC Glasgow Museums Collection

After his capture aboard the Ad-Vance *Wyllie outwitted the Federal marshals and returned to Britain. Just days later he was called to Glasgow to take command of another steamer for the blockade. This drawing, though slightly fanciful, shows the city at the time, with two grey steamers ready to make for Nassau or Bermuda. The shipbuilders of the Clyde received a considerable economic boost from the construction and conversion of steamers for the blockade.*

© CSG CIC Glasgow Museums Collection

A view of Wyllie's second runner, the Susan Beirne, *which he took from Glasgow to Bermuda in November 1864. The flag on the foremast would appear to be that of the Blue Cross Line, operated by the known Confederate sympathiser Henry Lafone. This is the only known depiction of the steamer.*

Courtesy of PBA Galleries / Chad Mueller

Wyllie's final command after 15 years at sea was the Stag, *a former blockade runner which during the war had been known as* Kate Gregg. *This is the fine scale builder's model held by Glasgow Museums.*

© CSG CIC Glasgow Museums Collection

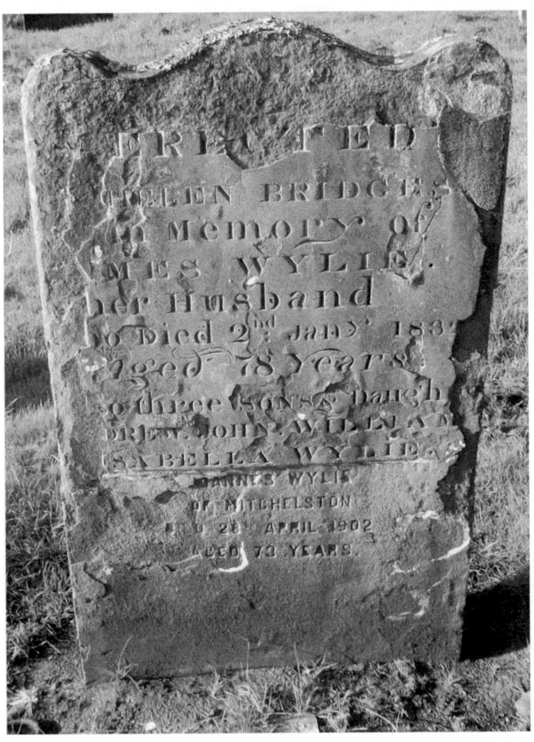

Wyllie is buried in his family lair (Scots for a family plot) in Kirkcaldy, Fife. The inscription at the bottom of the stone includes no mention of his time as a mariner. This basic burial may be an indication of Wyllie's lack of wealth later in life. His name is spelled with a single 'L' and the date of death is ten days late. Why these errors were engraved is a mystery.

© CSG CIC Glasgow Museums Collection

Today there is nothing left of Wyllie's farm except its name – now given to the industrial estate built in the mid-20th century. Wyllie might approve of the Kart Centre now on the site as well, having always been a supporter of the betterment and entertainment of the youth of his area.

© CSG CIC Glasgow Museums Collection

A previously unpublished view of the USS Frolic *in Naples Bay with a smoking Mount Vesuvius in the background. After its capture the* Ad-Vance *was commissioned by the Union Navy, renamed* Frolic *and went on to serve for another ten years.*

Painted by famed Italian maritime artist Tommaso de Simone.

Courtesy of Rick Burton

> reported that the yellow fever is in Bermuda and a man died on the *Mary Celestia* this morning, it is thought from yellow fever ... The *Helen*, which had been lying near us all day, went out, and as no guns were heard and no news from the ship, it is supposed that she escaped uninjured. Today, three more cases of yellow fever were reported on the *Mary Celestia.*

But once again the *Ad-Vance's* deep draft caused it to ground on the bars, preventing its escape.

On 10 August Mary recorded the third attempt by Wyllie and crew to run out their cargo:

> Last night, we made a last effort to run the blockade and were over the rip, and it was thought that we would get out without much difficulty, but they did not steer properly and we missed the channel and fastened in the sand.

The shifting sands had foiled them yet again. The steamer was marooned there until the morning, when with the incoming tide they were able to make it back upriver to Wilmington. By now the moon was near-full, and Wyllie thought better of running in those circumstances: the steamer would await a more favourable opportunity rather than rushing out.

Mary wrote that her father had left Smithville for Wilmington, then continued to their home in Warrenton, expecting to be back the following week. Then, with the wait for the darker nights, came a change of destination, as Mary recorded on 15 August:

> This morning the pilot of one of the ships lying in the river died of yellow fever. Ships that came in the last few days, say that yellow fever is raging in Bermuda, so the *Ad-Vance* will not touch there but proceed to Halifax.

The yellow fever in Bermuda, worse in the hotter summer months, had changed the destination of the steamer. The thought of another outbreak in Wilmington had put fear into the minds of owners and captain alike, and the news of the outbreak brought about a rethink about sailing to St George's. A journey to Halifax would avoid the yellow fever in Bermuda – but it would take longer, compounding the delays already experienced in trying to leave Wilmington.

The repaired *Ad-Vance* had yet to repay the expense lavished on it in Liverpool, and all involved began to feel disheartened. A new manifest was drawn up on the 19th with the Canadian port listed as the destination. It recorded that the steamer was loaded with 688 bales of cotton, valued by the Wilmington collector at $688,258 Confederate.[238] It was a smaller number of bales than carried on the previous runs from Wilmington, but given the continued issue with the steamer's deep draft and the sandbars it seemed a prudent decision.

During this time Mary had been staying in Smithville with her family, along with the family of Dr Boykin, the *Ad-Vance's* former purser, also heading for England. John White returned after a week in Warrenton, arriving on board the *Ad-Vance* as it made its way back downstream from Wilmington. As it approached its anchorage near Smithville it again grounded, this time in mid-river and had to await the high tide to start afresh for the Atlantic. The luck of the steamer and crew now appeared gone: four times the run had been attempted, and all four had been foiled by the shifting sands of the Cape Fear inlets. The moon was now full – but Wyllie was hard pressed to get the steamer out. The fifth attempt was made on the night of the 22nd, two weeks after the first, and this time into what appeared to be the jaws of the waiting Union fleet. Mary once again recalled the event, the ever-calm 15-year-old describing in her matter-of-fact way the force that now confronted the crew:

> Another attempt will be made tonight to run the blockade. About 13 steamers are in now. Eight large Yankee ships are so near that we can distinctly see them with the naked eye, but we will not encounter them as we go in the opposite direction, but there are five where we will have to go.

When they did start their run, their progress was initially better than before, but yet again they grounded: fate again reached up from the Cape Fear sands to hold the steamer back and halt its dash towards the open sea:

> Last night at about 8:30 we started off to make the attempt. We went very well until we got to the inner bar and there, as usual, we got aground and while we were vainly attempting to get off … the moon rose and shone very brightly and then of course we were effectively prevented from trying any more. After a while, we got off and got back to Smithville, where we are lying now.

Five attempts, five failures. The moon now full, Wyllie decided to wait until the month turned. A telegram was sent to Governor Vance informing him of the continuing difficulties. Power, Low & Company updated the governor, telling him that the steamer had again been denied exit and that they were sending 25 more tons of coal as requested by Wyllie: the attempts would have burned through a fair amount, and the distance to Halifax required full bunkers.

The coal that was now carried by the *Ad-Vance* was to become the source of serious disagreement between the owners and the Confederate officials. This new supply of coal was not the fine-grade steam coal preferred by blockade captains, which burned cleaner and gave greater efficiency to the engines. It was the poorer grade North Carolina coal, prone to launching huge black plumes into the sky and reducing the performance of the machinery. The finer coal usually reserved for runners had been commandeered by the Confederate government for the CSS *Tallahassee*, a steam cruiser recently returned to port. The cruiser being deemed a higher priority than the runner by the Confederate officials, and over Vance's vocal objections, the coal was loaded into the warship. Notwithstanding the low-grade coal supply, Wyllie and the Cape Fear pilot, C.C. Morse, confirmed White's telegram to Vance that they would now try every night until they were out, hoping to catch the end of the darker nights before the moon grew full again.

Mary observed several other blockade runners in the river while she waited in Smithville with her family. She watched as the *Lillian* left on 24 August, passing out of sight – and then saw, as she sat atop the cotton bales on the *Ad-Vance's* deck, the flares sent up by the Union warships to mark the position of a runner and heard the reports of 15 guns. Two mornings later she awoke to find that the Liverpool-built *Hope*, which had joined the blockade-running fleet in August, was aground on the sand near Fort Fisher. Union ships were firing at it, and the crew had abandoned ship before its impending destruction. But the guns at the fort kept the warships at bay; eventually the *Hope* was refloated, and made it to Smithville.

On the 30th Mary wrote that the people of the town were expecting an attack on Wilmington any day and that 19 blockaders now lay within sight – how many more beyond the horizon was anyone's guess.

Mary's father, too, was tired of their prolonged stay at Smithville and was eager to get himself and family away from the imminent dangers. He wrote to Vance on 1 September:

> We are all greatly disappointed in not getting out which we failed to do after making three attempts. The tides have not been high enough for the ship draft of water. The pilot thinks we will certainly succeed tonight, he at least will make another trial. The numbers of blockades we understand has been considerably increased within the last few days and one or two monitors has been added to the fleet. All feel confident that we will go out safely.[239]

John White's listing of just three attempts conflicts with his daughter's diary. No explanation is known why this should be the case; maybe John did not count some of the failed attempts when the steamer ended up on the bar.

As the nights grew darker and as the passengers' patience ebbed away, Wyllie was ready to head out once again, on the night of 1 September. This time the shoals and the tides were on their side, and Mary was thrilled that she and her family were finally able to leave the boredom of Smithville behind – but still they could not escape. Just as the dangers of nature were conquered, the might of the Union Navy became the obstacle to their success. On 2 September she wrote:

> Last night we got up steam about twilight and started out. We went splendidly, got over the rip as nicely as possible without touching and thought we would certainly go through, when the 1st Officer discovered something on the bar, and when the glasses were turned on, a large blockader was distinctly seen lying directly in our path. She saw us and flashed her light, so of course we had to put back to Smithville. It was supposed to be a monitor,[13*] as no masts were seen, and if it was, we would have passed so near that we would have been blown to atoms.

Unbowed, Wyllie was determined to make another attempt as soon as possible and the evening of 2 September was marked as the next window for escape; but yet another obstacle prevented them leaving:

> Last evening we got up steam, heaved the anchor and were just on the point of starting, when Capt. Wylie had a telegram sent him by a physician on shore, saying that he might not be well enough to navigate today if we got out to sea and consequently just had all the steam turned off and the vessel anchored again.

The physician must have presented a very powerful argument to persuade Wyllie, who had for the past month been stuck inside Cape Fear, to sit tight for yet another night. Might it have been the same illness that had prompted him to buy his medicines in Liverpool? If it was affecting his ability to command his ship, it must have been serious. By the night of the 3rd his condition was severe enough for him to get someone to help him con the ship. Mary noted:

> Last night we started out, as Capt. Wylie is still unwell, with another navigator to steer in case our Capt. should have a relapse. We got beyond the bar and the range lights were set, so we had to tum back, intending to try again, but the ship was so hard to tum that she had to be anchored and let the tide swing her around. We started out again, but by the time she got to the rips the tide had gone down so much that we could not cross them, so are back again for the night.

13* A heavily armed ironclad warship named after the USS *Monitor*, designed for working in shallow waters in order to help enforce the blockade.

The tally was now up to seven attempts, and providence appeared to be completely against the success of the steamer. Nature, the Union fleet and finally illness had combined to stop the *Ad-Vance*. But Wyllie pressed on and tried again the very next night. Their luck, however, fell to a new low, as Mary wrote of a terrifying collision in the river between the *Ad-Vance* and another runner, which almost sent both vessels to the bottom:

> We got to the rip, got aground and had just started off and were going at half speed, when the *Old Dominion*, which had started a little after us, actually ran into us. Mother and the small children were down between the cotton bales, while Mrs. Boykin and I were on top of them. One of the stewards, who was on the cotton bales with us, seeing the *Old Dominion* coming along at full speed, said, 'Look at the *Old Dominion*, she's coming into us. Get a hold, get a hold.' And with that he tumbled off. Mrs. Boykin and I were much nearer the shock, and we thought he was in fun and stayed up there. We saw the boat booming but thought, of course, that they would take care and not run into us, but the first thing we knew there was a most fearful crash ... The bow of the *Old Dominion* was very sharp and strong, but our ship was so strong that it did not run in until it had scraped the length of three feet and a half ... They say if this vessel had not been remarkably strong, it would certainly have gone down.

As morning broke on 7 September, Mary wrote, rather forlornly, that they had made it back to Smithville and 'anchored at our same, old place'. As a result of the collision, some 300 bales of cotton were removed, as recorded in a note on the manifest. This almost halved the cargo but would lighten the ship considerably, and it was hoped that this would finally overcome the problem of clearing the sandbars.

That night they would try again, but Mary wrote that their pilot, C.C. Morse, was 'ordered on another ship' and a new pilot needed to be found. Her description continues the theme of ill fortune for the *Ad-Vance*:

> another pilot was detailed to carry us out. He got on a spree and was not notified he was to go out on the *Ad-Vance* until about an hour before time for him to come on board. When he did come, the guard had to wake him up and bring him on board as drunk as a fish. Of course, we could not risk ourselves with him and have to wait until tonight.

Mary would be on board for one last attempt before her father decided to take his family off the steamer; the ill luck was just too much for him. She wrote:

> We got to sea that night and the pilot had just given the ship over to the Capt., when it was discovered that we were about to be surrounded … She was anchored in sight of the Yankees all day, and everybody thought it would be so perfectly desperate that Father and Dr Boykin took their families off.

Mary and her family would now need to find another steamer to take them through the blockade. She had spent a month hopping on and off the deck, watching as the many events of the blockade had played out in front of her eyes. She would at least see the steamer make its run, finally leaving the cursed sandbars behind. But its luck would continue to desert it, and Mary's last entry begins the tale of the ultimate chase and capture of the *Ad-Vance.* As she readied for bed the day after she stepped off the valiant steamer for the last time, she wrote: 'The *Ad-Vance* got out that night … 35 shots fired at her were heard at Smithville.'

The Chase and Capture of the *Ad-Vance*

The career of *Ad-Vance* on the blockade was now down to its last few hours. On the night of 9 September, on the ninth attempt, the steamer finally made it over the bar, as recorded by Mary, and out to sea. Its success however, was short-lived as it ran straight into the waiting Union fleet.

The details of the chase and capture of the *Ad-Vance* have over the years featured in many sources. Several first-hand accounts from crew members, notably engineer James Maglenn, were recorded, and set out the background to the chase and capture. However, one account has lain undisturbed and forgotten: that of Captain Wyllie himself. By far the most intimate and detailed of the accounts, it was featured in the pages of *The People's Friend* and provided insights that had never appeared before in histories of the Civil War. The author of the piece, Peter Anton, picked up the story where Mary White left off:

> It is night. His ship is chock full of cotton. Captain Wyllie is lying in Wilmington harbour all steam up, ready to proceed to sea. The night is clear – too clear for the work he has to do – but he has been so frequently successful, he is not now so easily daunted. His mind is not altogether at ease. President Davis sent an order commanding that all his coals should be transferred to the Confederate privateer *Tallahassee.* In place of his smokeless Welsh anthracite he received some horrid smoky shale. With his usual adroitness, however, he has saved a few tons of his good coal. They had no sooner crossed the bar than they received a fusillade from a Northern launch, which had been lying about on the look out for whatever might turn up in the course of the night. The balls rattled harmlessly about the boxes, and had evidently been meant for the pilot, helmsman, and captain. The small arms awoke the fleet. They had a smart

run, but with a speed of eighteen knots they were soon wholly out of danger. This run had exhausted the Captain's supply of good coal. With the new coal they could do nothing more than six knots. Getting into the Gulf Stream, Captain Wyllie shaped his course for Halifax, Nova Scotia. The morning dawned bright and beautiful and without a cloud in the sky. What was his chagrin, however, to see the dense black column towering up from the funnel – a very signal inviting reprisal, a very Jonah not to be thrown over board. In the circumstances, I think our captain hardly showed his usual resource in times of difficulty. He should have at once extinguished his fires, and taken the chance of being seen in the open sea, or he should have fed his fires with his cotton, saturating it with what oil he had aboard. At ten o'clock, worn out with the fatigue and excitement of the night, he was preparing for taking a rest for an hour or two. He had not lain for half an hour when the cry came from the crow's nest, 'something astern, sir.' With glass in hand, in a minute the Captain was up beside the look-out. He was far away, and no bigger than a sea gull. But he was without doubt a big bird of prey. The Captain's heart fell. The bird, the eagle was winging its flight down upon him. He regarded himself as good as captured. Barrels of turpentine were emptied on bales of cotton, the best coals were selected, but it was to no avail. What would he have given for a bit of London fog, or Jack the Giantkiller's coat of invisible green, or night, or Blucher? But there was no remedy. The ship's papers were burned; the secret despatches dropped into the sea. And this done, they sullenly waited for their fate. The eagle grew larger. By and by they could see the rage in his eye. She punched down. Captain Wyllie was disconsolate. Poor *Advance*, you are not yourself today, and your old captain cannot blame you. The American warship *Santiago de Cuba* brushed alongside and fired a blank cartridge. In a race for life a spavined old dray horse of Barclay & Perkin had been the winner of the Derby.[240]

At 4 P.M., through that mean order of President Davis, which was only one of a great number more of which the blockade-runners at the close of the blockade had bitterly to complain, the *Advance* became a Federal prize, and Captain Wyllie a prisoner. When he was boarded the muzzle of a pistol was kept in close proximity to his head, and the engineers and firemen were placed over the boilers in case of treachery on their part.

Brought before the captain of the *De Cuba* his flag was demanded. The English ensign was produced. It was galling they had not subjected them to the humiliation of hauling it down. 'Ship's papers?' 'At the bottom.' 'Letters?' 'Ditto.' This made the Yankee captain infuriated. But he was a gentleman, and

The Ad-Vance *was captured on the night of 10 September 1864 by the* Santiago de Cuba, *pictured here. The crew of the blockade runner lamented that their sleek greyhound had been caught by such a slow, lumbering vessel.*

Courtesy of the Library of Congress

> cooled down after he remembered he had the honour of taking the best prize of the blockade season, and the best-known captain.[241]

The commander of the *Santiago de Cuba* was Oliver S. Glisson, who just three days before this successful capture had lamented the fact that the runners could not be stopped no matter how much effort his squadron exerted. In his official report he noted that this success came as a surprise as his warship was, at the time of spotting the *Ad-Vance*, on its way to recoal at Hampton Roads, Virginia. After sighting the runner, he ordered full speed and prepared for the chase. In a fair contest the *Ad-Vance* would have easily outpaced the slower *Santiago de Cuba*, which was capable of only 14 knots. The *Ad-Vance*, sleek and recently repaired, could make 18 knots – but the poor coal had, from Wyllie's account, reduced the speed of the *Ad-Vance* by 66 per cent, and over a nine-hour chase the *Santiago de Cuba*, slowly but surely caught up. Glisson reported that after a shot was fired over the bow of the *Ad-Vance* the steamer surrendered without any resistance. The game was up.

In his report submitted on 20 September Glisson gave his details of the capture and discussion with Wyllie. He stated that Wyllie had told him that he:

> had captured one of the fastest blockade runners that they had; that his vessel costs $175,000 in gold two years since, and that since that time the owners had put on her in repairs $15,000, and to show me how highly he valued her he said he would give $100,000 in gold for her.[242]

The captain of the Santiago de Cuba, *Oliver S. Glisson, (1809–1890), was an experienced naval officer who had commanded blockaders since 1862. He chased the* Ad-Vance *for eight hours until finally catching the runner – slowed by the inferior coal it had been forced to use.*

NH 49337 Courtesy of the Naval History & Heritage Command.

Wyllie then told Glisson that 'if she was placed on the blockade she would be a great terror to the blockade runners', a prediction that would soon come to pass.

The fate of captured runners lay in the hands of the prize courts in New York and Boston. To the north was where the *Ad-Vance* would now head, bound for adjudication and if found a lawful prize to be auctioned to the highest bidder. Wyllie and several select crew members stayed with the ship in order to facilitate this journey; this was standard practice for captured vessels. Their fate, too, would be decided in a Yankee metropolis. The rest of the crew would be taken off and carried to a Union prisoner of war camp if they could not prove they were from neutral countries. Several of the Southerners on board attempted to fool their captors and avoid such a punishment. James Maglenn, *Ad-Vance*'s chief engineer, and of Irish birth, observed many of the Carolinian and Virginian sailors attempting to fake a British accent in order to claim protection by Her Majesty's Government, sounding the letter o in 'home' in a very broad manner. He himself would escape punishment, but many of the crew, broad o or not, were taken by the *Santiago de Cuba* to Norfolk, Virginia, to face a military tribunal.[243]

As the Union sailors were securing the steamer and making note of its cargo and fittings, they came across a forlorn passenger, one who had not been on the steamer by choice. He was found below decks, a prisoner locked tight in double irons. He was brought before Glisson, and he informed the captain that his name was Dr Orazio Lugo de Antonioni, he was an Austro-Italian, and he was being expelled from the Confederacy for espionage. He had travelled across the Southern states from Richmond to Wilmington, observing Confederate fortifications, railway lines and ordnance depots. Having been arrested as a Union spy he was to have been sentenced to death, but sufficient evidence could not be produced to warrant his hanging. The sentence was commuted and he was instead banished from the Confederacy, making this forced journey via the *Ad-Vance.* On release from his chains he informed his liberators that he had information concerning railways in the South that would be useful to the commanders of the Union Army. He was then conveyed on the *Santiago de Cuba* to Norfolk along with the crew. While on board that ship he wrote to Secretary of War Stanton that he could be a valuable resource; in response he was ordered to appear before General Ulysses S. Grant to offer his information and was told he would be granted a reward for his assistance. Not only was the steamer in Union hands, destined for possible use against its former fleet, but now its last passenger would further assist in the war effort against the Confederacy.[244]

The news of the capture of the *Ad-Vance* was splashed across newspapers in the North as early as 12 September. The *Daily National Republican* (Washington DC) had access to the official dispatches from Captain Glisson, and gave its eager readers the full details of the chase, capture and cargo. Soon the news spread to Philadelphia and New York, and then rapidly across the Atlantic to England, where on the 28th the *Liverpool Mercury* reported the latest news from the Civil War, culled from newspapers on board the recently arrived Cunard steamer *Europa*. The article reported that the *Ad-Vance* 'will be a most valuable prize, for, in addition to her size and speed, she underwent extensive repairs here in May and June last, and was perhaps one of the most efficient boats on the station'.

It took longer for the news to make it to the people of North Carolina than to those in Washington and New York. It wasn't until 16 September that Power, Low & Company sent a telegram to Governor Vance informing him that they had learned of the capture from a newspaper, writing '*Herald* 13th reports capture *Advance* Saturday last'. The capture was not only a great loss to the state, but a personal loss to Vance. The Fayetteville *Carolinian* said that the loss was a 'pretty severe blow to our State. She has done a noble service for our North Carolina soldiers, and has paid for herself twenty times.' The Raleigh *Weekly Standard* on 21 September echoed the sentiments from the Northern papers, to the effect that now the *Ad-Vance* was in their clutches it would make a formidable foe.

> The *Advance* was among the finest and swiftest vessels ever built on the Clyde … her capture, however, is a most unfortunate circumstance, as it furnishes the enemy with a sea going ship of greater speed than any they had yet captured, and faster, we think, than any they have in their blockade squadron. We presume it will not be long before she makes her appearance on our coast as a fully armed and exceedingly dangerous blockader.

Governor Vance was saddened by the loss of his prized steamer, and livid about the cause of its capture. His full response can be found in a message to the North Carolina State Assembly in which he informed the members of the capture. He remarked that this 'noble vessel, pride of the State, and benefactor of our soldiers and people' had only been taken due to the poor coal it had been forced to take, reducing its speed to half its normal maximum. His anger was focused on the decision to divert the fine steam coal to the Confederate Navy cruisers that had been despatched to the port of Wilmington. He also argued that hosting these Confederate warships at Wilmington meant that the Union forces had 'tripled the stringency of the blockade' which had 'already caused the loss of many valuable steamers, and ultimately provoke the utmost efforts of the enemy for the capture of Wilmington'. The effectiveness of the cruisers, in Vance's opinion, was of little help to the Confederacy, and he went on to damn their operations:

> These cruisers sally forth with the coal seized from steamers engaged in bringing us supplies of vital importance, thus ensuring their capture, destroy a few insignificant smacks which only serves to irritate the enemy, and then they steam back to Wilmington to seize more coal, bringing down upon the inlets a new swarm of the enemy's gunboats.

His frustrations peaked when describing the condition of the people of North Carolina, now left without a supply line. 'Where our supply of shoes is to come from this winter I do not know. I have an abundant supply at the Islands, but have now no means of getting them.' He concluded his remarks to the Assembly by stating that it was 'no exaggeration to say that the *Ad-Vance* alone in solid benefits has been worth more to our government than all the cruisers we have ever had afloat.'[245]

THE NEW YORK PRIZE COURT AND WYLLIE'S ESCAPE

The *Ad-Vance* now steamed north, bound for the naval yard at Brooklyn, New York. On board was a skeleton crew of Union officers and sailors, tasked with getting their prize to harbour safe and sound. It was indeed their prize, for if the steamer and contents were ruled as such, the money realised in the ensuing auctions of the vessel and its cargo and tackle would be divided between all those who had taken part in its capture. This could mean a very large payday for everyone involved, from the captain down to humble oilers and stokers. This was yet another way in which men could make money on the blockade, albeit one reciprocal to that of the men who were trying to run it and avoid capture.

On board with Wyllie were two former members of the crew: Charles Harris, the second engineer, and the purser, Thomas Carter; all three were to be questioned in front of the prize court judge once they had assisted in the safe delivery of the steamer.

Their testimonies were to be *prima facie* evidence in the adjudication of the court. All three were British subjects who would normally be released after interrogation, and if failing to be released in orderly manner would appeal to the representatives of the British government to request that pressure should be mounted for their release.

The steamer made New York a week after its capture, *The New York Herald* reporting on 17 September that it had come in under the prize crew led by Acting Master Josiah A. Hannum. Although adjudication had not yet taken place, the paper estimated the worth of the steamer and its cargo at 'half a million dollars'. As soon as the steamer arrived, Wyllie, Carter and Harris were made to appear in front of the prize court judge in an office on Wall Street. Despite Wyllie's claim that the ship's papers had been sent to the bottom during the capture, the acting master presented a bundle of items to the prize court, including the manifest for the last voyage, the ship's registry papers, mails and several bills of exchange. These would form vital evidence in the upcoming ruling on the fate of the steamer and its three former crew.

The process would be speedy, with the depositions of the three men required before the final decision could be rendered. Wyllie was the first to be questioned, and at the start he recalled that he had been shown a photograph of himself by the official as identification. The scene was described in *The People's Friend*:

> Wyllie was taken before the Marshall. He was shown his own photograph. The captain confessed the likeness was undeniable, and he ventured to hope that the Marshall might be pleased with the retention of the image, and let the reality go free.[246]

The 'Marshall' was United States District Attorney Edward Delafield Smith, and he would not take kindly to what he would probably have perceived as cheek. The photograph Wyllie mentioned might have formed part of the Union's files on vessels and crews known to be engaged in running the blockade, which were kept by officials at the Ludlow Street Jail in Manhattan, a vital archive in the wider fight against the runners.[247]

Delafield Smith was tasked by the prize court to gather evidence on the steamer and its crew and then present it to Samuel Rossiter Betts, the judge in charge of the case. Smith began by asking Wyllie the standard set of questions (known as interrogatories) used at the prize courts in New York and Boston. The answers would be legal testimony, and this was one of the most important parts of the whole process. The interrogatories began with questions about the person in question, their place of birth, citizenship and rank. Very quickly the questions turned to details of the captured vessel, its cargo, port of origin, owners and destination.

Wyllie's responses to these interrogatories can be described as at best basic. They were short and direct, and included the briefest of facts. He could not plead ignorance, for he was the master, but he was trying, based on his British citizenship, to extract himself from any

US District Attorney Edward Delafield Smith (1826–1878) took Wyllie's deposition for the prize court after the arrival of the Ad-Vance *in New York. An experienced lawyer of blockade cases, it was he who discovered that Wyllie, despite the Captain's careful testimony, was in fact a veteran runner.*

Courtesy of the Library of Congress

hint of guilt that might imperil his release. The responses of Harris and Carter followed a similar line; they gave the details of their employment and the ship's operation, doing their best to ensure that they would not incriminate themselves. All three gave almost exactly the same responses to the interrogatories, suggesting they might have conspired to get their stories straight while on the journey to New York (see Appendix 3).

After his deposition was complete, Wyllie made his way into the city. From his own recollections he was allowed to select his own hotel, but was ordered to appear at the marshal's office on Wall Street every morning at 10 a.m. He had almost nothing but the clothes on his back, because as a crew member of a captured runner he was only allowed to keep his own personal property. When he was asked if he had suffered any personal loss at the time of capture he claimed to have 'sustained no loss except the loss of my pay and my chronometer'. This was the watch that had been presented to him by the steamer's owners in Liverpool that summer. So important was the watch to Wyllie that he made a personal appeal for its return to Judge Betts. This request was lodged on 21 September and was sworn before the US Attorney. Wyllie's appeal claimed that as he had 'rendered every assistance in his power both by himself and crew to bring the said vessel and cargo into the port' he was entitled to the return of the chronometer and 16 bills of exchange totalling the substantial sum of £875 ($8,730 today; see Table 1). These bills, argued Wyllie, were not part of the steamer's business. In his request for their return he went as far as to describe these bills as 'entirely worthless' in the hands of the captors. If these were redeemable by Wyllie in some way, their total would be a vast amount, more than eight times the pay he usually received for a run. Due to the assistance Wyllie had rendered en route, Judge Betts consented to this motion, and a day later Wyllie arrived back at the office in Wall Street to collect his chronometer and the bills of exchange.[248]

With the full cargo listed and an estimate made of the value of the steamer submitted, the adjudication process was now almost complete. Judge Betts considered the evidence and ruled that the *Ad-Vance* had indeed been legally captured as a prize of war, and the steamer and its cargo could now be sold. The Union Navy had already made a bid by letter to Delafield Smith on the 19th, offering $120,000 for the vessel. The cargo and fittings went on to fetch $168,284 at auction, and after the deduction of court costs of $5,047 the grand total realised was $283,238. Under law, half would go to the United States government and half to all those involved in the capture of the steamer. The capture of such a valuable steamer would have life-changing effects on those involved. Since only the *Santiago de Cuba* had been present, $141,619 would be distributed between the commander of the squadron and Captain Glisson and his crew. Admiral S.P. Lee, commander of the North Atlantic Blockade Squadron, received 1/20th, and Captain Glisson was awarded 2/20ths, the staggering sum of $14,161. This was more than four years' pay for a commander at sea, whose usual remuneration was $291.67 a month. The *Santiago de Cuba*'s listed complement was 114 men, so the 113 crew shared out the remaining 17/20ths of the fund on a rate comparable to their monthly pay, meaning that a midshipman whose normal monthly pay was $41 might have taken home over $500 for his part in the capture – for what had amounted to less than two days' work. The business of blockade running could, for those who were successful, and regardless of which side they were on, be very profitable indeed.[249]

While the case was moving swiftly through Judge Betts' courtroom Wyllie was awaiting his expected release and his return to Britain. He was confident this would be the case, as he recalled that no flag other than the British ensign had been found on the steamer. But this faith would not be rewarded; he recalled that on the evening he was to be freed:

> a masonic friend came to him and told him that some of the crew having confessed they had sailed under the Southern flag, he was to be committed as a prisoner-of-war.[250]

Which of the crew members had talked is not clear, for both Harris and Carter had mentioned no Confederate flag in their depositions. The court recorded that they had both testified that the *Ad-Vance* had only sailed under 'English colors'. Wyllie, however, when asked under which flags the steamer had sailed, had replied, 'She had on board no other colors, but she had on board Confederate colors while she lay in Confederate waters.'

Whether this testimony led the judge and attorney to suspect Wyllie is not known, but what added to Wyllie's newfound fears for his freedom was that on 23 September Judge

Prize money paid to the complement of the Santiago de Cuba

Realisation from the sale of the *Ad-Vance*	
Cargo as auctioned	$168,284.00
Vessel and its tackle as purchased by US Navy	$120,000.00
Minus court and marshal costs	-$5,047.71
Total	***$283,238.78***

Distribution by court decree, 12 November 1864	
Half to be given to United States Government	$141,619.39
Half to crew of *Santiago de Cuba*	$141,619.39

Shares in 1/20ths as outlined by Congressional Act (17 July 1862) NB: these figures assume that the *Santiago de Cuba* was at the time under the direct command of the admiral; if not, the crew would have got 18/20.	
Acting Rear Admiral S.P. Lee, commander of fleet/squadron	***1/2*** ($7,080.97)
Captain Glisson, commander of capturing vessel	***2/20*** ($14,161.90)
Crew of the *Santiago de Cuba*: full complement listed at 114 'distributed and apportioned among all others doing duty on board … according to their respective rate of pay'	***17/20*** ($120,376.15)

Monthly pay for US naval crew at sea, 1864	
Captain	$291.67
Ensign	$100.00
Gunner (three years' service)	$95.83
Midshipman	$41.67

Betts issued a ruling that abruptly overturned his previous order for the return of Wyllie's chronometer and bills of exchange. The judge wrote that evidence had been provided to him by US Attorney Smith that Wyllie had 'repeatedly, prior to the present offense, and for a long period been engaged in running the blockade' and that his previous order to deliver to Captain Wyllie the chronometer found on the steamer was thereby rescinded.[251] Smith had obviously carried out further investigation into Wyllie's full career on the steamer and his relationship with the State of North Carolina – and might this also have been a response to the Scot's arrogance when he had first been interviewed, expressing the hope that he might be released and just his photograph retained? Judge Betts's new orders went out – but they would prove fruitless, as Wyllie had recovered his chronometer the previous day and had no intention of returning to the courtroom.

Less than a week after arriving in Manhattan, Wyllie made his way down to the docks. He did not show up for the required daily 10 a.m. check-in with the authorities. Now a fugitive, he would leave the city before Judge Betts, US Attorney Smith or any other law officers could apprehend him and take him to the waiting cells of a New York prison. His escape was speedy, as recounted later:

> Without waiting a moment, he went down to the wharf and got aboard a Halifax steamer which was just about to sail. The paddles turned and the Captain was out of the talons of the American eagle.
>
> The passage home was rough, but the Captain, notwithstanding his loss, enjoyed himself amazingly. To go to bed when he liked, to rise when he liked, to have no anxiety, no responsibility. What a glorious thing it was to be *a passenger*![252]

Wyllie made no mention of the name of the vessel he boarded, but his destination would be the safety of the neutral Canadian port of Halifax.

Just a month later RMS *Asia* arrived at Liverpool; it was a passenger and mail steamer from Boston which had called at Halifax on 14 October. The steamer's passengers had experienced easterly gales and stormy weather, to be reported, along with the passenger list, on 27 October in the *Liverpool Daily Post*. In this list are the names Captain Wyllie, Thos. Carter and Chas. Harris. The three crew members of the *Ad-Vance* who had brought the steamer to New York had made their escape together. Wyllie was now truly away from the 'talons of the American Eagle'.

While these former crew members of the *Ad-Vance* were making their escape, the steamer itself was being prepared for its new career. The day after Judge Betts had rescinded the order for the return of Wyllie's chronometer the steamer arrived at the Brooklyn naval yard to undergo repairs. As had been predicted by Wyllie, and feared by those in the South, the steamer, having been bought by the navy, was to be quickly converted into a blockader and renamed *Advance* (soon thereafter *Frolic*). Guns were mounted, machinery overhauled and upgraded, and with no low-grade coal reducing its speed it would return to the waters off Wilmington by mid-November. It arrived in time to take part in the long-expected assault and capture of Fort Fisher, the guardian of the Cape Fear River, finally closing Wilmington to blockade runners.

The *Frolic* would go on to have a long naval career, serving in the US Navy until 1883, when it was sold for scrap. After lying on the shore in Alexandria, Virginia, waiting to be scrapped, it was bought and converted into a coal barge, renamed *Maud Maclain*. The once proud and famous runner was relegated to a hulk. This news did not pass unnoticed by some of those that remembered the runner, as the *News and Observer* of Raleigh informed its readers on New Year's Day 1886:

> ALAS! To what base uses & … The famous blockade runner *Advance*, which during the war made many successful trips between Willington and Nassau is now but a barge, carrying coal between New Orleans and Galveston … She is now in her humiliation called the *Maud McLean* (*sic*).[253]

Poacher turned gamekeeper: after its capture the Ad-Vance *was commissioned into the US navy as a warship and it joined the blockade fleet. Here, moored in Naples Harbour in 1867 as part of the European Squadron.*

NH 53957 Courtesy of the Naval History & Heritage Command.

Five years hauling coal in the Gulf of Mexico followed, until one stormy night in November 1891. The tug hauling the *Maud Maclain* was forced to cut its lines when the barge became waterlogged, and the crew abandoned the hulk as it disappeared slowly beneath the waves. No Union warships near, no reports of cannons fired, no cheers of the crew as it escaped the hounds – just the roars of the storm (see Appendix 4).

WYLLIE'S RECORD

Wyllie's time on the *Ad-Vance* had spanned 17 months. He had been there when it had been purchased by Crossan, and as it made its way from Glasgow across the Atlantic. He was ever-present during its career on the blockade, right up to the very moment when he turned it over to Captain Glisson. His achievements during this time can be quantified as well as qualified. The *Ad-Vance* made 15 successful runs through the blockade as well as two transhipments between Bermuda and Nassau. Wyllie was on board for all of these, taking full command of the final four runs and the last transhipment. He was a steady hand at the wheel, knowledgeable of modern steam propulsion, and by all accounts a jovial, friendly face for both crew and passengers. The success of the steamer was in large part down to Wyllie.

The accomplishments of the steamer can be charted from customs records and contemporary newspaper reports. The main export was of course cotton, and the total number of bales carried on the seven successful runs out from Wilmington can be calculated. Adding the numbers of the runs listed as from Bermuda, itemised in the newspaper reports from North Carolina and mentioned in government records such as letters and telegrams to Vance, the number of cotton bales carried totalled 4,281, an average of 611 per trip.

Quantifying the materials imported to Wilmington is harder, as often the contents of items such as 'packages, crates, kegs' were not fully listed. But one significant listing does exist, and it comes from what can only be described as the highest and most reliable source, Governor Zebulon Vance himself. It was included in a speech he gave on North Carolina's record during the war, ten years after the fighting stopped. He could not give a complete manifest of the items, but his listing shows the huge contribution this one vessel made to the welfare of the soldiers and people of North Carolina. The steamer carried:

> Large quantities of machinery supplies, 60,000 pairs of hand cards, 10,000 grain scythes, 200 barrels of blue stone for the wheat growers, leather and shoes for 250,000 pairs, 50,000 blankets, gray woollen cloth for at least 250,000 suits of uniforms, 12,000 overcoats readymade, 2,000 best Enfield rifles, with 100 rounds of fixed ammunition, 100,000 pounds bacon, 500 sacks of coffee for hospital use, $50,000 worth of medicines at gold prices, large quantities of lubricating oils, besides minor supplies of various kinds for the Charitable institutions of the State.[254]

Vance also commented that it was not only North Carolina that benefited, but as the steamer had brought in many items such as blankets, shoes and clothing that were turned over to the national Confederate government, this aided the other Southern states and their regiments as well.

Wyllie was a respected member of crew, with never a bad word said about him. Despite the worry amongst some in Wilmington about a 'furriner' in command, Wyllie had earned the approbation of both his superiors and his charges. Through the actions and words of John White, Thomas Crossan, Joseph Flanner, Captain Guthrie, the partners at Power, Low & Co and of course Governor Vance it has been shown that Wyllie was a competent, intelligent, jovial and, above all else, dependable master of the *Ad-Vance.*

6

RETURN TO THE BLOCKADE: WYLLIE'S LAST TWO RUNNERS

> Captain Wyllie had seen the beginning of the blockade running, and now he had seen the end of it. And at the end of it he was again a prisoner in the hands of the victorious North. How would it go with him this time? Would he again slip his leash?
>
> – From 'Risen from the Ranks: Captain Wyllie, the Great Scottish Blockade Runner', *The People's Friend*, July 1889

Wyllie returned to Liverpool in late October 1864 with no firm plans as to what he would do next. He had spent the last two years involved in the blockade trade, but after his capture he might have felt that a black mark would be placed by his name if he were to apply to command another runner. Might he have wondered if his stint on the blockade was over?

It would appear, however, that any such introspection did not last long, because he soon took up command of another paddle steamer being made ready for a transatlantic trip. The Confederate agents in Britain were still ordering new ships, and experienced captains were still in demand, captured or not. Anton later wrote:

> What was his astonishment to find that when the capture of the *Advance* became known they had set to work fitting out another steamer for him, and at that moment it was lying at the Broomielaw with all steam up, ready to sail! In seventeen hours after his arrival in Liverpool he was again afloat and bound for Bermuda.[255]

This new vessel was the *Susan Beirne*, recently launched by the yard of Aitken and Mansel of Whiteinch, Glasgow. The firm had been established by James Aitken and Robert Mansel in 1863; both men were experienced maritime engineers. From the start the firm built paddle steamers to run the blockade, beginning with the launch of the *Arrow* in November of that year, latterly known as the *Florie*, noted as making 14 successful runs in 1864. In 1864 alone the company launched eight steamers, six of which were to be used as runners, including the *Banshee*, sister ship to the *Susan Beirne*.[256]

As a purpose-built blockade runner, the *Susan Beirne* was designed with the latest technology and features for the trade, including a steel hull, engines capable of 250 horsepower, and holds dedicated to cargo. The designs had been perfected over the previous two years by the Clyde builders to suit the trade, and a description of this steamer sums up how these vessels appeared:

> Built of one-eighth of an inch steel, for space and speed, she was too frail for service at sea, and quite unfit for heavy weather. To look upon, she was a beautiful specimen of marine architecture, long and narrow, with speed of fourteen knots – a type of the latest design for blockade-running, regardless of the lives on board.[257]

Wyllie made his way from Liverpool to Glasgow by train. It would appear that his claim of 17 hours from arrival to setting sail on the *Susan Beirne* might have been a bit of understatement, as the steamer would not leave Glasgow until mid-November. Once he had arrived in Glasgow he would be told that his job was to deliver the vessel to Bermuda, navigating it on the dangerous Atlantic crossing. He was of course an old hand at this, having made three such trips as master of *Lord Clyde/Ad-Vance* during the past year. The *Susan Beirne* was operated by the Importing and Exporting Company of Georgia, which had been set up in 1863 and was employed by the State of Georgia to slip goods in through the blockade. The company had formed a partnership with Henry Lafone, a Liverpool businessman involved in transporting cargoes from Liverpool to neutral ports like Bermuda in the ships of his Blue Cross Line; the partnership was to order six paddle steamers for use as runners.[258]

On 11 November the *Susan Beirne* steamed out of the city and down the river towards the Firth of Clyde, then to the open ocean, just as the *Lord Clyde* had done a year and a half before. This time there was less fanfare – just the briefest of mentions in the local press that the steamer was leaving port. The *Susan Beirne* was not a 'suspected *Alabama*', as Wyllie's first runner had been – it was just another Clyde-built steamer making for the blockade, and by the autumn of 1864 this had become a pretty regular occurrence. It carried machinery destined for Confederate torpedo boats. But once again the voyage would be far from routine as it would be a stormy crossing, and on the way Wyllie would speak publicly for the first time about his fame as a blockade runner.

The *Susan Beirne's* maiden voyage ran into trouble from the start. As it left the Clyde and turned south towards the Irish Sea it was hit by rough seas and sustained damage to its paddle boxes – damage that would obviously endanger it during the long Atlantic voyage. So Wyllie sought refuge at Belfast for repairs. The local papers mentioned the steamer and its damaged state, and also stated that a 'Captain Wyllie of the Confederate States of America' was a guest at Jury's Imperial Hotel in the city. At the time Jury's was listed as 'one of the best in Ireland and best in Belfast'. So while the repairs were being made, it would appear that Wyllie was sitting out the weather in a fair bit of style.[259]

The next leg of the journey was almost as short as the first, as the steamer made it only as far as Queenstown, putting in there for coaling. While in port Wyllie spoke to a local reporter, doing a bit of what today might be termed PR. The subsequent article features the first recorded narrative given by Wyllie as captain of a runner.

> RUNNING THE BLOCKADE
>
> There is now lying at Messrs. Robinson's yard a blockade runner called *Susan Beirne*, undergoing some slight repairs. She is commanded by Captain Wylie, and takes the place of the *Lord Clyde*, lately captured by the blockading squadron off Wilmington. Captain Wylie made in the *Lord Clyde* twelve voyages in and out of Wilmington, and on the thirteenth was captured. The risk in these feats was not trifling. Sometimes it happens that the vessel can slide in unseen, and then of course her task is easy. But, it does happen frequently that they are observed, and then they are made targets for as many of the blockading squadron as are within range. Captain Wylie in the *Lord Clyde*, has had as many as a hundred shot and shell flying about his vessel without being hit, her low lines and great speed rendering her a difficult object of aim. Captain Wylie has received from his owner, as a testimony to his boldness and success, a gold chronometer watch, bearing on one side an engraved picture of the ship in which he had been so fortunate and on the reverse the arms of North Carolina.[260]

Once again there would appear to be no concealment of the role that *Susan Beirne* would play: similar arrivals and sailings from that port were widely reported. In fact a local paper, the *Southern Reporter and Cork Commercial Courier*, made comment in its edition of 30 November that 'no fewer than four steamers intended for the hazardous enterprise of running the American blockade arrived at Queenstown last week.' This didn't even include *Susan Beirne*, which was listed separately in another brief article.

Wyllie didn't shy away from recounting his tales, and the facts he offered up for the article were accurate. He had retained his gold chronometer, hard won from the prize court officials in New York only two months previously, and appeared to wear it as a badge of honour. But as with many sailors' tales and stories, it can be interesting to examine what it *doesn't* say: there is, for example, no mention of his absconding from custody in New York, although to an Irish audience that might have been an exciting finale to his first stint as a runner. It is a short report, but does give an insight into the mind of Wyllie as being not afraid or shy to tell his story as a blockade runner, something that would continue later in life.

The *Susan Beirne* left Irish waters on 29 November, its destination given in the newspapers, incorrectly, as Nassau – Wyllie was to make for Bermuda. His command was to be a short one, as his job was merely to deliver the steamer to St George's then turn it over to another master to attempt to run the blockade.

There was an intriguing aspect to the voyage, as one of the crew was Eugene Anderson Maffitt, son of famous Confederate naval officer and blockade runner John Newland Maffitt, who had been the captain of the warship CSS *Florida* as well as the runner *Owl*. Eugene, meanwhile, had served on the famed warship CSS *Alabama* and had been on board at the time of its sinking in June 1864 off the coast of France by the steam-powered sloop of war *Kearsarge*. After that he made his way to Britain and was ordered to join his father on *Owl*, at that time docked in Nassau, which was why he was now on the *Susan Beirne*.[261]

Wyllie brought the *Susan Beirne* into St George's, Bermuda, on 17 December and there it was to be made ready for its initial run. The cargo, which had not been altered since leaving Glasgow, had been listed as general merchandise. A closer examination of the cargo manifest for its departure from St George's on 24 December reveals that it was a more or less standard cargo for a runner: it included 90 cases of shoes, 60 boxes of bacon, 100 barrels of copperas, 30 coils of rope, and over 150 boxes of 'merchandise'.[262]

Alas, *Susan Beirne*, the purpose-built, powerful runner, was destined never to make it through the blockade. After leaving Bermuda under the command of Captain D.S. Martin, the steamer encountered stormy weather that put a strain on the hull, possibly exacerbating the damage sustained after it had left Glasgow. A leak developed and the crew began to fear the worst. The captain decided, with the safety of crew and steamer paramount, to head back to Bermuda. As they started limping back to St George's it became clear that the steamer would require extensive repairs, but with no yard capable of making the repairs at St George's the *Susan Beirne* made for Nassau instead, and there it was laid up until the end of the war.[263]

Wyllie, having fulfilled his mission, would not wait long for another command. His next steamer's first and only voyage would turn out to be one of the most dramatic of all the events he ever experienced at sea, and would be the final trip of the 'Great Scottish Blockade Runner'.

Wyllie's Last Run: The *Deer* and the Fall of Charleston

Wyllie's last ever attempt to run the blockade would be different from all those that had preceded it. Unlike all his other runs where he had made for the Cape Fear River and Wilmington, this time he would be making for the port where the war had begun: Charleston, South Carolina. After the fall of Fort Fisher on 15 January, Wilmington had been cut off from the runners. Now Charleston was also under siege from Union forces, by both sea and land, and its fall was anticipated daily. Wyllie felt, nevertheless, that there was time for a few more runs, given the right conditions and a new moon. Although it was the dying days of the runners' trade, and indeed of the war itself, the chance was still there for one last voyage and its promised profit.

His final steamer would be the *Deer*, which like *Susan Beirne* was a newly built, purpose-designed runner. It had been built by the firm of W.H. Potter & Company of Liverpool to the order of Fraser, Trenholm. At 465 tons and with an engine of 180 hp, it was slightly smaller and less powerful than Wyllie's previous runners, but it had all the latest features to make it a sleek, fast steamer, ready to evade any Union warships.

The *Deer*, had only recently been brought over from Liverpool, under the command of Captain J.B. Butler, arriving at Bermuda a month after Wyllie had arrived in the *Susan Beirne*. While Wyllie was waiting at St George's, he and his fellow runners would have learned of the assault and ultimate fall of Fort Fisher, closing the port of Wilmington to their trade. The options were now even more limited and the risks even higher, but the chance for profit still existed. After spending both Christmas and New Year on dry land, Wyllie was ready to head out to sea, and he took command of the *Deer* at some time before 26 January; on that date it steamed from St George's bound for Nassau with a cargo of 123 packages of merchandise.[264]

At Nassau the situation for blockade running looked bleak. Even so, on 13 February Wyllie took the *Deer* out for the 500-nm voyage to Charleston. Wyllie himself recalled the events leading up to this voyage, recounted fully in *The People's Friend*:

> Wilmington having fallen, the only port now open was Charleston. Both at Bermuda and Nassau there was, however, among the shipping agents a strong suspicion that Charleston had fallen also. Startling rumours had come that Sheridan and Sherman were making forced marches to reach Charleston by land, and attack it from the rear, while the Union fleet were pounding Fort Sumter from the sea, and that by means of mounds and sand batteries the iron ring was being drawn closer and closer about the doomed city.
>
> The *Deer* and the *Stag*[265] were chosen to carry all the dispatches and news that had arrived from Europe at Bermuda down to Nassau and to forward

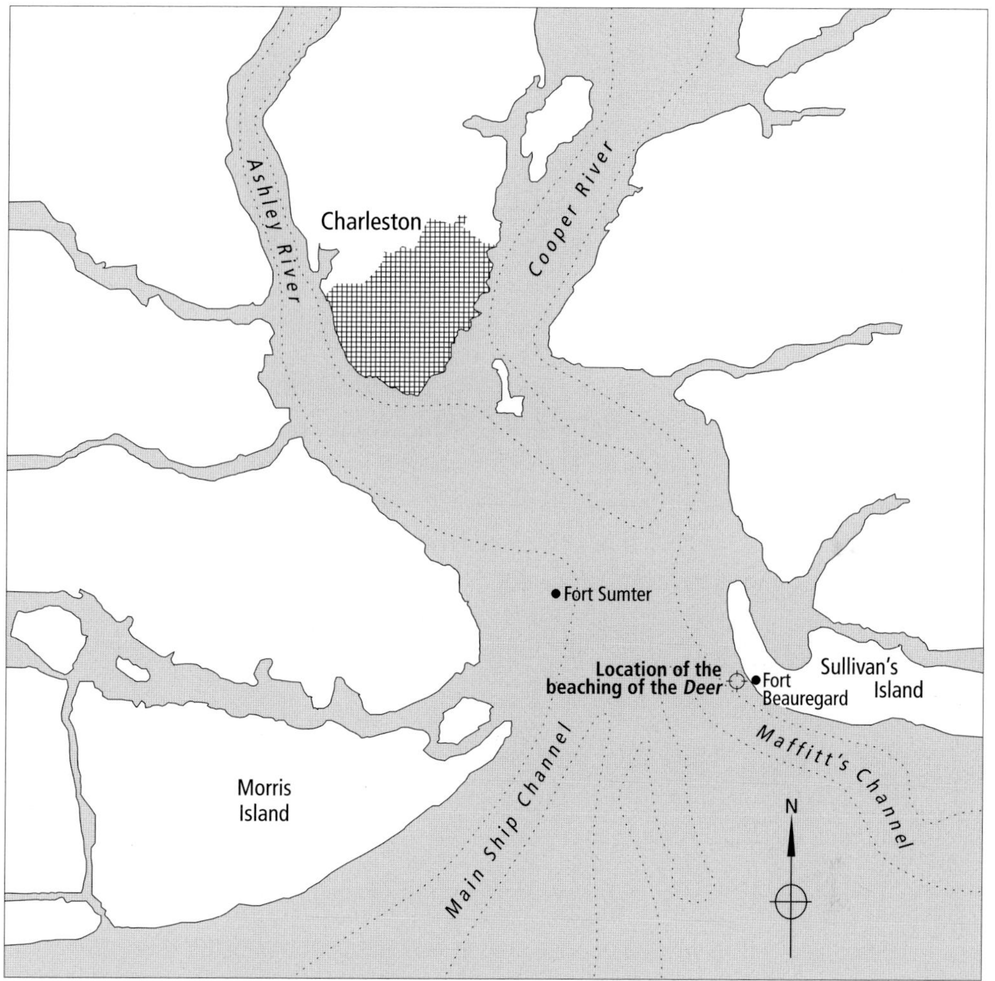

Charleston and its approaches

the despatches from there to the Confederates. To the first that reached Nassau was to be given the commission, along with the honour and danger, to discover whether or not Charleston had fallen. The sister ships steamed away from the Bermudas together. The sky soon grew troubled, both wind and sea rose together, and the barometer began falling fast. It was evident that a hurricane would immediately sweep the islands from the W.S.W. The *Deer* and the *Stag* were of the last class of blockade runners built. They were constructed for speed, not with a view to contending with the boisterous weather. By keeping straight on his way, Captain Wyllie – for he had given much attention to studying the nature and laws of storms – knew he would soon be in the heart of the cyclone. Turning his bow S.E. he ran 30 miles out of his course, by this means he escaped the fury of the tempest, and only, so to speak, received the wind caused by the passing waft of its wing. The barometer beginning to rise and the sea to calm down, which it continued to do until it was as smooth as oil, he turned his bow for Nassau, and gave the *Deer* all the steam she could take. It is needless to say he was anxious to win the race. He arrived twelve hours before the *Stag*, which came into the harbour with bulwarks, &c, gone, and in a dreadful plight.

Having earned the honour of steering into the jaws of the lion, his bunkers were filled to the brim with the best coal. Then, having received his despatches and orders, he was ready to go. He had no cargo. He merely ran in the interests of the other blockade runners. His orders were to run to Charleston and back as quickly as he was able. If he could not get in, or if the place had been taken, he was to get what news he could, and return with all speed.

Blockade running was for a time paralyzed, and there was (*sic*) about fifty ships engaged in the trade, one way or other, lying at that moment at Nassau. As Captain Wyllie steamed out, these vessels manned their yards, flew all their bunting, and gave cheer after cheer in his honour. All went well during the passage Northward. When they got into dangerous waters there was an ominous silence prevailing everywhere. They pushed right on, and did not halt until about a mile from Fort Sumter. The Captain was walking the bridge with the pilot, wondering whether the fort had been silenced and Charleston had fallen. The silence was occasioned by the preparations being made for a final assault. It was now broken. The ironclads began pouring broadsides and broadsides into the fort. Land batteries everywhere were showing their teeth. The whole time Sumter kept replying with wondrous briskness. The marines had determined to take Charleston from the sea before Sheridan and Sherman came up in the rear. In the midst of the fierce cannonading there was a tremendous report that drowned it all, and shook the *Deer* from stem to stern. This was followed by another and another and another, all equally powerful. What could it be? It was the Confederates driven to the desperate plight of blowing up their own ironclads.[266]

Suddenly the heavens became coloured a dark, bloody red. Of what new horror was this the sign? The town had taken fore in a certain quarter, cannonading went on without ceasing. But every now and then – drowning all – there was a fearful report, showing that some arsenal or powder magazine had exploded,

> or some warship had blown in the air. It was an awful sight, and captain and crew of the *Deer* gazed on its lurid glories with astonishment.
>
> To think of running into the harbour in the circumstances was madness. When it was drawing to the day the *Deer* ran twenty miles out to sea. When fifteen miles off shore one of the engines broke, and for some hours the ship was a helpless cripple. By six in the evening the steam was again up, and the *Deer* once more headed to Charleston. When they neared the place they found all quiet. They saw easily the dark masses of the ironclads. The nerves of the pilot had been utterly unstrung by the cannonading of the previous night. He took the *Deer* so closely in shore that he ran her aground. When they were preparing to get her off they were boarded by the Yankees. CHARLESTON HAD FALLEN that morning with the coming in of daylight, about an hour after the *Deer* had put to sea. Sheridan and Sherman had entered the city, and the mouth of Fort Sumter was shut. The South had been beaten, the war was at an end, and blockade running, with all its perils and excitements, its losses and fortunes, was over. Captain Wyllie had seen the beginning of the blockade running, and now he had seen the end of it. And at the end of it he was again a prisoner in the hands of the victorious North. How would it go with him this time? Would he again slip his leash?
>
> It was well that they had not been able to get the *Deer* afloat. She had been observed, and howitzers had been placed on shore which would certainly have blown her out of the water. After the boarding there was a terrible scene on board the *Deer*. The Yankees were drunk with victory and liquor. Of the former they could get no more, of the latter they were bent on making larger appropriations. The ship's stores were plundered. And there was not a teetotaller in the whole kit. In the midst of the headlong debauch, Captain Wyllie was afraid it would end in an infuriated attack on his person. After much clamour the crew were transferred to a Yankee man-of-war, with the exception of the captain, the first officer, and purser, who were allowed to remain aboard the *Deer*.[267]

The *Deer* grounded on 18 February, the night of the evacuation of the city, off Sullivan's Island, east of Fort Sumter and just off the main ship channel, Maffitt's channel.[268] There it was spotted by the crew of the *Catskill*, a single-turret monitor armed with two guns; it had been commissioned in February 1863 and since that date had been on station off Charleston. Its primary duty was to assist in the bombardment of coastal batteries and offer protection for the other Union vessels off the port. It formed part of the picket for the blockade line, but its low speed would not have allowed it to chase a runner.[269]

Wyllie's second capture came at the hands of the Catskill, *a monitor class warship that on the open sea would have been no match for a sleek purpose-built blockade runner. This etching shows the* Catskill *(left) in action in Charleston Harbour near Fort Sumter in 1863.*

Harper's Weekly

Sailors from the *Catskill*, led by Lieutenant-Commander Edward Barrett, made for the stranded runner in the monitor's boats. The *Deer* was caught. It was an ignominious ending, as in open water the tortoise-like monitor would have been no match for the sleek hare runner. But caught it was, and now Wyllie would once again have to answer to the Union officers. When Barrett came aboard, Wyllie was quoted as telling him 'Well, we give it up, she is your prize. Strange we did smell the rat, as we could not make out your signal at Fort Marshall.' This would appear to refer to the lights on Sullivan's Island that Barrett had ordered to be placed there earlier in the evening, in the hope of luring runners in. After speaking with Wyllie, Barrett would claim in his report that he'd had reason to suspect that Wyllie was not the captain's true name, as he had 'hesitated to tell it' to him. This hesitancy might have been because Wyllie, having been captured once before, was nervous of revealing his true identity in case his captor sent him in chains to a Yankee prison.[270]

The news of the capture of the *Deer* quickly made it to the Northern newspapers. A report in *The New York Herald* confirmed Wyllie's account, stating that the steamer had made the run in but then, on discovering the blockading fleet to be so far up the harbour, the officer (Wyllie) had ordered the ship to come about and when attempting to run out had stuck fast on the sand. The newspaper also reported that the cargo was 'principally of liquors', an assertion that would later be refuted at the prize court, which gave a full listing

The crew that captured Wyllie; the officers of the Catskill *are on the deck of their vessel. They had come upon the beached* Deer *during its attempted run into Charleston Harbour on the night of 18 February 1865.*

Courtesy of the Library of Congress

of the cargo.[271] The most significant item was 18 cases of sheet copper, with one barrel of brandy and a keg and barrel of whisky being the only alcoholic liquids present. The mention of liquors in the *Herald's* report might refer to the liberation of some of these casks by the sailors, explaining Wyllie's remarks about the Yankee boarders being drunk 'with victory and liquor'.

Wyllie was now once again in the clutches of the Union Navy. As with his last capture, he would stay on his steamer as it was taken north for adjudication at the prize court. This time, though, as this was his second offence Wyllie might well have believed that he would be unlikely to get off lightly, even with the protection offered by his status as a British subject. So as the *Deer* began its voyage northwards Wyllie's mind must have raced with thoughts of possible punishment. How was he to avoid it this time, and would the authorities know of his previous escape from the New York prize court officials? The events that followed, as recalled by Wyllie, would at first glance seem fanciful, whimsical and perhaps just the tall tales of a sailor. Yet the true story of Wyllie's last run through the blockade would not be about carrying cargo but escaping from the clutches of Federal marshals and detectives, and getting himself out of American waters to freedom.

THE GREAT SCOTTISH BLOCKADE RUNNER'S GREAT ESCAPE

Wyllie was joined on the *Deer* by just a few former members of the crew as well as the Union naval officers tasked with delivering the steamer to the prize court. The steamer was not to make for New York like the *Ad-Vance*, but farther north, to Boston. For Wyllie it was a painfully familiar task, under the watchful eye of his captors as his vessel steamed towards its fate. It turned out to be quite a slow voyage, as the *Deer* only made it to Boston on 6 March, over two weeks after its capture. Once there, however, events moved swiftly, as Wyllie again faced the court.

Wyllie recounted that on arrival he had been allowed to find his own accommodation but was under orders to appear before the marshal every morning. He recalled that 'The meeting with the Marshall in the morning was of the pleasantest kind. They chatted gaily for an hour, usually.'[272]

On the morning after arrival Wyllie, with the first mate Frank Ranger and the purser John Southgate Lemmon, gave their formal deposition to John Lowell, prize court commissioner. As with the deposition after his capture on the *Ad-Vance*, Wyllie and his crew gave short, matter-of fact responses to the interrogatories. Wyllie and Ranger were both British citizens, so hoped to be released soon after completing their testimony.[273] But Lemmon was a native of Baltimore and, Wyllie noted, he came from a well-known pro-Confederate family. After his deposition, Wyllie stated that Lemmon 'made tracks' by finding work on a schooner that was just about to go to sea. The initial, easy relationship with the marshal was now over, and Wyllie and Ranger were to be kept under surveillance by a 'continual companion' in the form of a detective named Mr Stone. Stone kept the pair close, as he 'ate with them, walked with them, slept in the same room with them'.[274]

What would now follow, as recalled by Wyllie himself, was an escape so fanciful that it would be hard to believe if the facts had not borne out the events he related. But, as has already been proved with Wyllie's stories during his time at sea, even the most fanciful of his tales were rooted in fact.

CATALOGUE
—OF—
ASSORTED
MERCHANDISE
CARGO AND STORES OF
Prize Steamer DEER,
TO BE SOLD BY AUCTION,
THIS DAY,
Wednesday, April 26th, 1865,
At 12 o'clock, M.,
AT STORES NO. 23 AND 24 LEWIS WHARF,
PER ORDER,
JOHN S. KEYES, U. S. Marshal.

A blockade runner's career came to a full stop when it and its cargo were auctioned off. The Deer *was sold in Boston in April 1865 for $40,000. Wyllie himself was not there to read the news, having already succeeded in his elaborate escape.*

Courtesy of the National Archives at Boston

First Wyllie and Ranger received word that they were to be confined at Fort Warren on Georges Island, at the entrance of Boston harbour. During the war the fort was used as a prison for captured Confederate officers and for political prisoners from both the North and the South. Imprisonment, previously of little concern to British blockade runners pleading their case as neutrals, could now be expected, after a proclamation issued by President Lincoln on 14 March. This directed marshals of the United States to arrest and commit to military custody 'all non-resident foreigners who now are or hereafter shall be found in the United States, and who have been or shall have been engaged in violating the blockade' and who had not left the United States 12 days after the issue of the order. So as a twice-captured runner captain who had previously absconded from custody in New York, Wyllie now faced the prospect of actual imprisonment.[275]

He knew that he was not in the best of health – possibly from his suspected malaria – and feared he would not last a week in the prison. He now formulated his plan to evade the authorities and make his way back to Scotland. First he needed to slip past his shadow, Mr Stone. So Ranger and Wyllie decided 'they should honour Mr. Stone with a good liquor up'. At dinner Wyllie plied Stone with drink while he himself drank the strongest tea. He was assisted in this effort by his waiter, a 'keen Southerner'. The escape thus began:

> Wyllie thought the waiter also seemed to have grown weary of fetching and carrying to this Stone, to whom a glass of brandy seemed nothing more than a drop of rain to the great Sahara. The captain is of opinion that the

'Unadulterated Hard Shell Quaker': how Wyllie might have appeared in his disguise, topped by a 'wide-awake', during his escape from Boston.

Courtesy of the Miriam and Ira D. Wallach Division of Art, Prints and Photographs: Print Collection, The New York Public Library.

> wearied waiter gave the last glass a heavy drugging. Anyhow, he had not long swallowed it when he fell to the floor.[276]

Now free of their minder, Ranger and Wyllie decided to go their separate ways to increase the chances of at least one of them escaping. Wyllie was rushed away to a nearby barber by the waiter who, Wyllie stated, had become a friend. There he lost his full beard, whiskers and moustache. It may have been the first time that Wyllie had been smooth-shaven for many a year, as his photograph in 1862 shows him in complete Victorian facial hair glory. Next, the waiter took him to an outfitter in order to complete the disguise:

> he was dressed from top to toe as a genuine, pure and unadulterated Hard Shell Quaker. A pair of green spectacles on his eyes, and the disguise was complete. The coat was a narrow swallow-tail, like an Irishman's donned for a funeral. The choker was a white cravat, and the headgear a huge wide-awake.[277]

The next step was to leave Boston. He would not make for the harbour like Lemmon – maybe believing that the authorities would be looking for a mariner there. Instead his waiter friend got him to the 'New York cars' – railway carriages. The waiter then made his farewell to Wyllie, saying that he: 'hoped he would in the city have a tarnation large gathering of Hard Shell Brethren'.

There were one or two choices for Wyllie's rail journey. He could have taken the Boston and Worchester line, which advertised four express trains a day to New York. A second option was to ride the rails down on the Norwich Line to New London, Connecticut, then board a steamer for either Greenport at the eastern tip of Long Island or New York itself. This route was advertised as providing 'Speed, Comfort and Safety: THE FASTEST, SAFEST, and Most Reliable and Only New Boats on the Sound'. Wyllie recounts that he got a good, sound sleep and awoke at his destination, so it appears that the first option, the direct train, was his chosen route.[278]

On arrival in New York, Wyllie planned to lay a false trail to attempt to throw the marshals off his tail, as he was sure that they were in hot pursuit. So he made for the wharves in Brooklyn where British mail steamers docked. There he boarded one and met a captain and a mate he knew.

> At first they could not make out their craft (*sic*), but when they did the laughter was inextinguishable. Getting them at length to be serious, he got them to give out that they had seen him, and that he intended to make the run of the detectives in the rig of a fireman. Nothing, he thought, like a false scent. The hunt was up, and he knew before a couple of hours the hounds would be aboard that very ship.

Mail steamers left for Britain from New York on an almost daily basis, so identification of that particular steamer is nigh on impossible now. But the Anchor Line for Glasgow and the Inman Line for Liverpool, to name just two, had steamers departing New York during the first two weeks of March, when Wyllie could have been in the city.[279]

With the false scent laid, Wyllie was next to plan how he could successfully make his way aboard a vessel bound for Britain and freedom. He set about making his way to Manhattan. From there he would have easy access to the wharfs of the transatlantic steamers or the shipping offices where he could, in his guise of pious Quaker, purchase a ticket – perhaps, in keeping with his story, saying he was on a religious pilgrimage to Britain. So he decided that he would leave Brooklyn and head across the East River on a ferry:

> The steamers that cross the river are large, and put into little harbours on each shore made to hold them. The sides of the ferry boats are for passengers, and the centre for carts and waggons. There being little or no tide the boats seemed like floating connections of the common street.

But as Wyllie boarded the ferry, his suspicions were proved correct. He spotted, at least in his mind, a Boston detective, and suddenly his prospects of freedom appeared precarious.

Wyllie's frantic escape led him to Brooklyn, where he boarded a ferry to cross the East River to Manhattan. Though the ferries were numerous and busy, Wyllie was wary of the Federal agents that he was convinced were hot on his trail.

Courtesy of the Russell P. Granger Collection, www.WhitmansBrooklyn.com

He needed to quickly devise a plan, somehow evading the agent and making it across the river undetected. The encounter was described:

> Having got aboard when he arrived, he was about to be amongst the first to step ashore. When, oh, horrors! there was a detective he knew scanning every passenger. His heart quailed, but his presence of mind did not leave him. He turned to the back of the ship where the carts were. There was a cut throat looking fishcadger sitting on the front of his van full of empty barrels. 'Ten dollars,' said the captain to him, 'the moment you land me in the first street in New York.' 'I guess your money is all right.' 'Best gold, and no mistake.' In a second he was prostrate among the barrels. Gee, hip, whew! He was out of the boat and rattling up the wharf fast as the cadger's wheels would carry him. Captain Wyllie rose up, glanced back, and saw the Bostonian detective enter the ferry boat. The cadger pocketed his gold pieces with the nonchalance of a prince, hardly bestowing on the donor a glance.
>
> What a vast amount of bother people would save themselves if they would act like this philosophical fish seller – ask no questions about matters in which they have no concern.

Broadway, in the heart of New York. Wyllie hid in what he described as a 'French hotel', possibly the well-known French's Hotel (far left) or one of hundreds of other such establishments that operated in mid-town Manhattan.

Courtesy of the New York Public Library

So Wyllie made his escape by hiding between those reeking, empty fish barrels. Once again, it is impossible to determine the exact location of his crossing from Brooklyn to Manhattan, as there were at least ten ferry companies operating the route in 1865.[280]

Wyllie now dived into the heaving metropolis. He had visited the city twice before, once as just another anonymous mate aboard the steamer *Hope* in 1862, and more recently as a prisoner. He had already hinted, when up in front of the prize court there in September 1864, that his face was well known, so in order to evade immediate capture he would need to find a place to hide in order to await the most opportune moment to make for the docks and a passage home. He recalled:

> Captain Wyllie now plunged into the heart of New York, and entered a French hotel in the centre of Broadway. To his host he made a masonic sign, which was responded to. He got an attic room, and sat down to chew the cud of reflection. The hotel keeper being a native of Bordeaux, the captain knew many of his friends, and he was never tired talking of them. Captain Wyllie told him who he was, and the strait he was in. The Frenchman was as close as a cockle and as true as steel.

Friendships, both professional and personal, appear to have now given Wyllie some security. He had for years served on vessels that called at Bordeaux, and since 1863 he had been a member of the mariners' masonic lodge in Liverpool. The 'French hotel' could have been the well-known French's Hotel, on Broadway opposite the City Hall Park. It had been built in 1849, and by 1864 was operated by Richard French. Or the hotel Wyllie found might have been one of several operated by proprietors known to be originally from France, such as Henry Maillard, who ran a hotel at 619–621 Broadway.[281]

Wyllie stayed at his hotel for a fortnight, keeping a low profile. He would have been able to mark the sailing dates for British steamers, noting their captains. Some of these might be acquaintances; if he was pursued by the detectives and marshals, he might hope to be able to rely on a fellow countryman to keep his presence a secret. Finally, he made his way to the wharf of the Anchor Line, which operated fortnightly transatlantic services to Glasgow. It was located on the western side of Manhattan, just a few blocks from Broadway. Once again, the story that Wyllie himself told contains all the high drama of his previous blockade runs.

> After spending a fortnight in his garret, one night at eleven o'clock he stole cautiously down to the wharf, where an Anchor Liner was lying and making ready to set sail for Glasgow. The lumpers were busy at work completing the loading of the vessel. He managed to get aboard unperceived. He entered the cabin. It was empty. A great green cloth covered the table. He thought he heard footsteps about the door – he crept under the table. In a minute or two the captain and a gentleman entered and sat down at the table and began to talk. The gentleman was an old acquaintance – had been a blockade runner – has been captured and confined to Fort Warren, and had just been released.[282] Their conversation turned on Captain Wyllie and his prospects of success. He heard the captain of the liner say to the gentleman that the detectives had been twice aboard of him that day. Then an officer of the Customs entered and said to the captain that 'he guessed the detectives were on the scent of some poor soul who was going with the ship.' All agreed it was impossible Wyllie could get out of the States. The Custom House officer did not stay for long, and the captain and his friend retired for the night. Wyllie got into a cramped place under a passenger's berth, with a trunk in front of him.[283]

The Anchor Line's four steamers going out of New York in the spring of 1865 were the *Hibernia*, *Caledonia*, *Britannia* and *United Kingdom*. So if Wyllie's story was true, he would have stowed away on one of these. Dates of sailings and arrivals were recorded in local newspapers, but they did not give a full list of passengers. However, the lists of passengers

ANCHOR LINE
OF
TRANS-ATLANTIC
STEAM PACKET SHIPS
BETWEEN
NEW YORK
AND
GLASGOW,

SAILING EVERY SATURDAY FROM NEW YORK, and composed of the following well-known favorite Clyde-built IRON STEAMERS,

EURÔPA, HIBERNIA,
IOWA, CALEDONIA,
COLUMBIA, BRITTANIA,
ACADIA, UNITED KINGDOM.

The final leg of the epic escape. Wyllie claimed he stowed away on the United Kingdom, *an Atlantic liner operated by the Glasgow-based Anchor Line. Advertisements like this would have alerted him to the most opportune sailing.*

Courtesy of the Library of Congress, Chronicling America Newspaper Archive

arriving in the United Kingdom on vessels from the USA and Canada during the 1860s were recorded, and were sent on to the Office of the Chief Secretary for Ireland to be checked for the names of known members of the Irish Republican Brotherhood (known as Fenians) and other agitators whom the authorities considered dangerous. One such surviving passenger list is from the *United Kingdom*'s sailing from New York on 1 April. In the list of cabin passengers is noted a 'Captain Wylie, Ship Master, aged 40' with his nationality given as Scottish.[284] This would appear to be Joannes Wyllie.

The story of Wyllie's Anchor Line escape continued, Wyllie stating he had stowed away while awaiting the steamer's departure.

> In this hiding place he remained all Thursday, all Friday, and all Saturday. At about five o'clock in the afternoon of the latter day he heard the screw beginning to turn. He knew the vessel was then leaving the wharf. He was getting exhausted, but the sound was welcome and revived him. He knew when the pilot left his hour of escape had come. Two hours later the engine stopped. After a little time it began again, and with greater energy than before.

> He knew the pilot had now gone, and the ship was on the open sea. Soon after the steward and Bos'un came down for stores for the crew. From the midst of the brandy cases he shouted to them. They thought there was a ghost in the larder, and sprang up the ladder like cats. Soon lights were brought, and various voices called through the hatch asking who was there. 'Hark ye!' replied the Captain. 'Haul out another passenger, and a Britisher.' The mysterious voice in the larder was cleared up. The cases were rapidly removed. The Captain was unable to do anything for himself, but willing hands soon had him borne through the narrow hatch to the cabin, where all the passengers and crew were gathered. His legs were severely swollen, and he could not stand. The excitement was gone, and the reaction was overpowering. He was laid down in a faint, and helpless as any little child.
>
> A feeling of pride pervaded the whole Liner when they knew they bore home the valiant captain whose escape and possible capture was the talk and excitement of the hour.'[285]

A truly remarkable tale. But can any of this be corroborated by contemporary evidence? A timeline can be established that could ascertain whether the events described could have been feasible. It starts with Wyllie's deposition in front of the prize court in Boston on 7 March. The dates of the sailing of the Anchor Line steamers can be added, the *United Kingdom* sailing on 1 April. This means that Wyllie would have had approximately 24 days to achieve his escape. If one night had been spent in Boston after the deposition, and two were spent travelling down from Boston and staying in Brooklyn, he would have made Manhattan on or about 10 or 11 March. A fortnight there, holed up at the 'French Hotel' preparing his final moves, puts the date at around 24/25 of March. He states that he stowed away on board the steamer in port for three days, going aboard at 11pm and staying all of Thursday–Saturday, and it was on the Saturday that he heard the steamer's 'screw begin to turn'. The *United Kingdom* is recorded as leaving on 1 April, which in 1865 was a Saturday.

These movements could certainly have fitted within a timetable of 7 March to 1 April. But this is reliant on the 'Captain Wylie' on the passenger list of the *United Kingdom* being Joannes Wyllie the famous blockade runner. A check of British shipmasters and mates shows that there were ten men called Wylie or Wyllie, with a Scottish background, active in 1865. Of these ten, five were on vessels plying their trade in the East Indies, Australia or the Iberian peninsula, and five were in the Americas. Of those five, four have been located by noting the movements of their ships through sources such as Lloyd's List. So, for example, James Wyllie, born in Ayrshire, was master of the steamer *Nova Scotian* in 1865 and on 1 April of that year he was at sea on that vessel between Liverpool and New York; this eliminates him. It turns out that on 1 April 1865 only one Wyllie is recorded as being active in the Americas but neither at sea nor in port, and that was Captain Joannes Wyllie. Thus, by process of elimination, the 'Captain Wylie' in the passenger list of the *United Kingdom* must have been be Joannes.[286]

Up the Clyde on the morning of 17 April came the steamer *United Kingdom*. It carried with it a full cargo of American produce along with 65 passengers – one of whom was famous blockade runner and escapee Joannes Wyllie. He was now revisiting the country of his birth for just the third time since he had left it in 1852, the other two visits having been brief stops between voyages. His days of commanding sleek paddle steamers giving Union blockaders the slip were over.

7

FINAL YEARS AT SEA

> He was a frank open-hearted lad; and we think we now see him as the social, jovial Captain of the 'Carolina.' May success ever attend him!
>
> – From the *Fife Herald* of 6 December 1866, recounting the exploits of Joannes Wyllie during the Civil War.

On 9 April 1865, in a small courthouse in Appomattox, Virginia, Confederate General Robert E. Lee sat down with Union General Ulysses S. Grant and by surrendering his forces ended the American Civil War. The conflict had lasted four years, resulting in the deaths of approximately one million Americans, devastation of the infrastructure across the Southern states, and a war-weary nation suffering from loss and sorrow.

Less than a week after this meeting Abraham Lincoln was assassinated, shot while attending a play at Ford's Theatre in Washington DC by actor John Wilkes Booth, a Confederate sympathiser. The war was over, but the nation was still ripped apart. At sea, the steamers that had served as blockade runners were now superfluous, their crews returning to the commercial trade or their homes. Some of the steamers made for European waters, while other sat for sale, awaiting new owners, in the docks of Nassau, St George's or Havana.

Wyllie's career as a blockade runner had ended but there would still be a few more voyages for the captain. This next chapter in his story links to the previous one, as his next vessel, though not a runner, did play a part in the war. The cycle of blockade running had depended on these fast steamers, but they were just part of a much larger operation. After they had made their mad dashes from Wilmington or Charleston to Nassau or St George's, their cargoes of cotton and turpentine would be stacked along the quaysides. These were then loaded onto larger, slower vessels for the Atlantic voyage back to Liverpool, London or Glasgow. These ships were as important to the success of blockade running as the fast greyhound steamers, and they were not stalked by Union warships, as they were commercial merchantmen sailing under the Union Jack, just going about their normal trade. Thus the cycle of running the blockade was complete. At the end of the war, these vessels also needed to find new routes or owners. It was on one of these that Wyllie would soon find himself.

After his dramatic escape in New York and return to Scotland Wyllie spent almost a year ashore. What he did during that time is unknown and for the most part can only be speculated on. It appears that he made a visit home to Fife to see his father and extended family: the *Fifeshire Journal* reported that a Captain Wyllie of Pathhead had attended the Grand Annual Assembly of the officers and members of the 7th Fifeshire Rifle Volunteers (Kirkcaldy) Corps at the Corn Exchange, Kirkcaldy, on 22 December 1865. Captain Wyllie is described as being on 'merchant service', which indicates his occupation in the merchant marine. But as he is listed as an attendee rather than an officer, his relationship with the volunteers cannot be confirmed. This is the only recorded appearance of Wyllie between his return to Britain and his next command.

That December visit to Fife notwithstanding, Wyllie had not chosen to return permanently to Scotland and trade his sea glass for the plough just yet. The blockade would seem to have not afforded him the financial means to retire, and after 12 months he returned to sea. In February 1866 he signed on as master of the *Carolina*, a screw steamer operating out of Liverpool. It was 1,115 registered tons with engines capable of 50 hp, and like Wyllie the *Carolina* had a link to the conflict in America. It had previously been named *Palikari*, and during the Civil War had been part of the Blue Cross Line operating from Liverpool to Bermuda and Nassau, working the transatlantic leg of the Confederate trade. As mentioned earlier, this line was operated by Henry Lafone, the noted Confederate agent who, through the Importing and Exporting Company of Georgia, was the owner of Wyllie's second blockade runner, the *Susan Beirne*.[287]

The *Palikari* itself might not have been used as a runner but during the dying days of the war its captain had been master of three such vessels. Robert Algernon Sidney Pittmann, an American born in 1812, had held the command of the *Sirius*, *Nola* and *Atalanta*, each of which had completed voyages from Britain as part of the task of blockade running. He had joined the *Palikari* in late 1864, moving away from the dangerous side of running to the more sedate, and less lucrative, transatlantic voyages.[288]

After the war several of the steamers that had been owned by the Blue Cross Line, including the *Carolina*, became part of the fleet of the British and American Steamship Company Ltd of Liverpool. This company, too, was run by Henry Lafone, and it would appear that the wartime connections made by Wyllie now brought him another opportunity to command a vessel. By the autumn of 1865 the company was offering a fortnightly service from Liverpool to New Orleans, continuing to serve the American South, but in peacetime. The strong link to the South was evident in that seven of its ships were named for Southern states.

Wyllie joined as master of the *Carolina* on 27 February 1866. It would seem that he was a last-minute replacement for the steamer's previous master, Captain Edward Hairby. Hairby had been in charge for the previous two voyages to New Orleans, and it was he who had signed the agreement of foreign going ship as master on 26 February. But Wyllie took his place. On the agreement Wyllie's last vessel was listed as the *Deer*, and it was noted that he been discharged from the vessel in March 1865.[289] This confirms that he had been a landlubber for the previous 12 months, having not been in the crew of any ship since the *Deer*'s arrival at Boston. What this emergency appointment says is that by February 1866 Wyllie was in Liverpool and that either he was looking for work, or he could be called on at short notice by a former employer as a trustworthy and able ship master. It could also indicate that the amount of wealth he had gained from his time as a blockade-running captain had not allowed him to lead a quiet life away from the hectic and dangerous life at sea: if he had come back to Scotland with great riches, why would he return to the bridge of a steamer on the much lower wages of a humble peacetime captain? Another explanation might be that the old salt missed the waves of the open ocean and the hubbub of a steamer. Whatever the case, Wyllie was once again back in command.

The steamer set off for New Orleans on the day he joined the crew – although the change of captain had been so abrupt that the *Liverpool Mercury* still reported Hairby as captain. It had been a year since Wyllie's brush with the law in New York, and now he was returning to a reunified, but as yet unhealed, United States of America. What might have been going through his mind during the month-long voyage to New Orleans? Wyllie himself had never before visited the 'Crescent City' – might his fame and reputation gained from his time on the *Ad-Vance* have spread as far west as Louisiana?

The *Carolina* was reported as arriving at New Orleans on 2 April, and it soon began to discharge its goods. *The Times-Democrat* of New Orleans reported that the steamer had brought a wide range of assorted merchandise, including the 'latest styles of straw hats'. In addition 100 passengers had made the journey from Liverpool, almost all of them immigrants in search of a better life in the United States.[290] Two weeks were spent at the quayside on the banks of the mighty Mississippi, which might have allowed Wyllie the freedom to once again explore an unfamiliar city; New Orleans was one of the America's largest ports and so was a melting pot of cultures, languages and cuisines. It was a multicultural metropolis, with French, Creole, and African traditions. Before the war it had been the South's most important cotton port, exporting the crops of Texas, Louisiana, Mississippi, Alabama and Arkansas. It had therefore been one of the first ports captured by the Union forces.

This was Wyllie's first peacetime voyage since 1862, and it gave him the freedom that a normal maritime captain might have, except for the restrictions imposed by the schedule of the shipping line and any problems with the loading of the return cargo. On 13 April the *Carolina* steamed back down the Mississippi towards the Gulf of Mexico, carrying 1,797 bales of cotton and several passengers.[291] Although his ship had changed, as had the

Wyllie's first port of call in America after the Civil War was New Orleans. He arrived as master of the steamer Carolina*, operated by Henry Lafone. During the war it had been part of Lafone's Blue Cross Line which had carried supplies to the neutral ports of the Caribbean.*

Courtesy of the Library of Congress

destination, to Wyllie there must have been a certain sense of *déjà vu* in leaving a Southern port as master of a steamer fully loaded with cotton. But this time he would not need to sneak away from port under the darkness of a new moon to evade the blockade; this time tide and current would be his only concern.

After returning to Liverpool Wyllie went on to make two more voyages as master of the *Carolina*, both of the destinations familiar to him – one in the west, the other in the east. The first of these voyages was another transatlantic journey to New York. The British and American Steamship Company Ltd had recently expanded its routes, opening up a line to the Big Apple, despatching five steamers from Liverpool, with two more under construction intended for the service.[292] On 20 May the *Carolina* left Liverpool, this time carrying 263 passengers, mainly immigrants. After a trip of 17 days, the steamer made it to its dock along the East River. It was just under 15 months since Wyllie had slipped aboard the *United Kingdom* there. The *Carolina* then left its mooring at Pier 52 on 15 June, Wyllie at the helm. It carried a cargo of 36,938 bushels of corn, plus wooden pit staves and tobacco.[293] No harm or drama had come from this voyage to the west, and it is the last time he was known to set foot on American soil. It was a book end: his first journey to the United States had been to New York five years earlier, and now he would sail down the Hudson, past the forts and the lights at the narrows out into the Atlantic, never to return.

That voyage west was uneventful, but his next trip as master of the *Carolina* would be more memorable. For the first time since he had been the first mate of the steamer *Hope*, Wyllie found himself heading for the Mediterranean. He was joined by a familiar face from his blockade-running days; his former crewmate, Eugene Anderson Maffitt, signed on as his third mate while the steamer was tied up at Liverpool. Maffitt had served under Wyllie when he had taken the *Susan Beirne* from Glasgow to Bermuda in late 1864. At the end of the war Maffitt had been imprisoned for a short period in Boston, and after his release had made for Liverpool where he joined Wyllie again.[294]

The *Carolina* was bound for the Black Sea, leaving Liverpool on 10 August 1866, making a stop at Cardiff to pick up additional cargo. Difficulties would once again meet Wyllie in port at Cardiff, but unlike the time when the customs inspection and threat of seizure caused him to take the *Lord Clyde* away in 1863, this time it would be his crew that would cause him his headache.

The steamer had called to load fine-grade Welsh fuel coal and some iron rails to be delivered to Genoa (Genova), in northern Italy, en route to Odessa on the Black Sea coast. Just after the steamer had arrived at Cardiff seven of the crew deserted. The exact reasons for this mass departure from the *Carolina* are unknown and no documents that might shed light on the situation, such as the ship's log, have survived. What is known, however, is that at the time there were cholera outbreaks at several ports in the Mediterranean and

Eugene Anderson Maffitt (1844–1886) joined Wyllie aboard the Carolina *on its voyage to the Black Sea in the autumn of 1866. Son of famous Confederate captain and blockade runner John Newland Maffitt, Eugene sailed with Wyllie on the* Susan Beirne *in 1864.*

Courtesy of the University of Alabama Libraries Special Collections the Black Sea, some of which the *Carolina* was due to visit. So it might have been the threat of a painful death brought about by this notorious killer disease that had motivated the crew to risk punishment and imprisonment by breaking their contract with Wyllie and the shipping company.[295]

In addition to having to find replacements for a large percentage of his small crew, Wyllie was required to appear before the local magistrate after three of the deserters had been involved in a violent altercation with a local hotel proprietor. John Thomas Burt, a 26-year-old able seaman from Dublin, had been wounded when hotelier Tobias Anderson attacked him with a hatchet. This had come after a fierce exchange between the seamen and Anderson at his boarding house, the proprietor claiming that the seamen were intoxicated. Wyllie appeared in court to confirm the identities of the accused seamen, and although he played no further part in the tribunal, this delayed his departure. The hotelier received a sentence of nine months for his attack, and the sailors were each given 12 weeks' hard labour for desertion.[296]

The courtroom drama now behind him, Wyllie took the *Carolina* out of Cardiff Bay on 23 August, making Genoa in just under two weeks. There the rails from Cardiff were unloaded, possibly for the new railway then being constructed, stretching westwards along the coast of the Ligurian Sea from Genoa to Ventimiglia. After a ten-day stay in port the steamer was off again, now headed for the Black Sea. It would streak past the Greek islands, transit the Dardanelles and pass the great city of Constantinople and the Golden Horn. Northwards into the Black Sea the course was set for Odessa, where the steamer took on a huge cargo of wheat. Odessa was the main port for the southern plains of Ukraine and Russia, one of the most important wheat-producing areas in the world. The return voyage was quiet and smooth, and when they reached Dublin they were greeted by a great fanfare – due, however, not to the man at the helm but to the sheer volume of cargo that the *Carolina* was carrying.

On 13 November the *Saunders News-Letter* of Dublin reported the anticipated arrival of 'the largest steamer with grain that ever entered the port of Dublin'. The *Carolina's* cargo of 1,250 tons of wheat was a record-setter, making headlines even though the steamer was still some distance out from the Irish capital. When it finally arrived on 25 November, its cargo and its captain's name were noted by several Irish newspapers and some from further afield as well: on 6 December the *Fife Herald* noted:

> The commander of the vessel, captain John Wylie, is the son of a much respected and enterprising farmer in the neighbourhood, Mr A Wylie, of Mitchelston and Pathhead. Many of our Markinch readers will recognise in Captain Wylie an old friend, who, when a stripling – and he is yet a young man – was teacher of Balgonie Square School in their neighbourhood. Then, he was a frank open-hearted lad; and we think we now see him as the social,

It was after Wyllie had arrived in Dublin as master of the Carolina *in December 1866 that the first account of his exploits as a blockade runner appeared in British newspapers.*

Courtesy of the Library of Congress

> jovial Captain of the 'Carolina.' During the American war, Captain Wylie performed several clever feats by frequently running the blockade. May Success ever attend him![297]

This brief article is notable for two reasons. First, Joannes is still referred to as John when the newspaper asked its readers to cast their minds back to remember him, indicating that his formal switch to the name Joannes would appear to have taken place after he had gone to sea, so the 'Markinch readers' would still know him as John. Secondly this is the first recorded mention in Scotland, and possibly in the whole of mainland Britain, of Wyllie being a lauded and a celebrated blockade runner. He had of course had his name associated with the *Ad-Vance* while in port in Liverpool, but there is no record of any newspaper at the time celebrating his success. This new report would indicate that his time in the conflict was a mark of respect, success and crafty adventure, at least amongst the locals in Fife.

THE LAST VOYAGES OF THE GREAT SCOTTISH BLOCKADE RUNNER

After the conclusion of the Civil War the docks in Liverpool and Glasgow were strewn with many of the steamers that had been sold or built for the blockade, their steel hulls rusting and their powerful engines sitting idle, slowly wasting away from exposure to the elements. This was the fate of the fast paddle steamers that had been built in great quantities during the years 1863–1865. By the end of the conflict the supply vastly outstripped the demand and the shipbuilders' and ship owners' profits vanished. When the peace agreement was signed the last few vessels ordered had not even left the yards. The hugely exaggerated prices once expected for them had dropped like a stone, and now many could only be sold at a loss, if indeed any buyers at all could be found. Some of these vessels returned to their previous jobs as ferryboats across the Irish Sea or up the west coast of Scotland. Others would sit for years awaiting a new owner and a new occupation. It was one of these steamers – a greyhound without a race – that would next take Wyllie out to sea.

The *Georgia Belle* had been launched by Jones, Quiggin & Company in October 1864 and registered in Liverpool that December.[298] It was one of ten vessels built by the firm in 1864 that were intended for use on the blockade. Although designed as a runner and reported locally in the press as 'the famous blockade runner', it had never actually left the Mersey.[299] It had attempted a maiden voyage in mid-December, but a fault had been found in the machinery and before it had even left the estuary it was forced to turn back to seek repairs. By the time it was ready again to attempt the transatlantic voyage the war at sea was all but over. Wilmington was still open to runners in December, but when Fort Fisher was captured on 15 January 1865 the entrance to the Cape Fear River was sealed. Although it had been reported that the *Georgia Belle* was loading for Nassau and ready to make the long journey across the Atlantic, it was destined to stay in the Liverpool docks until the war finally finished. For the next year it stayed in the same condition awaiting another role – one that would prove eerily similar to the one it had been designed for.[300]

For 28 months the *Georgia Belle* continued to sit in a Liverpool dock while advertisements were run in the local papers offering it for sale or alerting prospective buyers to a proposed upcoming auction, describing the vessel as 'the magnificent paddle wheel steamer' and as being 'fitted out with the latest improvements' in engine and boiler technology.[301] On 5 May 1865 the *Liverpool Mercury* ran a story about the fate of the blockade-running fleet, and there it was noted that the *Georgia Belle* was 'a magnificent looking vessel' but that it 'has failed somewhat in the engine room. She has never been at sea'. For the rest of 1865 and the whole of 1866 no buyer could be found for this state-of-the-art steamer. But as luck would have it, the spring of 1867 brought a new conflict that once again called for fast, shallow-draft steamers. The *Georgia Belle* and many other former Civil War runners were suddenly in demand again, and would finally make that Atlantic trip towards the Americas.

At the end of 1864 the dictator of Paraguay, Francisco Solano López, had declared war on the Empire of Brazil and then on the Argentine Republic as well. Uruguay would later join forces with Brazil and Argentina in what would become known as the Paraguayan War.[302] It lasted five years and was one of the bloodiest conflicts that took place between the end of the Napoleonic wars in 1815 and start of the First World War a century later.

Although almost all fighting took place on land, a key to the outcome of the conflict was the control of the Plate and Parana rivers, which allowed the transport of people, goods and military cargoes in towards the landlocked Paraguay. It was once again a perfect situation for sleek, powerful paddle steamers and from 1865 many former Civil War runners found themselves being piloted towards South American waters.[303]

The *Georgia Belle* would be the first of two such steamers that Wyllie would sail towards the River Plate that year, although he himself did not set out from Liverpool. Listed as master of the *Georgia Belle* was James Alexander Duguid, a 50-year-old experienced mariner from Cornwall. He had been a master since 1851, and during those years he had been involved mainly in the North American trade.[304] He too was a former blockade runner, having been during the course of the war master of four steamers: the *Oreto*, the *Giraffe* (also known as *Robert E. Lee)* the *Lucy* and the *Juno*.[305] He was obviously an experienced and trustworthy captain of such vessels, and he sailed the *Belle* out of the Mersey on 15 March 1867 with its destination set as Buenos Aires.

But for some reason, Duguid would not stay captain for long. As the steamer made its way down the Irish Sea a storm blew up. Damage was sustained from the force of wind and waves, and the steamer, its foremast-head gone, was forced to put into Queenstown. Immediate repairs were needed and the steamer was forced to spend the next two weeks in port. During that layover some sort of rebellion took place on board that would lead to the change of many of the crew, including the captain.[306]

The logbook of the *Georgia Belle* survives, and in it are recorded some of the details of the commotion. Captain Duguid entered on 19 March at 9 a.m. that 'All the firemen and seamen refused to proceed with the vessel'. Duguid didn't record why the crew refused, but possibly the damage sustained while leaving Liverpool might have convinced many that a transatlantic voyage might prove deadly and they had best not chance it.

Also of note is that the crew agreement stated that the voyage was to be to Buenos Aires and that the steamer would return to a British port within six months. In fact, this was to be a one-way trip, as the *Georgia Belle* was actually being taken to be sold at its final destination. Might the crew have been inveigled into their contract under false pretences, and perhaps rumbled the deception? Whatever their reasons, it is evident that a majority of crew were not for continuing.

The next entry regarding the crew was not made until 27 March, and this time not by Duguid but by Joannes Wyllie.[307] Until this point he is absent from any records of the steamer, so he must have been called upon by the vessel's owners to take command at very short notice. It is known that after his return to Liverpool in December 1866 on the *Carolina* he had travelled home to Fife. There he stayed with his father, Alexander, at the family farm. He was there until at least the end of February, when it was noted in the *Fife Herald* that he had acted as croupier at a supper that had been arranged by his father to reward local farmers who had assisted him with ploughing his fields. The word from Queenstown must have made its way to him in Scotland, and he would then have made a quick dash by railway and steamer to southern Ireland.[308]

As Wyllie was rushing from Scotland to Queenstown, Duguid awaited his replacement while repairs were made to the *Georgia Belle.* No reason is given for Duguid's ultimate removal and replacement, so only speculation can be attempted: illness, unwillingness to make the transatlantic journey himself, the possibility of receiving a better offer for command of another vessel? Whatever the case, once the repairs were complete, the *Georgia Belle* set off on 4 April 1867 for the River Plate with a new crew and a new master in charge.[309]

The steamer made it to Buenos Aires by the middle of May after an uneventful trip, and there most of the crew were discharged. Wyllie stayed on, and noted in the log that the steamer had sailed from Buenos Aires to Montevideo, Uruguay, by 31 May where he had effected its sale and delivered it for purchase. His note that he had 'effected the sale' indicates that he was not just there to deliver the steamer, but that he had played an active role in the transfer of the steamer to its new owners. Unfortunately, the history of the *Georgia Belle* after this point is lost and its ultimate fate is not recorded.

The members of the crew who had not been discharged – Wyllie, with his second engineer, the purser, the cook and several seamen – left the steamer a week later. He and these last few then needed to make their way back to Britain. The crew who had left at Buenos Aires had been shipped on the steamer *Cordova*, which arrived in Liverpool on 27 June. Wyllie found passage on another vessel back to Liverpool. He must have arrived on or before 27 July as well, as on that day he took the *Georgia Belle*'s agreement for a foreign going vessel to the superintendent of the Merchant Marine.[310]

When Wyllie arrived in England, he wasted no time. On 11 August he was once again at sea, headed back to the River Plate. On this transatlantic voyage he was taking the *Stag*, once again taking a steamer on a one-way trip which would end with its sale. The *Stag*, like the *Georgia Belle*, had been laid up in Liverpool for some time. But unlike the *Georgia Belle* it had been involved in the Civil War as a runner. It had been built in 1853 in Glasgow, and from that time had worked the passenger route from Glasgow to several Irish ports. It continued in this role until purchased in the summer of 1864 by the Atlantic Steam Packet Company of Charleston, South Carolina, for blockade running.[311] After leaving Glasgow in June and renamed *Kate Gregg*, it made eight successful runs through the blockade. After the war it returned to Liverpool in December 1865 and was listed for sale as early as 29 December.[312]

Wyllie's second voyage to South America went as smoothly as the first, with no storms nor any hint of trouble with the crew. No logbook survives, but the *Stag* was reported at Bahia in Brazil on 7 September and at its destination of Buenos Aires on 1 October. It is listed in the Appropriations Book as being sold at a 'Foreign Port', and as with the *Georgia Belle* its fate is unknown. For the second time in so many months Wyllie booked a one-way ticket on a steamer heading back to Liverpool.

Montevideo, Uruguay, from the River Plate. This was the last foreign port Wyllie visited during his maritime career.

Courtesy of the New York Public Library

WYLLIE'S TIME AT SEA DRAWS TO A CLOSE

The wind fills the sails while the engine turns the screw. The steamer makes good time as it heads away from the River Plate, out into the South Atlantic. At the taffrail stands a man more used to being awake on the bridge than sleeping all night, every night in his cabin as a humble passenger. Joannes Wyllie stares out at the waves and he ruminates … his 15 years at sea, the ports, the adventures, the trials he has faced, and the tales he can now tell.

This farmer's son from Fife had started on the lowest rung of the ladder and made his way to the very top. His last voyage as master took him along almost the same route as his first one, when he had been a mere apprentice on the barque *Hope*: both vessels sailed through the Irish Sea, then southwards, down past the west coast of Africa and across the South Atlantic to Bahia, then making for different destinations. His journey on the *Stag* was more peaceful than his leaky voyage on *Hope*, but for Joannes Wyllie both must have been memorable, even emotional. On his final voyage, as he left Bahia and turned south-west to the River Plate, did he recall the course that the *Hope* had plotted towards the Indian Ocean and how he had been witness to the death of a crew member at sea? – This was something that stayed with him for the rest of his days.

Wyllie had crossed the globe for a decade and a half, but now his time at sea was coming to an end. He had sailed on a humble barque, made the antipodes on a fast clipper, plied the gentle coastal seas of France on a screw-steamer merchantman, and been master of one of the most celebrated blockade runners of the American Civil War. Over those 15 years he had served on a total of 12 vessels, 2 of them sailing ships and 10 steamers, screw- or paddle-propelled. His promotions in the profession had almost always come at the first opportunity or on the first time of asking, showing both Wyllie's ambition and competence as a sailor. He had visited every continent where mercantile trade took place. He had experienced the impact of both death and birth at sea, seen true love bloom, been saved from sharks and poison, had weathered storms and had evaded the guns of blockaders hot in pursuit.

8

PLOUGHING THE SOIL: WYLLIE AS FARMER AND NEIGHBOUR

> In the district there is none more popular than 'the Captain', and well might it be so, not only because of the remarkable experiences he has come through, but because of the kindliness and culture which mark the true gentleman, and stamp him unmistakably as one of Nature's noblemen.
>
> – From *The Weekly Welcome*, 10 June 1896

After his 15 years at sea Joannes Wyllie settled down back at home in Fife. His father, Alexander, had taken on the tenancy of Mitchelston Farm, located a mile from Dysart, sometime before 1855. It had just over 60 acres of land, which was suitable for livestock and crops. Alexander had initially worked it with his eldest son James, then carried on alone after James took on his own farm near Galashiels, in the Borders. Joannes took up residence on the farm soon after his return from Buenos Aires.

He might have been the son of a gardener and farmer, but he had never worked the soil himself: cultivating the fields required a whole new set of skills, and for the first few years he worked alongside his father to learn his new trade. As with his maritime career, he was determined to learn quickly. In June 1868 it was reported that 'Mr Wylie, farmer of Mitchelston' had been successfully experimenting with the growing of California wheat. The seeds had been brought to Fife direct from the Southern states of America. With Wyllie's connections it seems he was able to combine old world knowledge with new world innovation.[313]

Wyllie was by no means the first sea captain to settle on the land. In fact it was a relatively common thing for seamen who had spent their lives on the rolling deck to root their feet in the soil when they came ashore. The *Farmer's Monthly Visitor* of August 1843 explained why these sailor farmers made such a success of their new calling:

> Of all the men not bred to farming, and when the earliest part of life is over, fancy retirement, green fields and singing birds, perhaps sea-faring men succeed the best. Your merchant buys a farm; spends his money freely; sets out his trees in avenues; has plenty of heads besides his own to direct him in the operations: and so with almost all other callings; but an exception has been noticed in the sea captain; he knows nothing of farming, but he comes to it naturally and kindly. In the first place, habits have been formed for anticipation; he is ever looking ahead of the time to be in readiness when the wind shifts, and generally anticipates the change. When he is so accustomed to command, and to feel that the responsibility is upon him, that he takes his own counsel only, and follows no advice but his own; and then the treacherous elements of winds and waves admonish him to have a place for everything and to keep everything in place – a practice that is both time and money with a farmer.[314]

The article went on to describe how many sailor farmers were distant in their manners and did not associate with their neighbours. But this was certainly not the case with Wyllie. Never was a bad word said about 'the Captain', as he was affectionately called, and it is a mark of his status and the appreciation of his fellow Fifers that the *Weekly Welcome* stated 'In the district there is none more popular than the Captain.'

WYLLIE'S FAMILY AND FARM

As part of his settling down process, Wyllie got married. In 1869, at the age of 41 he married 39-year-old Eleanor Brown Fraser at a ceremony in Glasgow. Eleanor was the daughter of Duncan Fraser who in the 1850s had been the tenant of a flour mill in the town of Markinch, near Coaltown of Balgonie, where Wyllie had been a teacher. So it is possible that Joannes and Eleanor had met in their younger days. In the marriage certificate she was listed as a spinster, indicating that she had never been married, so the romantic might imagine that they had been waiting for each other since that day in May 1852 when Wyllie had left home to join a ship. Eleanor would become a constant companion to Joannes at their farmhouse. There would be servants, milkmaids and farm hands to keep the farmyard bustling, but sadly the pitter-patter of little feet would not be heard in the house, as Joannes and Eleanor would have no children.

Wyllie's wider family was near him, too. His sisters Margaret and Isabel lived just down the road in Dysart. Margaret was the eldest of the family; she had been widowed at a young age but went on to run her own market gardening business, taking up the family business of supplying fresh fruit and vegetables to the villages near Kirkcaldy. When Alexander left the farmhouse in 1871 he moved in with Margaret, along with the unmarried Isabel and

The only known photograph of Wyllie's farm, Mitchelston, north-east of Kirkcaldy. Here he lived with his wife Eleanor as a tenant farmer until his death in 1902. This aerial photograph, taken in the 1930s, shows the area shortly before it was razed to be turned into an industrial estate. Boxed, the immediate vicinity of farm.

© HES (Aerofilms Collection)

several of his grandchildren. Isabel died later that year and Alexander died a year later at the age of 77.

Wyllie's youngest brother, William, was his only sibling to see more of the world than Scotland: at the age of 20 he had emigrated to Sydney, Australia, sailing on the clipper *Ben Nevis* from Liverpool on 29 March 1856. He too was following in his father's footsteps; his calling, as listed on his arrival immigration document, was 'gardener'. Though at the time of William's departure Wyllie called Liverpool home, the brothers were denied one last farewell as Joannes was at that moment sailing from Ireland on the *Hope*, to arrive in Liverpool just two days after William's departure.

One more family member is important in the story of Joannes Wyllie: his nephew George Porteous Scott. George was the son of Eleanor's younger sister, Agnes, and her husband James

Porteous Scott, a Glasgow iron merchant. It was George who donated to Kelvingrove Art Gallery and Museum (today part of Glasgow Museums) the oil painting of the *Ad-Vance* by the famed maritime artist Samuel Walters, which had once been owned by Captain Wyllie. As Joannes and Eleanor had no children, the painting went to his nephew, who donated it as a lasting legacy of his uncle and the Clyde-built steamer he had captained (see Appendix 5).

Over the years Wyllie became a successful farmer, regularly placing advertisements in the local newspapers for his bumper crops of swedes, turnips and potatoes. He also took an active role in local agricultural societies, attending their annual meetings, arranging ploughing matches and on numerous occasions entering – and frequently winning – their annual competitions: it was not rare to see the name 'Captain Wyllie, Mitchelston' amongst the prizewinners of the Windygates Agricultural Society, whether it be for 'Prize Bull', 'Best Five acres of Barley' or, at the 1878 Dysart flower show, when 'None could stand before the jolly captain in apples, lettuce and cauliflower.'[315]

His fame at sea and success on the land also led to Wyllie lending his name as a testimonial to a brand of livestock feed. In advertisements that appeared in Fife in 1874–1875 for Myer's Royal Cattle Spice, Wyllie's name appeared next to those of two of the largest landowners in Scotland, the Duke of Sutherland and the Duke of Buccleuch (pron. 'B'cloo'), as a patron for this supplement guaranteed to increase a farmer's return. Interestingly, although he was a successful farmer, it was not his adept hand at the plough that warranted the promotion, but his time at sea; his surname was always preceded by 'Captain'.[316]

WYLLIE'S FORTUNE

George Porteous Scott, writing in 1925, stated that 'he made a big fortune for the owners, and incidentally for himself'.

The records for the *Ad-Vance* in the state archives of North Carolina clearly show what Wyllie was paid for his part in bringing over the steamer from Glasgow as well as his pay as captain in 1864. These sums are noted in the surviving disbursement records for the steamer, which list all outgoings from the crew's pay to the purchase of provisions and new anchors to the repairs. His official pay as sailing master/first officer is not identified in the records, but as mentioned earlier it is known that state- and Confederate-operated steamers paid their first officers 25 per cent of what the captain received for a return trip. When he assumed full command his pay would have been the same as Guthrie's: £208 6s 8d per round trip. Details from his other enterprises are less clear, but we can estimate that during his 26 months on the blockade Wyllie was paid over £1,800, which equates to an average monthly wage of just under £70.

Comparisons cannot easily be made with other returning blockade captains, as very few ever told their stories or have ever been researched in depth. The best-known of these few was the aristocratic Augustus Charles Hobart-Hampden, a Royal Navy captain who

Estimated pay received by Wyllie as a blockade runner, May 1863–February 1865

Wyllie's pay while in the crew and as captain of the *Lord Clyde/Ad-Vance*	
Role/Rank	***Pay in Pounds Sterling*** (equivalent in US dollars)
One transatlantic voyage, taking *Lord Clyde* from Glasgow to Bermuda, plus one successful round-trip run	£230 9s 4d *($1,630)*
Sailing master/1st officer for **five** round trips *(based on 25% of captain's pay of £104 per leg)*	£260 *($2,590)*
Captain for **two** round trips (£104.3.4 per leg of trip)	£416 13s 4d *($4,150)*
Round-trip transatlantic voyage to Liverpool May/June 1864 *(estimated)*	**£352 12s 0d** *($3,510)*
Two trans-shipments between Bermuda and Nassau *(estimated)*	£130 *($1,300)*
	£1,389 14s 8d *($13,900)*

While captain of *Susan Beirne* and *Deer*	
One transatlantic voyage in command of *Susan Beirne* (estimated, based on pay received by Wyllie as captain of *Lord Clyde* across the Atlantic)	£176 6s 0d *($1,760)*
One inward run on the *Deer* (estimated, based on amount paid by private firms)	£250 *($2,500)*
	£426 6s **0d** *($4,260)*
Total	**£1,816 0s 8d*** *($18,160)*

*This total does not take into account any bonuses paid, which were not recorded in detail, nor the 16 bills of exchange that Wyllie kept after the capture of the *Ad-Vance,* nor any possible loss of money when both the *Ad-Vance* and *Deer* were captured.

Conversion from pounds sterling to US dollars: www.measuringworth.com/exchange/

The most famous British blockade runner was Augustus Charles Hobart-Hampden (1822–1886). An aristocrat, he ran the blockade under the pseudonym Captain Roberts and then published his memoirs in 1867. Shown here in the uniform of an admiral in the Ottoman navy, a role he took up after his time in America.

Illustrated London News

in 1862, under the pseudonym Captain Roberts, ran the blockade 18 times. After the war he served as an admiral in the Ottoman navy, and was granted the title of pasha. He went on to write two books that chronicled his time as a blockade runner, *Never Caught* (1867) and *Sketches of My Life* (1886). Hobart's experience was, however, very different from that of most mariners, as he belonged to the British nobility. The wealth he might have gained during the war was not discussed at any length in the books as – understandably in view of his background – it might not have had a significant impact on him.

William Watson is known for being the only Scottish captain to publish his story during his own lifetime. He was born in 1826, in the Ayrshire village of Skelmorlie. After training as a marine engineer he moved to the Caribbean in 1845 where he worked as a civil engineer. Sometime before 1850 he had moved to Baton Rouge, Louisiana, where he became a partner in several local businesses including the operation of steamships. When the war started he volunteered for the 3rd Louisiana Regiment and served in several campaigns. He then turned to the sea in 1862, when he became the master of vessels moving between the neutral ports of the Caribbean, and then master of the blockade runner *Jeannette*. The exact number of runs he made is unknown, as is his pay, but his three years involved with the blockade must have made him a pretty penny because after the war he returned to Scotland and invested in shipbuilding. His first company built small steamers, but he went on to purchase a factory in Greenock, the Ladyburn Boiler Works, which produced machinery for much larger vessels. He also invested in property, building two villas in Skelmorlie, called Oakhill and Pearidge, named after battles he had fought in during the war.[317]

David Leslie was a Dundee-born captain who was master of three runners during the war, the *Columbia*, the *Emma* and the *Helen*. Over the course of three years Leslie's steamers made a total of 17 successful runs through the blockade to Charleston and Wilmington. In all probability Wyllie and Leslie would have known each other during the war: on at least one occasion, in September 1864, *Helen* was at Wilmington at the same time as the *Ad-Vance*.

Leslie returned to Scotland in May 1865 and began investing significant sums of money in the construction of large villas in the resort town of Dunoon on the Clyde coast. These villas all had names related to his time as a blockade captain: Nassau, Bahama and Dixie, and his own villa, Bermuda. Later, he was elected local police commissioner, and he died a wealthy man in 1905.[318] He had been master of his steamer from the start, and as all of his steamers were private commercial ventures, not state-operated like the *Ad-Vance*, Leslie might have been making $5,000 per successful trip – five times Wyllie's earnings.

James Carlin was born in 1833 in the quiet village of Old Hunstanton, in Norfolk, England. He trained as a merchant seaman and in his mid-20s moved to America, where he worked for the US Coastal and Geodetic Survey Department. Carlin began his involvement in blockade running soon after the start of the war, when he took command of the steamer *Cecile*. His career looked to be cut short after he was captured on the steamer *Memphis* in July 1862, but he was freed following appeals to British officials. After more success through the blockade he became the superintending captain of the South Carolina Importing and Exporting Company, overseeing the procurement of more steamers. This took him to Scotland in 1863, where in Glasgow he partnered with Patrick Henderson, a Confederate agent in the city. He ordered four purpose-built blockade runners, which made 12 successful runs through the blockade. Carlin's ownership and management of runners meant he would be exposed to great financial loss if they were captured or if the war went badly for the Confederacy, and his overall gain from the conflict reflects this risk. At the end of the war he moved back to England, and although the collapse of the Confederacy and his company meant that in the end he did not make a fortune from the war, he and his family were at least able to purchase a house in Liverpool's new and leafy suburb, Everton.[319]

Wyllie may have been rewarded handsomely for his service by the State of North Carolina, but his rewards were modest compared to those operating on their own account or working for a private firm. He had sent his first payments from the State of North Carolina home to Scotland almost immediately, in order for them to be kept safe with his father, but what happened to any other payments we do not know. The details of the personal bills of exchange that were returned to him from the New York prize court after the capture of the *Ad-Vance* remain a mystery. In any case, if those and his pay, at least latterly, had been in Confederate currency, then at the end of the war they would have been virtually worthless.

Wyllie's wealth, what there was of it, appears to have been hidden away. He was not ostentatious in his manner; it was only on very rare occasions that his 'fortune' from the war was ever mentioned, and never by him. He made no major purchases of land or property. He remained a tenant farmer rather than a landowner, and as far as we know he never invested in any other business ventures. The only property we know that he owned was a small house and garden in the neighbouring village of Gallatown, giving him an annual rent of just £4 10s.[320] The only indications that betray any kind of wealth come from his financial support for friends and family and his charitable contributions to the local community.

A GOOD FRIEND AND NEIGHBOUR

Captain Wyllie was a man who made many friends easily; at his farm he hosted popular ploughing competitions, cricket games and curling matches. Wyllie's neighbours had a good opinion of him, and he was so well liked that he was made their representative at important events in the local town or ones that involved their landlord, the Earl of Rosslyn, Wyllie's personal history – his university education, his background as a teacher and of course his maritime career – elevating him to a position of spokesperson.

During his time at Mitchelston Wyllie become more than just a tenant of the earls of Rosslyn but also a personal friend. The 4th earl, Robert St Claire Erskine, was a Conservative politician and a member of the Privy Council as well as being a published poet. It was under his tenure that Wyllie had taken on the tenancy at Mitchelston. For over 20 years

James Francis Harry St Clair-Erskine, 5th Earl of Rosslyn (1869–1939), was not just Wyllie's landlord but also a friend.

Courtesy of the National Portrait Gallery, London

Wyllie served him as a loyal tenant, attending events in honour of the laird and his family. The 4th earl's death in 1890 elevated his son, James Francis Harry St Claire-Erskine, to the title, and it was the nature of the captain's meetings with the son that indicates their close relationship; for example, Wyllie was amongst the few who were invited to greet James and his new wife off the train when they visited Kirkcaldy on 14 August 1890. Then in the evening, as the couple and guests sat down for a banquet, it was Wyllie who presented the bride with a silver bowl and tea set on behalf of the tenantry of the Rosslyn Estate: in his toast to the couple he outlined the high respect in which the groom was held.[321]

Wyllie's oratory skills were highly regarded, and it was said that he 'is qualified to speak eloquently on any subject under the sun'.[322] These skills were once again called upon by the earl when two of the most senior members of the British establishment visited him at home on his Dysart estate. In November 1892 the earl entertained the Duke of Cambridge with a day's shooting. The duke, a cousin of Queen Victoria, was commander-in-chief of the British army and a veteran of the Crimean War. Captain Wyllie was a guest at the luncheon held in his honour, and was called upon by the Earl of Rosslyn to offer the toast to His Royal Highness. Wyllie's visit to the Crimea on the clipper *Indian Queen* as well as his role on the *Ad-Vance*, formerly named after Lord Clyde, a fellow officer to the duke, would no doubt have been a topic of discussion between the two men.[323]

Wyllie's gift for delivering toasts was again prevailed upon two years later when the Earl of Rosebery, at the time the prime minister, visited Rosslyn at Dysart House. After a morning of shooting pheasants – and, interestingly, rabbits – the earl and his guests sat down for a luncheon in a large marquee. Rosslyn offered a toast to his tenants, several of whom were present, and the captain responded on their behalf.[324]

Wyllie was also a man to repay past kindnesses. In 1889 he attended the jubilee of the City Line, a Glasgow-based shipping company. He had been invited by a very old friend – the first friend he had ever made as a mariner. This was John Smith, the captain on his first voyage in 1852, who had now become part of the company. At the banquet Wyllie offered his thanks to his old captain, and mentioned that several of the young men on the *Hope* all those years ago had gone on to successful careers as masters themselves. The respect and fraternity once shown by Smith to the young Wyllie was being returned.[325]

Wyllie's friends were not all in high places. His mentorship of the young Reverend Peter Anton, who had first met Wyllie when he was 25, had led to a lifelong friendship. It's not hard to imagine Anton being stirred by Wyllie's tales, to use them as inspiration as he set out to establish a career in writing. Although Anton had been a neighbour for just his six years at Sinclairtown Church, his admiration led him to seek out his old friend in 1889 for his seminal piece on Wyllie in *The People's Friend*. This is the only example of Wyllie's adventures being spread to an audience outside his native Fife. The publication of the piece came at a time when the exploits of blockade runners were once again fresh in the minds of many Scots; in December 1888 the first chapter of the fictional story *Jamie's Venture* had

Left: Rev. Peter Anton (1850–1911) was a prolific writer of biographies of well-known Scottish heroes and notables in articles for The People's Friend.

Newspaper image © The British Library Board. All rights reserved. With thanks to The British Newspaper Archive (www.britishnewspaperarchive.co.uk)

Below: Wyllie's story is given top billing amongst stories of adventure, love, helpful recipes and cheerful songs.

Newspaper image © The British Library Board. All rights reserved. With thanks to The British Newspaper Archive. (www.britishnewspaperarchive.co.uk)

THE PEOPLE'S FRIEND,

No. 1018, Ready, Monday, July 1, 1889, contains—

CAPTAIN WYLLIE: the Great Scottish Blockade Runner.

THE DAY WILL COME.

By M. E. BRADDON.

SOME MODERN POETS.

ALISON'S HERO.

A Romance of Factory Life.

THOUGHTS O' LANGSYNE.

THE MAKING OF JAMS AND JELLIES.

A WOMAN: Complete Story.

SEASONABLE RECIPES.

TWO SONGS, WITH MUSIC.

'TWEEN THE GLOAMIN AND THE MIRK: Complete Story.

16 PAGES—ONE PENNY.

appeared in several newspapers across Scotland. Serialised into 21 chapters and appearing until March 1889, this story stirred the minds of its readers, harking back to the reports of the chases and escapes that had appeared daily in the newspapers during the war. Yet this yarn could not compare to the life story of Joannes Wyllie.

Their friendship continued until Wyllie's last days. When Anton gave a lecture on Robert Burns in late December 1901 at the Sinclairtown Established Church, Wyllie was in the chair. As he introduced the speaker, the captain noted that the honour had fallen to him as it was 'because he had known Mr. Anton perhaps longer than anyone present that he had been asked to take the chair that night'. [326]

WYLLIE THE CITIZEN

Wyllie played an active role in local politics and government, and became a respected and veteran member of several organisations in Sinclairtown and Dysart (see Appendix 7). As early as November 1868, he was in listed as one the notable attendees in a crowd of 1,000 in Kirkcaldy who had come out to hear Sir Robert Anstruther MP pitch for their vote in the upcoming general election. Sir Robert was a member of the Scottish Liberal Party, the dominant force in mid-19th century Scottish politics.

As Wyllie didn't speak on behalf of the candidate, his own politics remain unknown to us. But he went on to be present at events linked to elections in Scotland over the next 30 years, from meetings hosted by the Conservative Party to those by the Liberal Unionists. In 1873 he was one of five men elected to the Dysart Landward school board. He would assist with the governance of the schools, including appointing teachers and seeking funding for projects. It was a role he relished, and over the next 25 years he was re-elected seven times to the post. For a man who had begun his career in the classroom, it was a fitting relationship. Wyllie's task was not just a matter of overseeing budgets and building improvements: he would also appear at events to award prizes to the students, a role he cherished. At Christmas 1883, when visiting Boreland School with the Countess of Rosslyn, he spoke of the:

> happy faces he saw around him that night, and said it gave him great pleasure to be present. He urged upon the scholars to continue their efforts to do well, and no doubt at some future time many of them would shine as stars in the firmament. It always gave him great pleasure to come to Boreland, and, as a member of the Board, he now had a greater interest than hitherto.[327]

Over the years he was also linked to several societies and clubs dedicated to the observation and study of nature, his favourite being the Kirkcaldy Naturalists' Society. The group arranged annual outings to visit local areas of interest, from the University of St Andrews to view fossils in 1885, to plant-gathering expeditions in 1886.

The excursion made by the Kirkcaldy Naturalists in 1894 along a recently opened branch railway line. The close-up could be the 66-year-old Wyllie.

© CSG CIC Glasgow Museums Collection

Wyllie was called upon many times to give toasts at the associated dinners, a task he completed with humour and wit. On one such outing in June 1894 the group set out by train to explore the recently completed Kirkcaldy and District Railway. The construction of the line had meant the exposure of layers of rock which the group could explore. Accompanying the group were members of the photographic group of the society, who documented the trip. One photograph survives, showing the group posed atop the train. In the background can be seen an elderly man, with a full beard and bowler hat. Matching the description as well as a sketch published in 1896, this might just be the second known photograph of Joannes Wyllie.[328]

As Wyllie approached his twilight years he continued to support those friends and neighbours who, like him, were of the greying generation. He was active in the Third Ward Old Folks festivals, annual events usually held near Christmas to support the older people in the district. The Third Ward was an area of Dysart that included Wyllie's farm. From as early as 1889 (at the age of 61) Wyllie chaired the events, which would include songs, speeches and a meal. Wyllie's association with this event continued throughout the 1890s. It was popular day in the calendar for the older members of the community, so much so that in 1895 the report for the dinner noted that it 'is looked forward to with so much pleasure by the *auld* folks in the Third Ward district long before the event comes off'. Wyllie would speak to the assembled crowd, who would enjoy pies and what was described as the 'usual bag of eatables' and a packet of tea. Although the costs of these events are not recorded, Wyllie's involvement in them for close to 15 years suggests he could have contributed more than just his oratory skills.[329]

Wyllie the Philanthropic Speaker

On several occasions his name was associated with the delivery of coal to the poor of his district, and in addition he would dress up as Santa Claus to award gifts to local schoolchildren at Christmas, preside over concerts and lectures in aid of groups or individuals, and offer his fields to host gymnastic games and races. In 1872, he allowed the Gallatown foot and horse races to take place at Mitchelston, an annual event that had suffered in the previous years from not having a suitable track due to police objections after serious injuries had been sustained on the old course. After the event, Wyllie was presented with a silver-mounted gig whip by the organisers in appreciation of his generosity, for if he had not provided his land the Gallatown Derby might have well faded from local memory.[330]

By far the most prolific of his philanthropic acts were the lectures he gave in aid of local charities or those who had fallen on hard times. There are 26 known lectures, given over a period of 33 years (see Appendix 6). All of them dealt with his time at sea, the main focus being his time as a blockade runner. The title was always 'Reminiscences of Sea Life, and Running the Blockade' or a shorter variant. The first lecture took place at the local primary school in December 1869; memories of his time on the *Ad-Vance* were still fresh, and his audience were keen to hear the details of his adventures. It was reported in the *Fife Herald* on 23 December that:

> On Friday evening Captain Joannes Wyllie, of Mitchelstone, who since he gave up his adventurous life as a sailor, we should rather say modern 'sea king' has betaken himself to the ploughshare, delivered a lecture on his 'Reminiscences of sea life, and running the American blockade' in St Clairtown School.

He spoke for an hour and a half and he was 'listened to with deep attention by a numerous audience, the school room being crowded to excess'. The lecture was in aid of the school, raising funds for improvements. The newspaper reported that his lecture had raised £8, almost £725 in today's money (see Table 1).

That first lecture set the tone for all those that would follow: a packed audience, entertaining tales, and money raised for a good cause. In each instance Captain Wyllie was offered a vote of thanks by the organisers and cheered loudly by his audience. Many of the newspaper articles contain some of the details contained in his oration. Although a full transcript has yet to be uncovered, these reports offer a good history of his upbringing and his time at sea. By 1874 his tales were in great demand; he gave three lectures in eight weeks. The second lecture, given on 27 January in the village of Thornton (just north of Mitchelston), was the first whose report mentions the name of Wyllie's steamer, and the audience reaction gives an indication of just how powerful his reminiscences were:.

> Having, in a very spirited manner, narrated some of his perilous voyages in tropical lands, the Captain then proceeded with the interesting account of some of the stirring times at sea during the great American civil war. Breathless silence reigned throughout the audience as he spoke of the capture of himself and his gallant vessel, 'The *Advance*' after all efforts to escape which nautical skill could devise had failed. His after fate, his ingeniously contrived escape, and his return homeward only to run the blockade again, were all told in an exceedingly pleasant way. Several allusions, during the course of the lecture, to love of home and country, showed what fine feeling reigns often in the warm hearts of a rough sailor.[331]

Over the years, his presentations became grander, with local musicians and singers adding 'songs appropriate to the graphic narrative', such as 'The Voyagers', 'Anchored' and 'A Sailor's Joy'. Several even featured lantern projections of sea views, the history of cotton, and of ships and sailing. His audiences were made up of men and women, young and old, and often children as well. His charity extended farther than just the time he gave to speak, as he also was known on at least one occasion to bestow a photographic print of his blockade runner to a schoolboy in the area: around 1870, possibly even at one of his lectures, Wyllie gave a print, which at the time was quite a valuable thing, to a young William Pirie. In 1937 Pirie recalled this in a letter to his grandson, noting that his love of all things sea-related had drawn him to the captain, and described him as 'a big, robust, breezy fellow and liked by everyone'.[332]

The fact that Wyllie did speak in public was rare in a former blockade-running captain. There are no recorded lectures by the other well-known Scottish captains such as David Leslie or William Watson. Although blockade running was viewed as adventurous, a modern take on the high seas swashbuckling tales of old, very few former officers went on to speak, brag or explain their time in the war at public events. One exception was William Allan, who during the war served as an engineer on a runner and later became a Member of Parliament for Gateshead, in the north-east of England. Born and educated in Dundee, Allan gave a series of lectures in that city in the 1890s to large crowds, speaking about his time at sea, the capture of his steamer, and his imprisonment in a 'Yankee prison', finally being freed after appeals to the British government – and it is not beyond the bounds of possibility that Wyllie would have attended such an event, enabling the two to compare notes.

A thoughtful gift to a grateful admirer. This photograph of the painting of the Ad-Vance *was presented to local schoolboy William Pirie sometime in the 1870s.*

© CSG CIC Glasgow Museums Collection

It was the power and emotion of Wyllie's tales that kept bringing back the crowds. The subject matter never changed, yet his adventures and oration continued to fascinate. Though most of his lectures were given at regular intervals, the longest drought being five years, it was in what turned out to be his last year of life that Wyllie was most prolific. Over those 13 months Wyllie gave five lectures, including the important one at the Adam Smith Hall in November 1901; more about this below. The final appearance on stage of the Great Scottish Blockade Runner was on 7 March 1902 at the Public Hall in the coastal town of East Wemyss, a three-mile train journey from his farmhouse. As in his first lecture some 33 years earlier, Wyllie described his life at sea, and the proceeds went to a good cause:

> To a large and appreciative audience captain Wyllie re-delivered his thrilling 'Running the Blockade,' on Friday evening in the Public Hall, Dr A Watson presided; and music, vocal and instrumental, was contributed by the local artistes. The proceeds were for the lighting of the street lamps.[333]

Wyllie passed away just a month later.

Though his many lectures were obviously popular events, the tales of his exploits remained local. He never spoke outside of Fife; indeed, the farthest he ever travelled from his home was just 13 miles. Wyllie's story, told in his own words, would only be heard by those in his immediate area, a fact that once again would conceal his role in the Civil War from the wider world.

FAMOUS BLOCKADE-RUNNER DEAD.

HIS THRILLING EXPERIENCES

THE LATE CAPTAIN WYLLIE, KIRKCALDY.

The death of Joannes Wyllie was marked by several poignant tributes. This drawing, one of only three detailed likenesses of him known to exist, appeared in an obituary in the Weekly News *of 26 April 1902.*

By kind permission of DC Thomson & Co Ltd

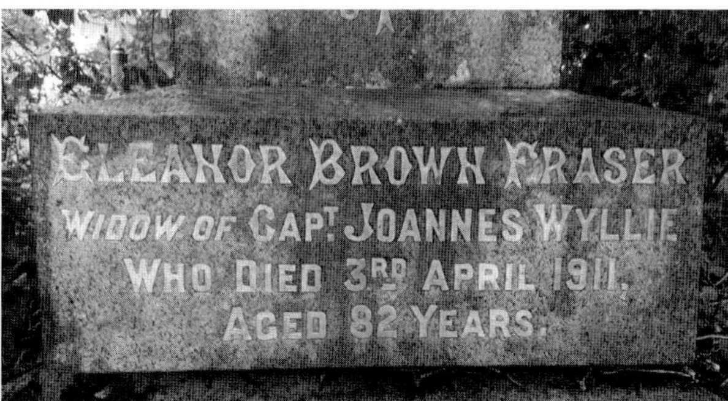

The only known physical reminder of the maritime career of Joannes Wyllie was found on the gravestone of his wife Eleanor (1830–1911). She is buried at Cathcart Cemetery on the south side of Glasgow.

© CSG CIC Glasgow Museums Collection

The task of crafting an obituary fell to his old friend Peter Anton. Although he was not identified as the author, it was he who wrote the article in the *Fife Free Press & Kirkcaldy Guardian* on 19 April, a week after Wyllie's death. The obituary is full of powerful and vivid imagery of the man, but Anton's best description of Wyllie can be found in *The People's Friend*; Anton's words roll along the page like a ship upon the sea; gracious and serene, in this description of the man he had called a friend:

> Looking at the 'cut of his jib,' one could not at the first take him for a sailor. He does not roll as he walks, but is remarkably light on his feet. He is tall and powerfully made, and in the region of the chest, shoulders, and neck there is a wonderful concentration of force. The head is Jovian. The locks are luxuriant and hyacinthine. The growth that fringes the lips is knightly, and if left to itself would evidently soon attain 'cathedral' proportions. The eye is the distinguishing feature. It lights up like a lamp all the face. It has often a far-away look, as if scanning something on the sea line where sky and ocean meet. Oftener, however, it brims with kindliness, and twinkles with racy or

> pawky humour. Altogether the Captain is a notable man, and no one can see him for the first time without pausing to inquire who he may be.[334]

Wyllie's estate was valued at £1,302 7s 1d, primarily made up of money in the bank and investments (£443), the value of his farm implements and tools (£691), and his household furniture and effects (just over £50). Against this was a non-itemised debt of £853 17s 9d. Wyllie's overall estate was therefore worth just £448.[335]

Wyllie's death in April 1902 marked the beginning of the fading of his story from memory. His exploits at sea, from his days as apprentice on the *Hope* to the escapes from the Union ships as master of the *Ad-Vance*, would soon just become just wispy recollections of his friends, his neighbours and those who had the pleasure of hearing him speak. Eleanor, his wife of 33 years, no longer able to work the farm as a widow, moved to Glasgow to be closer to her sister, Agnes, and there she died in 1911.

CONCLUSION: THE LEGACY OF JOANNES WYLLIE

> Captain Wyllie was a fine type of the leal hearted gentleman for he was always ready with kindly word or happy smile … he was also a good specimen of the kindly Scot – an experience which was felt, we believe, by all who had the pleasure of his acquaintance.[336]
>
> – From the obituary of Captain Wyllie.

On the cold winter's night of 26 February 1902 a group of men, tenants of several nearby farms, trudged along the muddy roads on their way towards Mitchelston Farm. They were heading to the home of a man that some local people knew as a celebrity and others as a famous speaker, but to most of these he was just a humble farmer and their neighbour. To the members of the delegation, however, Joannes Wyllie was more than just these things: he was their friend and a man of substantial local standing who had for over 35 years had been a pillar of his community.

They were welcomed into the farmhouse by Joannes and Eleanor. They had brought with them a gift, described as a 'tangible expression of their esteem', and that many local people had contributed to the gift. The presentation was made by their leader, the local magistrate, Dean of Guild McKenzie, whose speech, though brief, spoke volumes about the respect that Wyllie was held in:

> I have the very great pleasure in being a member of the deputation who are acting as the servants of a number of your very good friends, who, through their appreciation of your worth as a neighbour, instructed us to present you with a small token of respect. Sometimes it is said testimonials are very much

> overdriven, and in many cases it is somewhat difficult to understand how they originate, or for what particular reason they are given. In this case it was well known who were the originators, and the reasons were fully expressed and explained as a heading to the subscription book, all of which I need not now repeat. With these few remarks, I, in the name of the subscribers, beg your acceptance of this bank cheque, value sixty guineas, and, I may add, it is our fervent prayer that Mrs Wyllie and yourself may be long spared to enjoy the tenancy of Mitchelston Farm.

The gift was indeed a generous and substantial one. By 1902 the golden guinea coin had long ceased to be legal tender, but the term lived on as an amount equal to 21 shillings, or £1 1s 0d.[14*] So 60 guineas equated to £63, which today would amount to just under £7,000 (see Table 1). Humbled by such a generous gift, Wyllie's response to the presentation is telling, illustrating the situation that he found himself in:

> [P]ermit me to thank you from the bottom of my heart for coming up to my house to-night and presenting me with such a handsome gift as sixty guineas. Were it possible to enhance such a gift I would say the subscribers had done so by selecting a deputation so well known to me as kind friends and neighbours since I retired from the sea in 1868, and I am certain it will continue so until I cross the narrow span that lies between me and the unknown. I also appreciate the chivalrous feeling of delicacy in making the presentation in private. To have done so in public would to me been a thousand times more difficult than running the blockade … Now, I am old, nervous, and booked as a passenger for a land where there will be no more sea. Your very kind wish that Mrs Wyllie and myself may remain on Mitchelston Farm until the end is a wish probably as dear to us on our estimation as your very great and generous gift.

Wyllie was 73 years old and, it would seem, in poor health. The gift of money, rather than a tangible, physical memento, along with the fact that it had been just four months since Wyllie's lecture at the Adam Smith Hall in Kirkcaldy where the proceeds had gone to him instead of a charity, would indicate that late in life Wyllie found himself without the comfort of riches or luxuries that other well-known former blockade-running captains had enjoyed. It is noteworthy that he himself made reference to his days as a blockade runner in response to this generous gift. It was obviously the aspect of his life that he felt defined him.

14* The concept still exists in the 21st century; at the time of writing the guinea, worth 105% of £1 sterling, is still used as currency in many British livestock and racehorse auctions.

By far the most notable vessel he served on during his 15 years at sea was the *Ad-Vance*. No other vessel matched its importance or its fame. From May 1863 until September 1864 the *Ad-Vance* made 19 distinct voyages as a runner: 15 of these voyages were through the blockade itself into Wilmington, from either Nassau or Bermuda. The other four were journeys between neutral British ports with all the hazards of the open sea but none of the dangers posed by the blockading fleet. Official documents, diaries and other primary sources note that Wyllie was the master for nine of these voyages, while Thomas Morrow Crossan commanded six and John Julius Guthrie four. Even if some of these listings were part of the campaign to obscure the role of the *Ad-Vance*, Wyllie was far from being just a peripheral member of the crew or a minor footnote in its operation. He was a constant presence and the most important officer on the vessel from its departure from the Clyde until its surrender to the Union Navy off the coast of North Carolina.

Wyllie's impact on the circumvention of the blockade was significant. The *Ad-Vance*'s 15 successful runs through the blockade, 8 inward and 7 out, were made in 17 months, giving a rate of one complete run for just under every two months in service. The two successful trans-shipments between Bermuda and Nassau and the transatlantic round trip to Liverpool for repairs were also made during this period.[15*] Compared with other vessels employed on the trade during the war the *Ad-Vance's* success rate was high, but nowhere near that of steamers such as the *Syren* (33 successful runs), *Denbigh* (26), *Herald/Antonica* (24) and *Alice* (24). Yet the *Ad-Vance's* record far exceeds the average lifespan of blockade runners: just over 4 runs, or 2 complete round trips.[337] What made Wyllie's success even more important was its impact on the people of the State of North Carolina.

From cargo manifests, newspaper reports and Governor Vance's papers the number of bales of cotton carried out of North Carolina aboard the *Ad-Vance* can be established at 4,281. The inward supplies are more difficult to quantify, given the lack of detail on official documents. What can be shown is that large quantities of blankets, shoes, cloth and the carding combs used in textile production were brought in. Beyond the contemporary records, there also exists a listing of the cargo carried by the *Ad-Vance*, written 30 years after the end of the war by William H. Oliver, who was tasked by Governor Vance during the war to purchase cotton on the state account. In a letter to James Sprunt, a former crew member of the steamer who later went on to become a historian of the conflict, Oliver listed, according to his recollection, the full cargo delivered by the steamer, which included 275,000 yards of cloth of various widths and material, 25,887 pairs of grey blankets, 37,092 pairs woollen socks, 46,096 pairs of army shoes, and over 7,000 pairs of combs for carding cotton and wool.[338] Added to this were various quantities of medicine, machinery, paper, pens and lead. These huge numbers show that the success of the *Ad-Vance* made

15*Stephen Wise listed the number of successful runs for the *Ad-Vance* at 17; this number must take into account both transshipments between St George's and Nassau. In addition, Wise lists an estimated run in August of 1864, but the vessel at this time was confined to the Cape Fear River and although it made several attempts to leave it would not actually do so until the night of 9 September.

a considerable impact on the ability of the State of North Carolina to clothe and arm its soldiers as well as supplying materials for its civilian population and industrial production.

The contribution Wyllie made on his two other runners should also be noted. Though neither the *Susan Beirne* nor the *Deer* had any meaningful impact on the outcome of the war, Wyllie's command illustrates that to the owners of both vessels he was a trusted captain. If Wyllie's command at the helm of the *Bonita* is included as part of his record as a blockade runner, then the total number of voyages he completed rises to 24 and would indeed rank high amongst other captains employed in the trade.

The comparisons that can be made with other successful blockade-running captains are limited, as many never recorded their own stories. Certainly Wyllie was not the most successful captain either in terms of number of runs or fortunes amassed: David Leslie completed more runs and would appear to have returned with more spoils, while William Watson equally returned a wealthy man having completed fewer runs than Wyllie. The careers of other British captains like John Burroughs (of the *Cornubia)*, Thomas Gilpin (*Minnie* and *Talisman*), James Alexander Duguid (*Oreto*, *Giraffe/Robert E. Lee*, *Lucy* and *Juno)* can be hinted at, but their full stories remain uncovered. What is certain, however, is that the *Ad-Vance* was one of the more successful runners, so Wyllie's record in that area stands up to most.

How then best to summarise the life of Joannes Wyllie? Perhaps the most appropriate description comes from Peter Anton's obituary in the *Fife Herald*:

> Widely read, he could quote from the great authors, ancient and modern, with the most perfect case. He had a vast fund of humour, which was always agreeable; and the best of good himself, he could readily suit himself to the company of others. He was intensely sympathetic, and when a kind or encouraging world could help a brother he could be trusted to speak it … by his death we all today feel poorer.[339]

Many of those who attended Wyllie's lecture at the Adam Smith Hall in November 1901 would have wholeheartedly agreed with this sentiment. In front of his largest crowd and the biggest stage from which he would ever speak, he was frequently applauded and kept his listeners in the best of spirits with a 'fine spice of humor'. As he concluded, the crowd rose to their feet, and he was saluted by both the audience and from the chair by the Earl of Rosslyn. This would turn out to be the last great lecture he would give, as well as a last opportunity for many to hear his grand stories of adventure, daring, and danger. During his own lifetime he had been called the 'Great Scottish Blockade Runner', but to most he was just a true and loyal friend, known for his reliable, honest, knowledgeable, and kind nature.

His legacy at the helm of the *Ad-Vance* may not have been widely known or appreciated during his lifetime, but now the record can be put straight and his great importance to the operations of the State of North Carolina during the Civil War can be recognised. He may not have acquired great wealth as a blockade runner, but there can be little doubt that a great fortune of friendship and warm feelings was accumulated by Wyllie through his 72 years. His accomplishments certainly make him one of the great blockade runners of the American Civil War.

APPENDICES

APPENDIX 1

Full listing of sailings of the steamer *Lord Clyde/Ad-Vance* as a blockade runner

This is a detailed listing of all movements completed by the *Lord Clyde/Ad-Vance* during its time as a blockader runner from May 1863 until September 1864. To give as complete a history of the vessel as possible, it was compiled from a variety of sources including: the list of incoming and outgoing vessels from Wilmington from *Lifeline of the Confederacy*; lists of Bermuda cargo manifests compiled by Frank Van Diver; the Governor Vance papers archive; contemporary newspapers from North Carolina, Bermuda and Britain; official US Naval correspondence; first-hand accounts and diaries; prize court documents; and Joannes Wyllie's own recollections.

The exact number of runs completed by the *Ad-Vance* has been a matter of debate since the time of the blockade. Even today the number varies from source to source. Using the sources listed above, the exact number of voyages made by the steamer is known to have been 19, of which 15 were runs through the blockade itself and 4 were trips between other ports.

Full listing of the sailings of the Lord Clyde/Ad-Vance *as a blockade runner, May 1863–September 1864*

Blockade run	*Sailed from*	*Date*	*Arrived at*	*Date*	*Captain*	*Notes*
	Dublin	13 May 1863	Glasgow	13 May 1863	John Stephen Byrne	Last voyage of Lord Clyde as passenger steamer
	Glasgow	21 May 1863	Cardiff	22 May 1863	Joannes Wyllie	Left Greenock on the Clyde and sailed south through Irish Sea. Stopped at Cardiff to load coal for transatlantic voyage, where briefly boarded and searched for contraband.

Full listing of the sailings of the Lord Clyde/Ad-Vance *as a blockade runner, May 1863–September 1864 (cont.)*

Blockade run	*Sailed from*	*Date*	*Arrived at*	*Date*	*Captain*	*Notes*
	Cardiff	30 May 1863	Madeira	4 June 1863	Wyllie	Brief stop, possibly to take on extra coal
	Madeira	4 June 1863	St George's, Bermuda	14 June 1863	Wyllie	Transatlantic voyage
	St George's	20 June 1863	Nassau, Bahamas	22 June 1863*	Thomas Morrow Crossan#	Wyllie still listed in official documents as master
1	Nassau	22 June 1863	Wilmington	26 June 1863	Crossan#	Arrival at mouth of Cape Fear River. Arrived at Wilmington proper on 28 June. First run through blockade
2	Wilmington	24 July 1863*	St George's	27 July 1863	Crossan#	Wyllie listed as master within documents at Bermuda
3	St George's	14 August 1863	Wilmington	16 August 1863	Crossan	Daylight run described by John Baptist Smith
4	Wilmington	23 September 1863*	St George's	26 September 1863	Crossan	Captain Justus Scheibert, Prussian army officer observer, is a passenger
5	St George's	6 October 1863	Wilmington	12 October 1863	Crossan	Passengers include Reverend Moses D. Hoge and James H. Burton
6	Wilmington	23 October 1863	St George's	26 October 1863	John Julius Guthrie	First voyage under Guthrie
7	St George's	3 November 1863	Wilmington	9 November 1863	Guthrie	Cargo included 18,000 pairs of shoes and 17.500 blankets
8	Wilmington	19 November 1863*	Nassau	23 November 1863	Crossan	Crossan once again in command
	Nassau	4 January 1864*	St George's	9 January 1864	Crossan	After long lay-up at Nassau, the steamer headed to St George's. This was not a run through the blockade

Full listing of the sailings of the Lord Clyde/Ad-Vance *as a blockade runner, May 1863–September 1864 (cont.)*

Blockade run	***Sailed from***	***Date***	***Arrived at***	***Date***	***Captain***	***Notes***
9	St George's	11 January 1864	Wilmington	18 January 1864	Crossan	*Ad-Vance* listed as beaching on 18 January, finally refloated 24 January. This run is described by signalman John Baptist Smith
10	Wilmington	6 February 1864	St George's	9 February 1864	Guthrie	Guthrie again in command. Over 700 bales of cotton carried
11	St George's	13 February 1864	Wilmington	16 February 1864	Guthrie	Run described by W in North Carolina papers. Ran aground on the 'Rip' at mouth of Cape Fear River
12	Wilmington	8 March 1864*	Nassau	10 March 1864	Wyllie	Wyllie takes command. Largest cargo of cotton, 820 bales
	Nassau	15 March 1864*	St George's	19 March 1864	Wyllie	Not a run, but a voyage between Nassau and St George's to collect cargo
13	St George's	26 March 1864	Wilmington	1 April 1864	Wyllie	Stormy passage with long chase by a Union blockader
14	Wilmington	14 April 1864	Nassau	16 April 1864	Wyllie	Start of trans-Atlantic trip to Liverpool for repairs
	Nassau	21 April 1864	Halifax, Canada	26 April 1864	Wyllie	Arrived in ballast, took on more coal for transatlantic crossing to Liverpool
	Halifax	3 May 1864	Liverpool	17 May 1864	Wyllie	Called at Cork, southern Ireland, on 16 May, arriving with six bales of cotton
	Liverpool	28 June 1864	St George's	14 July 1864	Wyllie	Six weeks in dock at Liverpool undergoing repairs. Three-day stop at Queenstown, Ireland, to re-coal

Full listing of the sailings of the Lord Clyde/Ad-Vance *as a blockade runner, May 1863–September 1864 (cont.)*

Blockade run	***Sailed from***	***Date***	***Arrived at***	***Date***	***Captain***	***Notes***
15	St George's	25 July 1864	Wilmington	30 July 1864	Wyllie	Last inwards run.
Several attempts	Wilmington	6 August 1864	Smithville, mouth of Cape Fear River	8 September 1864	Wyllie	Multiple failed attempts to leave Cape Fear River. Chronicled in diary of Mary White
Capture	Wilmington	9 September 1864	Halifax	10 September 1864	Wyllie	Captured by *Santiago de Cuba* off Cape Hatteras
Journey to Prize Court	Off Cape Hatteras	10 September 1864	New York	17 September 1864	Josiah A Hannum, US Navy	Taken by US Naval crew to prize court at New York with Wyllie on board. Stopped at Norfolk, Virginia, to unload prisoners

* estimated date
# Wyllie listed in official documents as master

Voyages commanded by captain, as listed in official documents

Wyllie	9
Crossan	6
Guthrie	4

APPENDIX 2

Crew list of the blockade runner *Ad-Vance*, February 1864

This listing comes from a handwritten note found in the John Julius Guthrie papers held at the state archives of North Carolina. It is one of only three known crew listings from the *Ad-Vance* during its career as a blockade runner. Its official title as listed on the outside of the document is *Officers and Crew list of the Ad. Vance, Feb 1864, Inward List.* Two voyages were made by the steamer in February of that year, so this list might refer to its arrival at either St George's on 9 February or Wilmington on 16 February.

It is not known who wrote the list; possible authors include Captain Guthrie, the ship's steward George Hunt, the purser Thomas Boykin, or a customs official in St George's. One person who can categorically be ruled out is Joannes Wyllie, as it is highly unlikely that he would have incorrectly spelled his own name as 'Johanes Wilie'. The crew consisted of 56 men, with Wyllie's role listed as first officer.

A NOTE ON 'NATIVITY'

Each crew member's nativity is shown next to his position. Of the 56 crew, 21 are listed as being born in the United States while 35 are listed as foreign born. 'Nativity' in this context refers to the place of birth, but may not necessarily reflect the citizenship in February 1864 when this list was compiled. For example, William C. Jones, the 2nd officer, was born in Scotland but must have emigrated to the United States sometime before 1860 as he is listed in that year's census as living in North Carolina. Other crewmen listed as being of Scottish, English etc birth may also have been residents of the United States when the war began.

Officers and crew of the Ad-Vance, February 1864

Complement of the* Ad-Vance *under Guthrie, 1864		
Name	***Rank***	***Nativity***
J J Guthrie	Captain	North Carolina
Thos. Boykin	Pusser (purser)	North Carolina
Johanes Wilie	1st officer	Scotland
Wm C Jones	2nd officer	Scotland
B Taylor	3rd officer	Norfolk, Virginia
Jn Carrow	4th officer	North Carolina
Wm H Jones	Boatswain	North Carolina
J B Robertson	Carpenter	North Carolina
C C Morse	Pilot	North Carolina
C L Neil	Signal officer	Virginia
E F Wicks	Watchman	New York
Wm Barry	Watchman	Ireland
P G Gilligan	Seaman	North Carolina
Rob Brantburg	Seaman	Sweden
Charles Johnson	Seaman	Sweden
Anthony Silva	Seaman	England
Benj Smith	Seaman	England
Jn. Stewart	Seaman	Scotland
Geo. Peters	Seaman	Portugal
Andrew Hay	Seaman	England
R Houll	Seaman	Ireland
T.L. Jefferson	Seaman	Ireland
W. Costin	Seamen's mess boy	North Carolina
J Venerman	1st cook	France
W W Bell	2nd cook	England
Wm Fenton	3rd cook	England
Geo Hunt	1st steward	England
T.D. Willson	Purser's steward	North Carolina
Robt. Young	2nd Steward	Scotland
W C Mews	Captain's clerk	Virginia
A Sholar	Officers steward	North Carolina
Engineering Department		
Geo Morrison	Chief engineer	Pen (Pennsylvania?)
J Maglen	1st assistant engineer	Ireland

Officers and crew of the Ad-Vance, February 1864 (cont.)

Name	***Rank***	***Nativity***
A J Barnes	2nd assistant engineer	St Johns, New Brunswick, Canada
Geo Curtis	3rd assistant engineer	Virginia
T W Hill	Greaser	Maryland
D G Hamlen	Greaser	North Carolina
W C Swan	Greaser	Rhode Island
Geo Murphy	Greaser	Ireland
S Roland	Fireman	Ireland
Jn Moss	Fireman	England
P Riley	Fireman	Ireland
Wm Gill	Fireman	Ireland
W Quinlinan	Fireman	Ireland
W Barnes	Fireman	Ireland
W Palmer	fireman	Ireland
W Furlong	Fireman	Ireland
J Blossom	Fireman	Portugal
P McGrath	Fireman	Ireland
J Britton	Fireman	Ireland
Geo Stapleton	Fireman	England
J S Sholar	Storekeeper	North Carolina
Alex May	Engineer's steward	France
C Rankin	Coal heaver	Maryland
Jn Battle	Coal heaver	France
W Colrane	Coal heaver	England

Nativities as listed

American	***21***	***Foreign***	***35***
North Carolina	12	Ireland	14
Virginia	4	England	9
Maryland	2	Scotland	4
New York	1	France	3
Rhode Island	1	Portugal	2
Pennsylvania?	1	Sweden	2
		Canada	1

APPENDIX 3

Prize court deposition of Captain Joannes Wyllie after the capture of the *Ad-Vance*

On 10 September 1864 the *Ad-Vance* was taken, along with Captain Wyllie and several other members of the crew, to New York to be legally adjudicated as a lawful prize. There Wyllie appeared before officials of the prize court of Judge Samuel Betts.

The record of the answers given by Wyllie are in the prize court files held by the national archives in New York. The questions, known as 'Interrogatories' are not listed on the document as they were a standard set asked of all captured blockade-running crew.[16*]

Here is the full transcription of the answers that Wyllie gave in New York on 17 September 1864:

DISTRICT COURT OF THE UNITED STATES

FOR THE SOUTHERN DISTRICT OF NEW YORK

Deposition of *Joannes Wyllie (master)* a witness produced, sworn and examined *in preparatorio*, on the *Seventeenth* day of *September* in the year eighteen hundred and sixty *four* at the *office* of *E.H. Owen, Prize Commissioner, Number 72 Wall Street, New York City.*

On the standing interrogatories established by the District Court of the United States, for the Southern District of New York; the said witness having been produced for the purpose of such examination by *E Delafield Smith, United States Attorney.*

In behalf of the captors of a certain ship or vessel called the *'Ad. Vance' her tackle etc.*

1. To the 1st Interrogatory he says.

I was born in Kelsey *(sic)* Scotland. I now live in Liverpool England and have lived there for the last twenty years. I am a subject of the Queen of Great Britain and owe her allegiance. I am not a citizen of the United States of America. I am not a married man.

16* For a full listing of the Interrogatories see *The Law of Nations Affecting Commerce During War* by Francis H. Upton, published in 1863.

2. To the 2nd Interrogatory he says.

I was present at the capture of the above named vessel and of the merchandise on board thereof.

3. To the 3rd Interrogatory he says.

The capture was made on the 10th of September 1864 at 7 o'clock pm in North Carolina 35 degrees and 74.30' west longitude, Cape Hatteras, bearing North 78° West. The vessel and cargo were first carried to Norfolk and thence to this port of New York. The vessel captured had no commission or letters authorising her to make prizes. The reason for making the seizure was that the vessel had run the blockade.

4. To the 4th Interrogatory he says.

The vessel sailed under English colors. She had on board no other colors, but she had on board Confederate colors while she lay in Confederate waters.

5. To the 5th Interrogatory he says.

No resistance was made except an effort to escape capture if possible by running away. There was one gun fired by the capturing vessel. The capture was made by the '*Santiago de Cuba*'. There were no other ships in sight at the time. The *Ad. Vance* was a merchant vessel and belonged to Power Low & Co of Wilmington, North Carolina.

6. To the 6th Interrogatory he says.

The *Santiago de Cuba* was a ship of war belonging to the government of the United States, and she made the capture. I don't know by what authority she acted. The *Ad. Vance* has never been seized or condemned before.

7 To the 7th Interrogatory he says.

The name of the vessel taken was the '*Ad. Vance*' and I was her master and commander. I was appointed to that command by the before named Power, Low & Co at Wilmington. I have known the '*Ad. Vance*' for fully twelve months, and have known that firm for the same period. I took command of the vessel first in Wilmington. I was sailing master of the vessel from England to Wilmington and subsequently became master. She was delivered to me by that firm.

8 To the 8th Interrogatory he says.

The *Ad. Vance* is 475 tons English measurement, as near as I recollect, excluding the Engine Room. The vessel's company all told was about sixty and all were on board at the time. They were English, Irish, Scotch, and Dutch. There was a boy on board who was the son of the late Commodore Meuse. The crew were shipped at different times and in different places, at Liverpool and Halifax. They were generally shipped by the Purser or chief officer of the ship.

9 To the 9th Interrogatory he says.

I did belong to the ship's company at the time of the capture. I was the master thereof. I had not any interest, nor do I know that any of the officers, mariners or company had any interest in the vessel or any part share or interest in the merchandise on board of her.

10 To the 10th Interrogatory he says.

I have already stated how long I have known the vessel, as when I first saw her, which was at Clyde Scotland. She carried no guns. She was built at Clyde and her first name was '*Lord Clyde*' and afterwards it was changed to the '*Ad. Vance*'.

11 To the 11th Interrogatory he says.

The vessel at the time of capture was bound for Halifax. That voyage began at Bermuda and was to have ended at Halifax. When she sailed from Bermuda she had on board a general cargo, consisting principally of clothing and bacon – provisions; when captured she had on board cotton and turpentine. This last cargo was taken on board in August last, 1864. I have stated her cargo and don't know whether the same was contraband or not.

12 To the 12th Interrogatory he says.

The vessel had no passport or sea brief on board. She sailed from Bermuda to Wilmington, North Carolina, where she discharged her inward cargo and took aboard the aforesaid cargo of cotton and turpentine. The vessel has been running between Nassau, Bermuda and Wilmington ever since I have been connected with her and has carried the same kinds of cargoes above mentioned. Those cargoes were delivered at Wilmington and Nassau and Bermuda. The vessel last sailed from Bermuda in July last, and from Wilmington on the 9th of September instant.

13. To the 13th Interrogatory he says.

I have already stated what lading the vessel had on board when she sailed from Bermuda on her last voyage and what she had when captured. She had on board, as nearly as I know, fully 400 bales of cotton and ten barrels of turpentine – no resin.

14 To the 14th Interrogatory he says.

I have already stated what the persons having charge of the vessel were Power Low & Co of Wilmington, but I don't know that they were the owners of the vessel, nor who the owners were. They had the entire management of the vessel and could displace me if they pleased. One of the members of that firm and perhaps both were Englishmen. It was an English house establishment there. I believe they were married but I don't think they had their families there. I don't know how long they had resided there, nor where they resided previously.

15 To the 15th Interrogatory he says.

I know nothing about any bill of sale of the vessel nor of any engagement to purchase the same.

16 To the 16th Interrogatory he says.

I have already in part answered this interrogatory. The laders of the cargo were the before named Power Low & Co. I don't know whether they had any interest therein or not. If the cargo were delivered up I suppose it would belong to them.

17 To the 17th Interrogatory he says.

I don't know that there were any bills of lading for the cargo. I never signed any thereof. I don't know that there were any bills of lading signed by any one.

18 To the 18th Interrogatory he says.

There were not on board of the vessel at the time of capture, nor in my possession any bills of lading, invoices, letters, or other writings to prove or show my own of any persons interest in either the vessel or cargo as far as I know.

19 To the 19th Interrogatory he says.

I have already stated the latitude and longitude of the place where the capture was made, which was off Cape Hatteras. There was no charter party for the voyage that I know of – there was none.

20 To the 20th Interrogatory he says.

I can't state what letters, papers, bills of lading or other writing were on board, when the vessel left Wilmington, relating to her or her cargo. I don't know that any papers were burnt, torn or attempted to be concealed, but I believe some papers or letters were thrown overboard while attempting to escape capture, but I don't know to what they related. I don't know by whom they were thrown overboard. They were not thrown over by me, but I think they were thrown over. I can't say who was present. I did not see them thrown over. This was just before the capture and after we had given up all hopes of escape. The letters were in two loaded cases, that is, loaded for the purpose of sinking them, and were placed at my room door to be thrown over if necessary.

21. To the 21st Interrogatory he says.

I knew and all on board knew that Wilmington was in a state of war with the United States and was held by the naval forces of the United States under blockade. This had been known for a long time while we had been entering and departing from that port on the voyages before mentioned.

22. To the 22nd Interrogatory he says.

That port was in fact under blockade at the times the vessel entered and departed therefrom as before I stated. I have been warned of the blockade by being shot at when entering and leaving. I knew there was danger in entering and departing from that port while so under blockade. There was no notice by any endorsement on the ships papers.

23 To the 23rd Interrogatory he says.

The register of the vessel has never been examined by any officer of the United States navy or revenue.

24 To the 24th Interrogatory he says.

I have already stated that the vessel, while I have been connected with her, has repeatedly entered Wilmington while blockaded and departed therefrom.

25 To the 25th Interrogatory he says.

The vessel has never before been seized as prize.

26 To the 26th Interrogatory he says.

I have sustained no loss except the loss of my pay and my chronometer. I have no indemnity therefor.

27 To the 27th Interrogatory he says.

I don't know whether the vessel or goods were insured or not.

28 To the 28th Interrogatory he says.

I don't know anything more about the ownership of the property than what I have already stated. I don't know to whom it would have belonged on delivery at the destination port.

29 To the 29th Interrogatory he says.

The growth and manufacture of the cotton and turpentine on board of the vessel was of the Confederate States, but whether it was from North Carolina or not I cannot say.

30 To the 30th Interrogatory he says.

The cargo was taken from the wharf at Wilmington.

31 To the 31st Interrogatory he says.

I don't know any such papers as are enquired of in the interrogatory.

32 To the 32nd Interrogatory he says.

There were no papers delivered out of the vessel or carried away except such as were delivered to the captors at the time of seizure. Where they now are I know not.

33 To the 33rd Interrogatory he says.

Bulk was not broken after the vessel sailed, nor since to my knowledge or belief.

34 To the 34th Interrogatory he says.

No passengers were on board except the boys and some persons who were working their passage as firemen or sailors, who were really of the ships company. There were no persons on board except the boy and those connected with the navigating the ship.

35 To the 35th Interrogatory he says.

I don't know how to answer this question whether the papers which were found on board were entirely true or fair. I don't know that they were false or colorable nor do I know of any matters or circumstance to effect their credit. I don't know what papers were found on board. I cannot answer the remainder of this interrogatory.

36 To the 36th Interrogatory he says.

The vessel was steaming for Halifax at the time she was first pursued. Her course was not altered on the appearance of the *Santiago de Cuba*. I put on all the steam I could to get away. The chase lasted from 11 o'clock in the forenoon until the time of capture, which was 7 p.m.

37 To the 37th Interrogatory he says.

I know nothing of any sale or transfer of the vessel and cannot answer this interrogatory any further. If restored I think she would belong to Power Low & Co, before named.

38 To the 38th Interrogatory he says.

I have already stated the cargo on board of the vessel – she carried no guns and had none of the property mentioned in the interrogatory, except she had some sky rockets for her own use.

39 To the 39th Interrogatory he says.

I have stated all I know or believe according to the best of my knowledge and thereof regarding the real and true property and destination of the vessel and cargo. The vessel was a side wheel steamer. Her engines was (*sic*) 300 horse power.

40 To the 40th Interrogatory he says.

The vessel has never sailed under convoy. I had instructions to destroy the papers if there was danger of being captured.

41 To the 41st Interrogatory he says.

I have already stated that the vessel has gone in and out of Wilmington in violation of the blockade of that port.

42 To the 42nd Interrogatory he says.

I have already said that the vessel carried no letter of license to act as privateer.

43 To the 43rd Interrogatory he says.

The *Ad. Vance* never sailed or acted in company or concert with any armed vessel.

Signed *Joannes Wyllie*

APPENDIX 4

A HISTORY OF WYLLIE'S SHIPS

During his 15 years at sea Joannes Wyllie served aboard 12 ships. These ranged from slow merchantmen to speedy clippers, from sturdy screw steamers to slippery paddle-propelled blockade runners. Below is a brief history of each of those vessels. The official number, O.N., was the unique identifier given to all British-registered vessels, as stipulated in the 1854 Merchant Shipping Act.

Barque *Hope* (Wyllie served in it from May 1852 to April 1856)

Official Number 3872

The barque *Hope* was Wyllie's first vessel, and he was a member of its crew for just over four years. His time on the *Hope* was his longest service aboard any single vessel during his career at sea.

The *Hope* was built in 1839 in St Johns, New Brunswick, Canada. By 1852 it was registered in Glasgow, and before Wyllie joined its crew it had made voyages from Liverpool to New Orleans and from Glasgow to Aden.

A year after Wyllie left it in 1856, it sank in a heavy gale off the west coast of France in the Bay of Biscay. On the night of 26 August 1857 it was en route from Cardiff to Cape Verde, loaded with patent fuel, when the storm hit. The crew of 17 were saved by the French brig *Amitie*; the *Hope*'s crew 'would not have lived through the night had it not been for courage and providential aid of the French crew'. The rescued seamen were then put ashore at Caen.[340]

Clipper *Indian Queen* (June 1856–March 1858)

Official Number 24006

The *Indian Queen* was a fast clipper that served both the tea route to China and the migrant service to Australia/New Zealand. It was built by Johnston & Mackie of Miramichi, New Brunswick, Canada, in 1852, and was registered in Liverpool. It was part of the fleet of the Black Ball Line, a successful shipping company engaged in the colonial trade from Liverpool. The *Indian Queen* was known for several fast sailings to Australia in the 1850s and would sail for 20 years.

In December 1872 the *Indian Queen* found itself caught in a fierce North Atlantic gale. It had left Quebec bound for Liverpool when it encountered 'fearful weather, with the whole of her deck furniture and deck being swept away'. Fourteen of the crew were swept overboard, including the master and first mate. On 3 December the floating hulk of the *Indian Queen* was spotted by the barque *Don Guillermo*, then on a voyage from New York to Liverpool. The remaining crew of the *Indian Queen*, some in a terrible state, were taken on board, and the crippled clipper was left to its fate.[341]

Screw steamer *Tamaulipas* (June 1858–December 1858, November 1860)

Official Number 1058

Wyllie's first Scottish-built ship was the *Tamaulipas*, a screw steamer launched by John Reid and Company of Port Glasgow in 1852. It mainly served the routes between Liverpool and French coastal ports such as Bordeaux. Wyllie served for over a year in the crew and it was on the decks of the *Tamaulipas* that he began his education in the operation of steam-powered vessels.

After a 25-year career it was wrecked during one of its regular voyages from Liverpool to Rouen, where it became stranded on the Berville Bank in the Seine near Le Havre on 17 December 1877. It could not be refloated and was subsequently broken up where it lay.[342]

Screw steamer *Nemesis* (January 1859–September 1860)

Official Number 27126

The *Nemesis* was an iron-hulled screw steamer built in 1858 by Denny & Rankin in Dumbarton, on the Clyde. Built for the James Moss & Company of Liverpool, it was employed between the Mersey and the coastal ports of France, primarily Bordeaux. Wyllie served as first mate for over 20 voyages, having joined in January 1859. He was on board the steamer on 13 September 1860 when it sank after striking a rock in the Rez de Seine passage, off Brest. All crew and passengers were saved by local fishing boats.[343]

Screw steamer *Hope* (November 1860–August 1862)

Official Number 4656

The *Hope* was built in 1853 by John Laird of Birkenhead, England. The iron-hulled steamer first served routes from Liverpool to ports along the west coast of Africa.

By the time Wyllie joined its crew in November 1860 it was plying the French coastal trade as well as visiting ports in the eastern Mediterranean. Like Wyllie's previous steamer, the *Nemesis*, it was operated by the Liverpool firm of James Moss & Company. After a relatively uneventful period of just under two years aboard *Hope* Wyllie left it, to take up command of his first steamer in August 1862.

The *Hope* was renamed *Luxor* in 1864 and it survived until 1898 when its then owners, the Clapham Steam Ship Company, sold it to the shipbreaking firm of Thomas W. Ward of Sheffield, for £1,625.[344] It had the longest career of any of Wyllie's former vessels, sailing for 45 years.

Screw steamer *Bonita* (September 1862–December 1862)

Official Number 29154

The *Bonita* was the first vessel that Wyllie commanded. It was built in 1860 by Archibald Denny of Dumbarton, and on launch was named *Economist*. It made transatlantic runs from Glasgow to New York as well as European voyages from Liverpool in 1861, before being purchased by Fraser, Trenholm & Company as a blockade runner. It made just one run, into Charleston, in early 1862. Returning to Liverpool that summer, it was sold and renamed *Bonita* in an attempt to obscure its previous activities. Wyllie was in command of it for just one round-trip voyage, sailing for Nassau in September 1862 and arriving back at Liverpool in late December.

In February 1863 it was sold to the Royal Netherlands Steamship Company and renamed *Cycloop*; it sailed from Liverpool for Amsterdam on 28 February. Over the next ten years it served routes in the Mediterranean, the North Sea and the Baltic. It was caught in a storm off the Polish coast on 22 October 1874, which caused it to list and its engine room to flood. The crew were forced to abandon ship, and it finally sank on 26 October 1874.[345]

Paddle steamer *Lord Clyde/Ad-Vance/ Frolic/ Maud Mclain* (May 1863–September 1864)

Official Number 44574

The *Lord Clyde* was built by Caird and Company at Greenock. It was first employed by the Dublin and Glasgow Steam Packet Company in September 1862 as a fast passenger and freight ferry between the two ports, setting speed records during its seven months on that route. It was purchased by the State of North Carolina in April 1863 and renamed *Ad-Vance*. It operated as a blockade runner until captured by the *Santiago de Cuba* off the Carolina coast on 10 September 1864. It was then purchased by the US Navy for $120,000 from the New York prize court and renamed *Advance*. After being refitted as a warship it steamed south to serve as part of the blockade fleet off Wilmington: poacher turned gamekeeper. It was part of the flotilla that took part in the bombardment of Fort Fisher in January 1865, which closed the Cape Fear River and Wilmington to all steamers trying to run the blockade.

After the war it was renamed *Frolic* and it served in the US Navy for the next 18 years. It made a transatlantic trip in the summer of 1865 to join the European Squadron as a dispatch vessel, where it served for the next four years. It accompanied the flotilla commanded by Admiral David Farragut, the 'Hero of the battle of New Orleans', as he toured Europe during 1867–68. The *Frolic* accompanied Farragut's flagship, the *Franklin*, and was used by the admiral for trips into smaller ports. Farragut's tour took him from St Petersburg in the Baltic to several of the warm water ports of the Mediterranean and as far east as the Ottoman capital of Constantinople. The movements of the fleet of this noted Civil War hero were often reported in British newspapers.

The *Frolic* returned to American waters in the spring of 1869 where on 8 May it was placed out of commission while at port in New York. The retirement was short-lived as it was returned to active service that September. Soon after the steamer visited Wilmington, North Carolina. The presence of the old runner was mentioned in the pages of the *Wilmington Journal* on 2 October: 'Her dimensions, capacity and speed are quite familiar to a large portion of our readers.' In 1870 it served along the north-western Atlantic coast, patrolling the fishing grounds off Nova Scotia. During 1875–1877 it was assigned to the South American Squadron. It was decommissioned in October 1877 and sat in the Naval Yard at Washington, DC, for several years waiting to be struck from the Naval List. It was sold at auction to the firm of J.P. Agnew & Company of Alexandria, Virginia, in September 1883 for $11,250.[346]

After its sale, the *Frolic* sat in the yard of J.P. Agnew, a company that built and broke ships. It had at first hoped to sell the vessel on, but then came a change of mind: an advertisement was placed in the *Alexandria Gazette* of 22 May 1885 for an auction of recoverable parts from the *Frolic*, including items of machinery, piping, lead, copper, chains and anchors. These items had been removed from the hull, which by April 1885 was sitting almost empty. At that time there was a change of plan: the iron hull remained intact and was converted into a coal barge. Its sale to a 'Southern Firm' was reported on 26 October 1885 in the local Washington, DC, papers, its price double what Agnews had paid the navy. It was renamed *Maud McLain* (also spelled *Maud Mclean*), and a full report of the hulk's metamorphosis was given in the *Alexandria Gazette* on 3 December. The vessel, now a barge, was towed to Baltimore to be loaded with coal for its first voyage to New Orleans.

The ignominious end of the state's runner was reported by the *News and Observer* of Raleigh, informing its readers:

> ALAS! To what base uses &.... The famous blockade runner *Advance*, which during the war made many successful trips between Willington and Nassau is now but a barge, carrying coal between New Orleans and Galveston … She is now in her humiliation called the *Maud McLean*.[347]

For the next three years the *Maud* worked in the Gulf of Mexico carrying coal from the Alabama mines to the ports of New Orleans, Galveston and Pensacola. Although some noises were made by the then owner, L.O. Desforges, Jung and Company of New Orleans, about restoring machinery to the old hull and making it a steamer once again, nothing came of this talk. Desforges, Jung and Company went bankrupt in 1889 and the barge was once again sold, this time to the Export Coal Company of Pensacola, Florida, for $9,700. It continued its life as a barge delivering coal to ports along the gulf for a further two years.[348]

During one of its regular runs in the gulf the *Maud McLain* was under tow from the steam tug *W.J. Keysar* on its way from Pensacola to Galveston on the night of 9 November 1891 carrying 900 tons of coal. It was a literal shell of its former, glorious self. Around 95 miles south-west of Pensacola the tug and barge ran into danger. The night was stormy with strong winds whipping and waves breaking over the rails, and the barge started taking on water. The barge's master made a distress call to the tug, which went about in order to take the crew of six off the foundering vessel. The towing hawser was thrown off and the barge began to list, and it finally sank. [349]

So ended the career of the *Lord Clyde/Ad-Vance/Frolic/Maud McLain*. Where so many other former runners had succumbed to the storms of the Atlantic, sandbars of Cape Fear or fire from Union warships, it was the waves of the Gulf of Mexico that took this former greyhound down. In a final insult to its illustrious history, the owners of the barge, the Export Coal Company, had seen fit to insure only the coal it carried; the vessel itself had been left uninsured, deemed not worth the premium to cover it in case of accident.[350]

Paddle steamer *Susan Beirne* (November 1864–December 1864)

Official Number 50355

The *Susan Beirne* was built by Aitken & Mansel of Glasgow as an iron-hulled blockade runner in the summer of 1864. It was the sister ship of the *Banshee*, the successful runner notably under the command of Thomas Taylor (not to be confused with the runner of the same name built by Jones, Quiggin & Company of Liverpool in 1863).

Launched on 31 August, it left the Clyde in mid-November bound for Bermuda and the blockade with Wyllie in command. It was forced to put into Belfast after severe weather in the North Channel caused some structural damage. It then sailed south to Queenstown, where it was repaired before setting off on the transatlantic voyage. Wyllie's role was to deliver the steamer to St George's, after which he handed over command to D.S. Martin. After Wyllie's departure Martin attempted to run the *Susan Beirne* through the blockade of Wilmington, but heavy weather forced the captain to turn back to Bermuda. It never again attempted to make a run and was laid up at Bermuda where it awaited new owners and a new role. It was sold in late 1865 and made its way from the Caribbean towards the River Plate, calling at Bahia and Rio de Janeiro along the way.[351] That year it transported

Brazilian troops during the Paraguayan War, fought by Paraguay against the combined forces of Brazil, Argentina and Uruguay. In 1871 it disappeared from the records, listed in the Appropriation Book as 'sold at a foreign port'.

Paddle steamer *Deer* (February 1865)

Official Number 51018

The *Deer* was a purpose-built blockade runner constructed by W.H. Potter & Company of Liverpool in 1864. Wyllie took command of the *Deer* at Bermuda in January 1865 and sailed it to Nassau. It made just one attempt to run the blockade, being captured by Union forces off Charleston on 18 February 1865. It was subsequently sold in April at the prize court at Boston for $40,000 to Nickerson and Company of that city. It was then renamed *Palmyra* and it served on the route from Boston to New Orleans for the following few years. It was last listed in *Lloyd's Register of American and Foreign Shipping* in 1873 as the '*Palmyra* (ex-*Deer*)' of Boston. Its ultimate fate is unknown.[352]

Screw steamer *Carolina* (February 1866–December 1866)

Official Number 29393

Built in 1860 by Richardson, Duck and Company of Stockton-on-Tees, the steamer was originally named *Palikari*. Although not a blockade runner it did make several voyages to Caribbean ports during the Civil War while under the direction of the Liverpool-based Confederate agent Henry Lafone. At these ports the steamer either delivered cargo intended to be run through the blockade or picked up items to be taken to Europe. Wyllie joined as master at Liverpool in February 1866, serving on it for three voyages: two to the United States and one to the Black Sea.

In subsequent years the *Carolina* made various voyages from Glasgow to India, and from London to Mediterranean ports. Its final port of registration was in Hull. It sank on 14 November 1872 while bound from Baltimore to Queenstown with a cargo of corn. It foundered after encountering heavy seas which filled its hold and extinguished its boiler fires. The crew were saved by the passing Norwegian barque *Magnus Lagaboter*, which landed them at New York.[353]

Paddle steamer *Georgia Belle* (March 1867–June 1867)

Official Number 51050

The *Georgia Belle* was the first of two former blockade runners that Wyllie took to the River Plate during 1867. It was built in 1864 in Liverpool by Jones, Quiggin and Company, and it never saw the blockade, having failed to leave the Mersey in late 1864 due to mechanical failures. After two years sitting in the Liverpool docks, it was finally taken to Montevideo,

Uruguay, to be sold. It was delivered to that port and sold there by Wyllie in June 1867.[354] It disappears from the records after that time. It is believed to have been used in some capacity during the Paraguayan War.

Paddle steamer *Stag* (August 1867–November 1867)

Official Number 3033

The *Stag* was launched in 1853 from the yard of William Denny & Brothers, Dumbarton. Originally used on Irish Sea ferry routes, it made its way to the blockade in 1864 where it was renamed *Kate Gregg*. Four successful runs were completed before it return to British waters. Like the *Georgia Belle* it sat after the war in the docks of Liverpool awaiting a new owner. After over two years in its mothballed condition it finally changed hands and was taken by Wyllie to South America in August 1867. There it was sold to foreign owners and it disappears from the records.[355] Like the *Susan Beirne* and the *Georgia Belle*, it is believed to have been used in some capacity during the Paraguayan War.

APPENDIX 5

THE HISTORY OF SAMUEL WALTERS' PAINTING *A.D. VANCE*

Perhaps the most evocative depiction of the *Ad-Vance* is the oil painting attributed to the famed maritime artist Samuel Walters; it is held in the collections of Glasgow Museums in Scotland. It was owned by Joannes Wyllie himself, and it came into the possession of the museum service when it was donated in May 1917 by Wyllie's nephew, George Porteous Scott, a successful Glasgow iron merchant.

The painting depicts the steamer at sea, its paddles turning, thrusting the vessel through the choppy waves. On its deck are crew members going about their duties as well as a figure standing near the paddle box, surveying the steamer's course; his attire would suggest an officer or even its master. Although other vessels can be seen in the background, including one flying the Stars and Stripes, they are not blockaders chasing the *Ad-Vance* as it makes a run into Wilmington. Far from it; the scene is in fact off Tuskar lighthouse on the south coast of Ireland, used by Walters as a backdrop for several of his paintings. The *Ad-Vance* is depicted in the drab greys of a blockade runner, with a turtle deck installed at the bow to help shrug off heavy seas. Flying from the masts are a flag depicting the seal of the State of North Carolina, and a red pennant with the steamer's name, *A.D. Vance*; on the ensign staff at the stern is the second national flag of the Confederate States of America.

Walters captured on canvas several vessels involved in the American Civil War which had connections to his home town of Liverpool. These included the blockade runner *Banshee* and the cruiser CSS *Florida*, both depicted at sea, these two paintings are now in the Merseyside Maritime Museum in Liverpool. Like many of the vessels depicted in Walters' paintings, those vessels had been built in that city, and he had easy access to the docks and wharfs to study his subjects.

Detail of Samuel Walters' painting: the prow with a demi-man *figurehead (possibly of Colin Campbell, Lord Clyde) and the wave-breaking turtle deck on the right.*

© CSG CIC Glasgow Museums Collection

From the foremast flies a flag featuring the seal of the State of North Carolina.

© CSG CIC Glasgow Museums Collection

The painting had originally been attributed by museum staff to the famous Scottish maritime artist William Clark who, from his home in Greenock, painted many ships built on the banks of the Clyde. It had been believed, wrongly, that this painting was Clark's painting of the steamer before its blockade-running days, when it was known as the *Lord Clyde*. Clark's painting was completed in 1862, just after the steamer's launch, before it left for Bermuda. That painting, yet another wonderful depiction of the steamer, was in fact owned by the Civil War historian and collector Charles Peery, and is now in the South Carolina Confederate Relic Room and Military Museum.

The painting of the *Ad-Vance* held by Glasgow Museums was positively identified by the Samuel Walters historian A.S. Davidson while researching his book *Maritime Art and the Clyde* (2001). Complicating the final decision was that the painting is unsigned, a common Walters trait. It is also undated, and does not appear in any inventory of Walters' works, but it probably dates to 1864, when it is possible that Walters saw the steamer in Liverpool's Sandon dock during its visit to the city for repairs in May and June. The use of the incorrect name of the ship, *A.D.Vance*, on the red pennant could be an indication of this; the local newspapers had reported the steamer's arrival using this version of the name, and Walters

From the stern flies the second national flag of the Confederate States of America.

© CSG CIC Glasgow Museums Collection

A figure, possibly the master by the look of the coat and hat, stands between the wheelhouse and the paddle box. Was this intended to represent Wyllie?

© CSG CIC Glasgow Museums Collection

could have used it on his painting. It was the only time that the *Ad-Vance* ever visited the Mersey and thus Walters' only opportunity to see the steamer at first hand and up close.

The history of the painting's ownership is clouded as well. When George Porteous Scott gifted it to Glasgow Museums, accompanying it was a photograph of Wyllie (dated 'about 1862') and a copy of Wyllie's 1862 master's competency certificate. After Wyllie's death in 1902 these items appear to have passed to Eleanor, his widow. Though no painting was itemised in Wyllie's will, it might have formed part of the larger, general listing of 'household furniture'; as the Wyllies had no children of their own these items stayed with Eleanor to be passed on through her family. Eleanor moved to Glasgow sometime after Joannes' death to be nearer her sister Agnes, George's mother. After Eleanor's death in 1911, these family heirlooms appear to have stayed in Glasgow with Agnes. When Agnes herself passed away in 1916, within a year the painting and other items were donated to Glasgow Museums by George.

Another mystery is exactly when Wyllie acquired the painting. It would have to have been some time after he had returned from sea, in late 1867. Details in the Glasgow Museums

24	a	Photograph of Captain Joannes Wyllie who ran the American Blockade 31 times successfully, once in daylight, which is the world's record.
	b	Certificate of competency as Master granted to Joannes Wyllie Twentieth day of August 1862.
	c	Oil painting of steam ship "A. D. Vance", Commander Joannes Wyllie. The painting of the celebrated blockade runner is is respectfully presented by his sincere friend Charles E. S. Rose.

The entry for the donation of the painting (item **c***). This brief mention is the only direct connection between Wyllie and Charles E.S. Rose. The 31 successful runs in the listing of photograph* **a** *would have been claimed by the donor, who appears to have inflated the number, as research has established this at 19.*

© CSG CIC Glasgow Museums Collection

accession register, recorded at the time of the donation, suggest that it was presented to him by a close friend by the name of Charles E.S. Rose.

Although we do not know for sure, it is most likely that this friend was Charles Edward Stuart Rose, a Scottish-born, Liverpool-based plumber and hydraulic engineer, who lived at 46 Boundary Street, the same street in which Wyllie had lived. In the early 1860s Rose was a partner in the firm Wilson and Rose, listed in the 1860 Liverpool Street Directory as 'Ironmonger, Brassfounders and ship painters'. In 1864 the partnership was dissolved and Rose continued on his own as a 'Brassfounder and tin and coopersmith, iron monger and plumber'.

Rose's company was one of those contracted to undertake repairs on the *Ad-Vance* in 1864 during its trip to Liverpool. The disbursements for the steamer survive, and indicate that Rose paid £968 for 'brass and iron work' for the steamer. Rose could have commissioned Walters to complete the painting in the summer of 1864 as a thank you to his friend for gaining the contract. Rose was unfortunately declared bankrupt in December 1868, and he died in 1870, aged 40.

There is evidence that Wyllie owned the painting by 1870. This evidence comes in the form of a photographic print of the painting, donated to the Glasgow Museums in 2018. A letter that accompanied the print, written in 1937, outlines how Captain Wyllie himself had given this print to the letter's writer, a William G. Pirie. In that letter, Pirie wrote to his grandson, who he was passing on the print, saying that the print was:

> given to me by Captain Wylie himself in memory of his prowess at sea during the American Civil War. He was a typical seafaring gentleman, and made a small fortune running the blockade with food etc. He was a brave fellow and in the nature of his career was twice caught, but always when he was leaving port with nothing on board.

Pirie was born in 1860, and in the 1871 census is listed as being at school in Dysart. A print of this type in 1871 would have been a gift indeed, as photography was still both exclusive and expensive. Wyllie's tales of adventure on the high seas would have fascinated the young Pirie; his letter to his grandson says that that as a boy he was 'keenly interested in all matters connected with sailing boats and ships of all sorts'. He may have attended one of Wyllie's lectures, two of which are recorded as taking place near Pirie's home while he was a student.

It is possible that Wyllie commissioned a local photographer to make copies of his painting to hand out as souvenirs at his lectures, but unfortunately there is no photographer's stamp on the back of the print to indicate when and where it was produced.

There is no doubt that the painting is the finest illustration of the *Ad-Vance* to have been completed and would have sat proudly on a wall in Wyllie's farmhouse, a fond reminder of days gone by and his adventures during the Civil War.

APPENDIX 6

LECTURES GIVEN BY JOANNES WYLLIE

Joannes Wyllie was a prolific speaker who delivered at least 26 lectures over a 33-year period, from 1869 to 1902. The first was given two years after he returned from sea, while the last took place just a month before his death. The title for his lectures was always *Reminiscences of Sea Life, and Running the Blockade* or a close variation.

All of his lectures took place near his home, and all within the county of Fife. Some were delivered in tiny school halls, others in grand theatres. Contemporary newspaper articles reported that his lectures were always well attended with the crowds enthralled by the captain's recollections of his stories of the sea and the blockade. When Wyllie spoke it was nearly always in aid of a local charity or good cause, and given freely. The one exception was one of his last lectures, given in November 1901 at the Adam Smith Hall in Kirkcaldy in front of his largest audience. It was recorded that by this time Wyllie was struggling as a farmer, and in thanks for his years of charitable offerings the proceeds were given to him.

The table and map give the exact dates, locations and venues for all of Wyllie's known lectures.

Lectures given by Joannes Wyllie, 1869–1902

	Date	Town	Venue	*In aid of*
1	17 December 1869	Sinclairtown	St Clairtown School	Improvements to school
2	2 January 1874	Gallatown	Gallatown South Public School	Supplying coal to the poor
3	27 January 1874	Thornton	Thornton Schoolroom	*Not listed*
4	27 February 1874	Markinch	Town Hall (Markinch)	Markinch Public Library

Lectures given by Joannes Wyllie, 1869–1902 (cont.)

	Date	Town	Venue	*In aid of*
5	18 December 1878	Coaltown of Balgonie	Coaltown of Balgonie Hall	The poor of Coaltown of Balgonie
6	26 January 1883	Coaltown of Balgonie	Coaltown of Balgonie Hall	The poor of the district
7	5 February 1884	Methil	Methil Parish Church	*Not listed*
8	13 March 1884	Leslie	Leslie Town Hall	Leslie YMCA
9	16 October 1885	Pathhead	Pathhead Public Halls	Reducing the debt of Sinclairtown Church
10	18 December 1885	Dysart	Normand Memorial Hall	Dysart Mechanical Institute
11	25 November 1887	Freuchie	Lumsden Memorial Hall	*Not listed*
12	2 December 1887	Auchtermuchty	Victoria Hall	Auspices of the Reading Room Committee
13	19 December 1888	Kingskettle	Location not recorded	*Not listed*
14	20 November 1889	Boreland	Boreland Schoolroom	*Not listed*
15	13 February 1890	Falkland	Location not recorded	*Not listed*
16	5 December 1890	Boreland	Boreland Schoolroom	*Not listed*
17	10 March 1893	Thornton	Strathore School	Auspices of Dysart Landward School
18	18 December 1896	Dysart	Normand Memorial Hall	Dysart Mechanics Institute
19	19 February 1897	Gallatown	Gallatown Free Church Hall	Working Men's Institute
20	3 February 1898	Pathhead	Pathhead Public Halls	The building fund of Dysart Parish Gospel Temperance Union
21	1 February 1901	Dysart	Normand Memorial Hall	William Simpson
22	27 November 1901	Kirkcaldy	Adam Smith Hall	Joannes and Eleanor Wyllie
23	6 December 1901	Cupar	Union Street Hall	*Not listed*
24	20 December 1901	Markinch	Markinch Town Hall	*Not listed*
25	27 January 1901	Wemyss	Victoria Hall	Coaltown Brass Band
26	7 March 1902	East Wemyss	Public Hall	Lighting of the street lamps

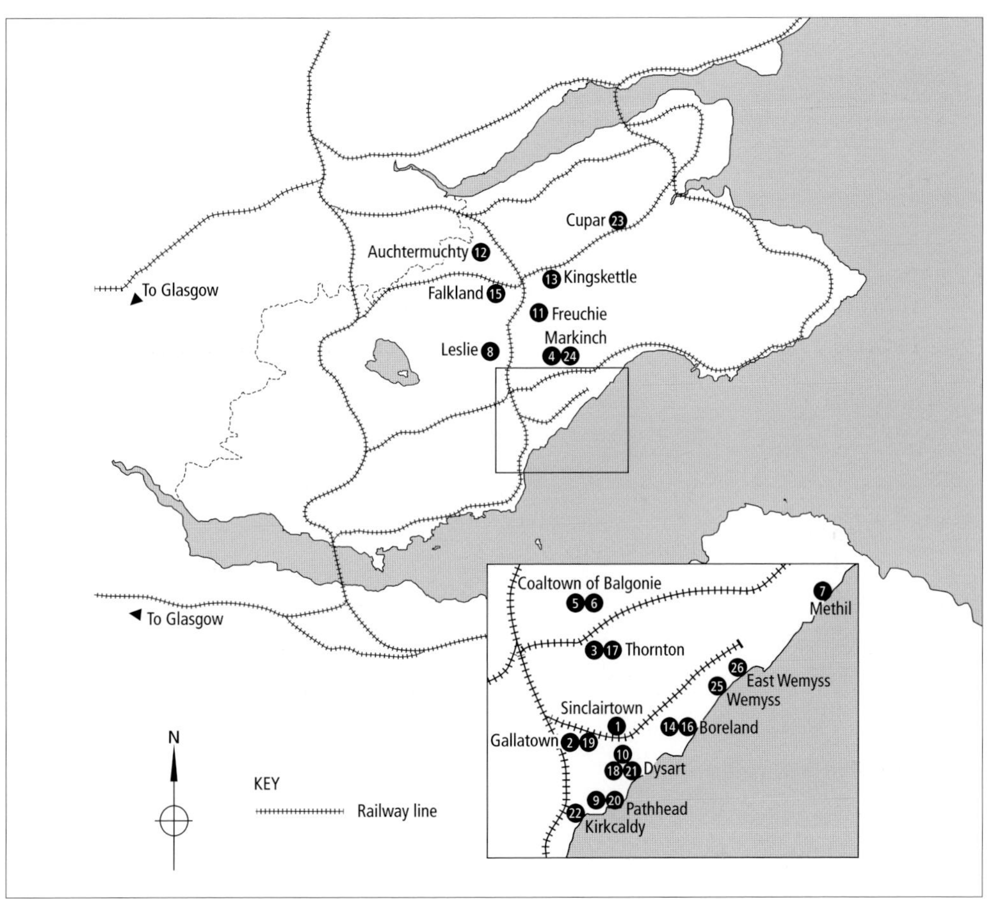

Locations of lectures given by Joannes Wyllie, 1869–1902

APPENDIX 7

Known Affiliations And Organisations

This is a list of Wyllie's known affiliations from his return to Fife in 1868 until his death in 1902, including memberships and associations, and his hosting of events and attendances. It shows that he was an active and valued member of his community, involved in many charitable events.

Educational organisations

- Student at the University of St Andrews, 1846–1849
- Teacher at Strathmiglo Subscription School 1846
- Teacher at Coaltown of Balgonie School 1849–1852
- Founder of Circulating Library at Coaltown of Balgonie, 1850
- Elected member of the Landward School Board, Dysart Parish 1870s–1890s

Agricultural organisations and events

- Dunnikier Agricultural Society 1870s
- Dysart Horticultural Society 1870s
- Kirkcaldy Naturalists Society 1880s–1890s
- Windygates Agricultural Society 1890s
- East of Scotland Union of Naturalists' Society
- Tenant farmer of the estate of the Earl of Rosslyn 1868–1902

Sporting organisations and events

- Founding member of Mitchelston Cricket Club 1870
- Hosting the annual Gallatown races and market on his land 1871, 1873, 1875
- Hosting local Gallatown gymnastic games and races 1872, 1889
- Hosting of the Gallatown 'Derby' horse race 1875, 1876

Church-related organisations and events

- Present at the ordination of Rev. Peter Anton at Dysart Parish Church 1875
- Benefit of new church in Sinclairtown 1877
- Present at laying of cornerstone of new Established Church, Sinclairtown 1877
- Search for new minister at *Quoad Sacra* Church of Sinclairtown 1880
- Convenor of the committee to find new reverend of the Sinclairtown Established Church 1883
- Other activities including events to help the poor, Sunday School services, benefit concerts, annual Christmas events for children, and the welcoming of new ministers.

Political events

Wyllie was listed as being in attendance at numerous meetings (known as hustings) for political candidates over the years 1868–1901. Some of these were for candidates for the Conservative Party, others for the Scottish Liberal Unionist Party.

Other local groups and activities

- Masonic Lodge St Clair of Dysart No 520 from 1876
- Acted in private theatricals at Dunnikier House, Kirkcaldy 1882
- Dysart Third Ward Old Folks Festival 1889–1901
- Attended the opening of the Adam Smith Hall, Kirkcaldy 1899

SELECTED BIBLIOGRAPHY

PRIMARY SOURCES

Australia

State Library of Victoria
Pictures Collection

Bermuda

Bermuda Archives, Hamilton
Bermuda Custom Manifests
St George's departure and arrival lists

Canada

Maritime History Archive, Memorial University of Newfoundland
Crew lists of British-registered vessels, 1857–1942

Ireland

National Archives of Ireland, Dublin
Shipping agreements and crew lists 1863–1921
Transatlantic Passenger Lists arriving from the United States and Canada, 1858–1870.

United Kingdom

British Library
The British Newspaper Archive
D.C. Thomson & Company, Dundee
Publication archive for *People's Friend*, *Weekly News* and *Weekly Welcome*

Fife Archives/Museums
Listings of known Fife photographers and *Carte de Visite* collection

Glasgow Museums
Accession register for transport and technology collection
Joannes Wyllie and Samuel Walters archive documents, 1917.24.a-c
William Pirie papers, T.2018.50

Mitchell Library, Glasgow
Glasgow Collection papers

The National Archives of the United Kingdom, Record Office, Kew, London
Crew lists and agreements and logbooks of merchant ships after 1861
Merchant seaman records 1858–1917

National Library of Scotland, Edinburgh
Newspaper and periodical archive

National Maritime Museum, Greenwich, London, England
Crew lists, agreements and official logs of British-registered ships;
masters', mates', engineers' and skippers' certificates.

National Museums Liverpool
Customs bills of entry, Liverpool
Ship registry for the port of Liverpool

National Records of Scotland, Edinburgh
Census returns
Legal records (wills and inventories)
Statutory registers (births, marriages deaths)
Valuation Rolls

Unpublished materials held in private collections
Minutes of Masonic Lodge St Clair of Dysart, No 520

United States

Boston Athenaeum
Journal of the House of Commons of the General Assembly of the State of North Carolina, at its adjourned session, 1864.

Cornell University
Official Records of the Union and Confederate Navies in

the War of the Rebellion Making of America website www.collections.library.cornell.edu/moa_new/index.html

Library of Congress, Washington, DC

Chronicling America: Historic American Newspapers Digital Collections

National Archives at Boston, Massachusetts

Prize court documents relating to the adjudication of the steamer *Deer*

National Archives at New York City

Prize court documents relating to the adjudication of the steamer *Ad-Vance*

National Archives, Washington, DC

Vessel papers for steamer *Advance*

State Archives of North Carolina, Raleigh, North Carolina

John Julius Guthrie papers

North Carolina Military Collection, Quartermaster Records

North Carolina Treasurer and Comptroller Records

Zebulon B. Vance Papers

University of North Carolina, Chapel Hill

James P. Beckwith Papers

University of Virginia Library, Charlottesville

John Smith Papers

SECONDARY SOURCES

Books, journals, magazines

American Lloyd's Register of American and Foreign Shipping. New York: 1873.

Anderson, James Maitland. The Matriculation Roll of the University of St Andrews 1747–1897. Edinburgh: William Blackwood and Sons. 1895.

Anton, Peter. 'Risen from the Ranks: Captain Wyllie: The Great Scottish Blockade Runner'. *The People's Friend.* Dundee: D.C. Thompson. 1889.

Balfour, C.B. 'Notes on Newton Don and its Former Owners' *History of the Berwickshire Naturalists Club*, Vol. 14, 1895, 291–313.

Bethell, Leslie. *The Paraguayan War (1864-1870).* London: Institute of Latin American Studies. 1996.

Captains Registers of Lloyd's of London, 1851–1869. London: Lloyd's.

Carlin, Colin. *Captain James Carlin: Anglo-American Blockade Runner.* Columbia, South Carolina: University of South Carolina Press. 2017.

Carr, Dawson. *Grey Phantoms of the Cape Fear: Running the Civil War Blockade.* Winston-Salem, North Carolina: John F. Blair. 1998.

Clark, Walter. Ed. *Histories of Several Regiments and Battalions from North Carolina.* Goldsboro, North Carolina: State of North Carolina. 1901.

Cochran, Hamilton. *Blockade Runners of the Confederacy.* Indianapolis: Bobbs-Merrill. 1958.

Dautremer, Joseph. *Burma under British Rule.* London: T. Fisher Unwin. 1913.

Davidson, A.S. *Marine Art and the Clyde: 100 Years of Sea, Sail and Steam.* Upton, Wirral: Jones-Sands Publishing. 2001.

---. *Samuel Walters – Marine Artist: Fifty Years of Sea, Sail and Steam.* Coventry: Jones-Sands Publishing. 1992.

Dictionary of American Fighting Ships. Washington: Navy Department. 1959.

Fonvielle, Chris Eugene. *The Wilmington Campaign: Last Departing Rays of Hope.* Mechanicsburg: Pennsylvania. Stackpole Books. 2001.

Gifford, John. 'Parish of Nenthorn,' *The New Statistical Account of Scotland; Vol II Linlithgow, Haddington Berwick.* Edinburgh, Scotland: William Blackwood and Sons. 1845.

Graham, Eric. *Clyde Built: Blockade Runners, Cruisers and Armoured Rams of the American Civil War.* Edinburgh: Birlinn Ltd. 2006.

Haldane, R. and Buist, George. 'Parish of St Andrews' in *The New Statistical Account of Scotland, Vol. IX.* Edinburgh, Scotland: William Blackwood and Sons. 1845.

Hallock, Charles. 'Bermuda in Blockade Times,' *New England Magazine,* New Series Vol. 6, 1892, 337–43.

Life in Bombay and the Neighbouring Outstations. London: Richard Bentley. 1852.

Lloyd's: *see under* American *and* Captains.

Lonn, Ella. *Foreigners in the Confederacy.* Chapel Hill, North Carolina: University of North Carolina Press. 2002.

Lyndenberg, Harry Miller. *Crossing the Line: Tales of the Ceremony During Four Centuries.* New York: The New York Public Library. 1957.

McKenna, Joseph. *British Ships in the Confederate Navy.* Jefferson, North Carolina: McFarland Books. 2010.

The Mercantile Navy List and Annual Appendage to the Commercial Code of Signals for All Nations. London: Bradbury and Evans. 1861

The Mercantile Navy List and Maritime Directory. London: Bradbury and Evans. 1852–1867.

McNeil, Jim. *Masters of the Shoals: Tales of the Cape Fear Pilots Who Ran the Union Blockade.* Southport, North Carolina: Southport Historical Society. 2014

McQueen, Andrew. *Echoes of Old Clyde Paddle Wheelers.* Glasgow: Gowans & Gray, Ltd. 1924.

Murray, Rev. David. 'Parish of Dysart,' *The New Statistical Account of Scotland: Vol IX FIFE.* Edinburgh, Scotland: William Blackwood and Sons. 1845.

Oliver, William H. *Blockade Running by the State of North Carolina.* New Bern, North Carolina: publisher unknown. 1895. https://repository.duke.edu/dc/broadsides/bdsnc061830

Peters, Thelma. 'Blockade Running in the Bahamas during the Civil War'. *Tequesta – The Florida Historical Quarterly* 25, no. 1. 1946.

Scheibert, Captain Justus. *Seven Months in the Rebel States during the North American War, 1863*, translated by Joseph C. Hayes. Tuscaloosa, Alabama: Confederate Publishing Company. 1958.

Smith, John. *The Rise and Progress of the City Line.* Edinburgh: Oliver and Boyd. 1908.

Smith, John Baptist. 'The Saucy Blockade Runner'. *The Guildford Collegian* 9, no. 1. September 1896.

Smith, Myron J., Jr. *Civil War Biographies from the Western Waters.* Jefferson, North Carolina: McFarland Books. 2015.

Sprunt, James. *Chronicles of the Cape Fear River 1660–1916.* Raleigh: Edward and Broughton Printing Company. 1914.

Stuart, Meriwether. 'Dr Lugo: An Austro-Venetian Adventurer in Union Espionage'. *The Virginia Magazine of History and Biography* 90, no. 3. July 1982.

Sutherland, Daniel E. and Toutziari, Georgia. *Whistler's Mother: Portrait of an Extraordinary Life.* New Haven, CT: Yale University Press. 2018.

Taylor, Thomas E. *Running the Blockade: A Personal Narrative of Adventure, Risks and Escapes during the American Civil War.* New York: Charles Scribner's Sons. 1896.

Vandiver, Frank Everson. *Confederate Blockade Running Through Bermuda, 1861–1865: Letters and Cargo Manifests.* Austin: University of Texas Press. 1947.

Wallace, Frederick William. *Record of Canadian Shipping.* Toronto: The Munson Book Company Ltd. 1929.

Watson, William. *The Adventures of a Blockade Runner: Or Trade in Time of War.* London: T. Fisher Unwin. 1892.

Wilson, Frank I. *Sketches of Nassau: to which is added the Devil's ball-alley, an Indian Tradition.* Raleigh, North Carolina: offices of the *Raleigh Standard.* 1864.

Wise, Stephen R. *Lifeline of the Confederacy: Blockade Running During the Civil War.* Columbia: University of South Carolina Press. 1991.

NEWSPAPERS

Australia

The Age, Melbourne, Victoria
Colonial Times, Hobart Town, Tasmania
The Tasmanian Daily News, Hobart Town, Tasmania

Canada

Halifax Citizen
Halifax Morning Sun

Ireland

Cork Examiner
Freeman's Journal, Dublin
Saunders's News-Letter, Dublin

Netherlands

Algemeen Handelsblad, Amsterdam

New Zealand

Daily Southern Cross, Wellington.

United Kingdom

Bolton Chronicle, England.
Caledonian Mercury, Edinburgh, Scotland
Cardiff and Merthyr Guardian, Glamorgan, Monmouth, and Brecon Gazette, Wales
Cardiff Times, Wales
Dundee Advertiser, Scotland
Dundee Courier, Scotland
Dundee Evening Telegraph, Scotland
Evening Mail, London, England
Fife Free Press, & Kirkcaldy Guardian, Scotland
Fife Herald, Cupar, Scotland
Fifeshire Advertiser, Kirkcaldy, Scotland
Fifeshire Journal, Kirkcaldy, Scotland
Glasgow Herald, Scotland
Glasgow Morning Journal, Scotland
Glasgow Saturday Post, Scotland
Gore's Liverpool General Advertiser, England
Greenock Advertiser, Scotland
Greenock Telegraph and Clyde Shipping Gazette, Scotland
Leicester Journal, England
Leven Advertiser & Wemyss Gazette, Scotland
Liverpool Daily Post, England
Liverpool General Advertiser, England
Liverpool Mail, England
Liverpool Mercury, England
Lloyd's List, London, England
Manchester Courier and Lancashire General Advertiser, England
Morning Post, London, England
Newcastle Chronicle, England
Public Ledger and Daily Advertiser, London, England
St Andrew's Citizen, Scotland
The Scotsman, Edinburgh, Scotland
Shetland Times, Scotland
Shields Daily News, Tynemouth, England
Shipping and Mercantile Gazette, London, England
Weekly News, Dundee, Scotland
Weekly Welcome. Dundee, Scotland

United States

Brooklyn Daily Eagle, New York
Carolina Watchmen. Salisbury, North Carolina

Daily Carolina Watchman, Raleigh, North Carolina
Daily National Republican, Washington DC
Evening Star, Washington, DC
Farmer's Monthly Visitor, Concord, New Hampshire
Fayetteville Observer, North Carolina
The Framer and the Mechanic, Raleigh, North Carolina
The Morning News, Savannah, Georgia
New Orleans Daily Crescent, Louisiana
New York Daily Tribune, New York
The New York Herald, New York
The New York Times, New York
News and Observer, Raleigh, North Carolina
Times-Democrat, New Orleans, Louisiana
Times-Picayune, New Orleans, Louisiana
Washington Evening Star, Washington DC
Western Confederate, Raleigh, North Carolina
Weekly National Intelligencer, Washington DC
Western Democrat, Charlotte, North Carolina
Wilmington Journal, North Carolina

UNPUBLISHED

Watts, George P. 'Phantoms of Anglo-Confederate Commerce: an Historical and Archaeological Investigation of American Civil War Blockade Running.' PhD dissertation. University of St Andrews. 1997.

WEBSITES

American Presidency Project **www.presidency.ucsb.edu**
Ancestry **www.ancestry.co.uk**
British Library Newspaper Archive **www.britishnewspaperarchive.co.uk**
Chronicling America **www.chroniclingamerica.loc.gov**
Crew List Index Project **www.crewlist.org.uk**
Clyde Ships **www.clydeships.co.uk**
Delpher **www.delpher.nl**
Grace's Guide **www.gracesguide.co.uk**
Internet Archive **www.archive.org**
Maritime and Historical Research Service **www.maritimearchives.co.uk**
Measuring Worth **www.measuringworth.com/exchange**
Mystic Seaport Museum, Collections and Research **www.research.mysticseaport.org**
National Library of Australia, TROVE archive **www.trove.nla.gov.au**
National Library of Scotland, Map collection **www.maps.nls.uk**
Naval History and Heritage Command **www.history.navy.mil**
National Library of Scotland, street directories **www.nls.uk/family-history/directories**
National Records of Scotland **www.scotlandspeople.gov.uk**
Newspapers.com **www.newspapers.com**
NCPedia **www.ncpedia.org**
Statistical Accounts of Scotland **www.stataccscot.edina.ac.uk/static/statacc/dist/home**

Wreck site **www.wrecksite.eu/wrecksite.aspx**

ENDNOTES

Chapter One

1 Rev. John Gifford, 'Parish of Nenthorn', in *The New Statistical Account of Scotland; Vol. II Linlithgow, Haddington Berwick*. William Blackwood and Sons, Edinburgh, 1845, pp. 215–222.

2 C.B. Balfour, 'Notes on Newton Don' in *History of the Berwickshire Naturalists Club*. Henry Hunter Blair, Alnwick, 1892, pp. 296–309.

3 'Alexander Don of Newton Don, Berwickshire', The History of Parliament, accessed 19 January 2018, http://www.historyofparliamentonline.org/volume/1790–1820/member/don-alexander-1779–1826.

4 Registry of birth of John Wyllie, 10/06/1828, WYLIE, John. Old Parish Registers Birth 753/2014 Nenthorn p. 14 of 108, Crown Copyright National Records of Scotland.

5 Peter Anton, 'Risen from the Ranks: Captain Wyllie, the Great Scottish Blockade Runner', *The People's Friend*, July 1889, 404.

6 Rev. David Murray, 'Parish of Dysart', in *The New Statistical Account of Scotland; Vol. IX Fife*. William Blackwood and Sons, Edinburgh, 1845, pp. 127–145.

7 Anton, 'Risen', 404.

8 *Dublin Monitor*, 17 March 1845.

9 Anton, 'Risen', 404.

10 *Fife Herald*. Cupar, Scotland, 20 August 1846.

11 The other universities in Scotland at the time, with dates of foundation, were Glasgow (1451), Aberdeen (1495) and Edinburgh (1583).

12 Rev. R. Haldane and Rev. George Buist, 'Parish of St Andrews', in *The New Statistical Account of Scotland, Vol. IX*. William Blackwood and Sons, Edinburgh, 1845, pp. 449–497.

13 James Maitland Anderson, *The Matriculation Roll of the University of St Andrews 1747–1897*. William Blackwood and Sons, Edinburgh, 1895, *lxii*, pp. 105–106.

14 *Fife Herald*, Cupar, 7 October 1847.

15 Records of the University of St Andrews. Letter from Rev James Landall Rose, 11 October 1848.

16 *Fife Herald*, 17 January 1850.

17 *Fife Herald*, 6 February 1851.

18 *Fife Herald*, 4 September 1851.

19 *Fife Herald*, 8 January 1852.

20 *Fife Herald*, 2 January 1851.

21 *Fife Herald*, 9 January 1851.

22 *Weekly Welcome*, Dundee, Scotland, No 14, 10 June 1896.

23 Anton, 'Risen', 405.

24 *Fife Herald*, 13 May 1852.

Chapter Two

25 National Archives, Kew, England. Agreement for a Foreign Going Ship, *Hope*, 18 May 1852. BT 98 3350.

26 *Public Ledger and Daily Advertiser*, London, England, 27 May 1852.

27 'Death of a West of Scotland Ship Owner', *The Scotsman*, 20 February 1915.

28 John Smith, *The Rise and Progress of the City Line*. Oliver and Boyd, Edinburgh, 1908.

29 National Archives, Kew, England. Agreement for a Foreign Going Ship, *Hope*, 18 May 1852. BT 98 3350.

30 Peter Anton, 'Risen from the Ranks: Captain Wyllie, the Great Scottish Blockade Runner', *The People's Friend*, July 1889, 405.

31 Richard Bentley, *Life in Bombay and the Neighbouring Outstations*, 1852, pp 5–6.

32 Lloyd's List, 15 December 1852.

33 Lloyd's List, 6 April 1853.

34 Anton, 'Risen', 405.

35 *Fife Free Press & Kirkcaldy Guardian*, 30 November 1901.

36 Harry Miller Lyndenberg, *Crossing the Line: Tales of the Ceremony during Four Centuries*. The New York Public Library, New York, 1957, pp. 129–130.

37 *Greenock Advertiser*, 16 August 1853.

38 Anton, 'Risen', 405.

39 Anton, 'Risen', 405.

40 The National Archives, Kew, England. Registers of Wages & Effects of Deceased Seamen; *Class:* BT 153; Piece: 1.

41 *Fife Free Press & Kirkcaldy Guardian*, 23 November 1889.

42 Joseph Dautremer, *Burma under British Rule*. T. Fisher Unwin, London, 1916. pp. 155–157.

43 Lloyd's List, London, 3 July 1855.

44 National Maritime Museum. Greenwich, England. *Master's Certificates*.

45 Anton, 'Risen', 419.

46 *New York Daily Tribune*, 22 March 1856.

47 Anton, 'Risen', 419.

48 Lloyds List, London, 19 March 1856.

49 National Museums Liverpool, England. Bills of Entry, Liverpool Customs, 2 April 1856.

50 Frederick William Wallace, *Record of Canadian Shipping*. The Munson Book Company Ltd., Toronto, 1929, p. 134.

51 *Liverpool Daily Post*, 22 May 1856.

52 First Mate Competency test application for Joannes Wyllie. List of testimonials and Statement of Service from time of first going to sea. Liverpool, 1858.

53 *Liverpool Daily Post*, 25 September 1856.

54 *The Mercantile Navy List and Annual Appendage to the Commercial Code of Signals for All Nations*. Bradbury and Evans, Whitefriars, London, 1861, pp. 12–14.

55 *Liverpool Daily Post*, 29 October 1856.

56 *The Age*, Melbourne, 14 March 1857.

57 National Archives, Kew, England. Births aboard the *Indian Queen*. Registers of Births, Deaths and Marriages of Passengers at Sea. BT 158.

58 'Sir John Batty Tuke (1835–1913)', Royal College of Physicians of Edinburgh, https://www.rcpe.ac.uk/heritage/art/tuke-sir-john-batty-1835-1913 < accessed csp 24/03/2021>

59 *Daily Southern Cross*, Wellington, New Zealand, 10 April 1857.

60 Anton, 'Risen', 420.

61 'Family Notices' *The Tasmanian Daily News (Hobart Town, Tas: 1855–1858)* 1 May 1857: 2. http://nla.gov.au/nla.news-article202989502 <accessed csp 24 March 2021>

62 'Shipping Intelligence', *Colonial Times* (Hobart, Tas: 1828–1857) 9 May 1857: 2 <http://nla.gov.au/nla.news-article8781937 . <accessed csp 24/03/2021>

63 Anton, 'Risen', 420.

64 Anton, 'Risen', 420.

65 Ancestry.com. *UK Roll of the Indian Medical Service, 1615–1930*. Roll of the Indian Medical Service, Wellcome Library, London, England.

66 *Leicester Journal*, Leicester, England, 1 January 1858.

67 *Bolton Chronicle*, Bolton, England, 17 April 1858.

68 Anton, 'Risen', 420.

69 *Ibid.*

70 *Liverpool Daily Post*, 17 September 1860.

71 *Liverpool General Advertiser*, 11 October 1860.

72 *Liverpool Daily Post*, 26 October 1860.

73 National Maritime Museum. Agreement for a Foreign Going Ship, *Indian Queen*, 25 October 1856. National Archives, Kew, England. Agreement for a Foreign Going Ship, *Hope*, 9 September 1861.

74 National Maritime Museum. Agreement for a Foreign Going Ship and logbook, *Hope*, 11 February 1861.

75 *Caledonian Mercury*, Edinburgh, Scotland, 30 July 1861.

76 National Maritime Museum. Logbook of Foreign Going Ship, *Hope*, 22 July 1861.

77 *Leeds Mercury*, Leeds, England, 1 January 1862.

78 *Liverpool Mercury*, 6 January 1862.

79 *New York Daily Tribune*, New York, USA, 5 February 1862. Library of Congress, Chronicling America https://chroniclingamerica.loc.gov/ .

80 *New York Herald*, 15 March 1862.

81 *Public Ledger and Daily Advertiser*, London, England, 5 April 1862.

82 *Liverpool Daily Post*, 21 April 1862.

83 *Liverpool Daily Post*, 5 May 1862.

Chapter Three

84 Abraham Lincoln: 'Proclamation 81 – Declaring a Blockade of Ports in Rebellious States', 19 April 1861. *The American Presidency Project* online, by Gerhard Peters and John T. Woolley, http://www.presidency.ucsb.edu/ws/?pid=70101.

85 Charles Hallock, *Bermuda and the Blockade*. Boston, Massachusetts: New England Magazine Company, 1892, 337. https://archive.org/details/bermudainblockad00hall . <accessed csp 24/03/2021>

86 Thomas E. Taylor, *Running the Blockade: A Personal Narrative of Adventure, Risks and Escapes during the American Civil War*. New York: Charles Scribner's Sons, 1896, pp. 86–87.

87 As many as 3,000 Scottish sailors were involved in blockade running, according to Dr Eric Graham.

88 Stephen R. Wise, *Lifeline of the Confederacy*, University of South Carolina Press, Columbia, South Carolina, 1988, pp. 98–111.

89 *Wilmington Journal*, 22 March 1862.

90 *Liverpool Mercury*, 3 May 1862.

91 *Liverpool Daily Post*, 15 May 1862.

92 *War of Rebellion: Official Records of the Union and Confederate Navies*. Government Printing Office,

Washington, 1921); Series I, Vol. XIII, pp. 331–332. Listed after this as *O.R.N.*

93 National Archives, Kew, England. Agreement and Account of Crew for a Foreign Going Ship, Steamer *Bonita*, 4 September 1862, BT 99/128.

94 *Liverpool Mercury*, 9 September 1862.

95 The cargo also contained a quantity of quinine, as reported in the *Nassau Guardian*,13 October 1862.

96 Wyllie states in the article that this ship was the *Ad-Vance* and not *Bonita*. The *Ad-Vance* would be Wyllie's first true blockade-running vessel, and it would not sail for the blockade until May 1863. The details in this first account match the *Bonita's* progress exactly from Liverpool to Nassau, while the *Ad-Vance* would make from Glasgow to Bermuda. This might be a confusion between Wyllie and the author, but it should not take away from the description of the voyage, as almost all major details in the *People's Friend* article can be proven with primary sources, including the voyage of the *Bonita*.

97 National Archives, Kew, England. Agreement and Account of Crew for a Foreign Going Ship, Steamer *Bonita*, 4 September 1862.

98 *New York Herald*, 2 November 1862.

99 *O.R.N.*, Series I, Vol. XIII, p. 445.

100 Sometimes spelled 'Whyte'.

101 Hamilton Cochran, *Blockade Runners of the Confederacy*, Bobbs-Merrill, Indianapolis, 1958, p. 172.

102 *Fife Free Press & Kirkcaldy Guardian*, 30 November 1901.

103 *Liverpool Customs Bill of Entry*. Bill A. No 13603, 24 December 1862, National Museums Liverpool.

104 State of North Carolina Archive. Governor Zebulon Vance Papers. Letter to Governor Vance from Thomas Crossan, 7 March 1863.

105 'Royal Netherlands Steamship Company', The Ships List http://www.theshipslist.com/ships/lines/knsm.shtml . <accessed csp 24/03/2021>

106 *Liverpool Mail*, 28 February 1863.

107 In the entry for Joannes Wyllie in Lloyd's Captain Register 1851–1869, he is listed as master of the *Bonita* in 1862 and *Lord Clyde* in 1863. The register does not include any voyages when the individual was qualified as master but served as mate, but Wyllie does not have such a voyage entry between these two ships.

108 State of North Carolina Archive, Zebulon Vance Papers, GP 182 Vance Papers, Steamer *Advance*, Letter to Governor Vance from John White.

109 State of North Carolina Archive, Governor Zebulon Vance Papers, Agreement between John White and Alexander Collie, 27 October 1863.

110 *Greenock Telegraph and Clyde Shipping Gazette*, 1 November 1862.

111 *Greenock Telegraph and Clyde Shipping Gazette*, 27 December 1862.

112 Clark's painting of the *Lord Clyde* was once owned by Charles Perry, a noted Civil War historian and collector. In 2001 he sold his vast collection, including many blockade-related items, to the State of South Carolina.

113 *Greenock Telegraph and Clyde Shipping Gazette*, 4 October 1862.

114 *O.R.N.*, Series I, Vol. XIV, pp. 234–235.

115 The listed sale price was given as £35,000 in a letter by John White to Governor Vance.

116 Andrew McQueen, *Echoes of Old Clyde Paddle Wheelers*, Gowans & Gray Ltd, Glasgow, 1924, p. 163.

117 Wise, *Lifeline of the Confederacy*, p. 304.

118 *The Scotsman*, Edinburgh, 9 May 1863.

119 *Greenock Advertiser*, 7 July 1863.

120 National Archives of Ireland, Dublin. Agreement for a Foreign Going Ship, *Lord Clyde*, 21 May 1863.

121 *Dundee Advertiser*, 1 May 1863, and *Dundee Advertiser*, 11 September 1863.

122 The Abden Ship Yard, as Key's yard was known, launched its first ship in 1864. Over 100 ships were built there until its final closure in 1920.

123 *The State – Down Home in North Carolina*, Vol. 35 No. 11, 1 November 1967.

124 *Brooklyn Daily Eagle*, 18 May 1863.

125 'Thomas Morrow Crossan', Dictionary of North Carolina Biography, https://www.ncpedia.org/biography/crossan-thomas-morrow . <accessed csp 24/03/2021>

126 *Dictionary of American Fighting Ships*, Navy Department, Washington, 1959, p. 267.

127 'CSS *Warren Winslow*', North Carolina Squadron Ships, https://northcarolinasquadron.wordpress.com/

128 The prize court document held at the National Archives of the United States at New York listed 21 May 1864.

129 *Greenock Advertiser*, 23 May 1863.

130 *Glasgow Morning Journal*, 26 May 1863.

131 *Greenock Telegraph and Clyde Shipping Gazette*, 30 May 1863.

132 *Cardiff Times*, 29 May 1863.

133 *Cardiff and Merthyr Guardian, Glamorgan, Monmouth, and Brecon Gazette*, 29 May 1863.

134 *Cardiff and Merthyr Guardian, Glamorgan, Monmouth, and Brecon Gazette*, 5 June 1863.

135 'Charles Dexter Cleveland 1802–1869', Dickinson College, http://archives.dickinson.edu/people/charles-dexter-cleveland-1802-1869 <accessed csp 24/03/2021>

136 Published again by *The New York Times*, 17 July 1863.

137 William Henry Seward, US Secretary of State, and Gideon Welles, US Secretary of the Navy.

138 *Liverpool Mercury*, 9 June 1863.

139 *Cardiff and Merthyr Guardian*, 22 May 1863.
140 *Greenock Telegraph and Clyde Shipping Gazette*, 27 June 1863.
141 *Cardiff and Merthyr Guardian*, 5 June 1863.
142 *The New York Times*, 17 July 1863.
143 Walter Clark, ed, *Histories of the Several Regiments and Battalions from North Carolina, in the Great War 1861–'65*, State of North Carolina, Goldsboro, North Carolina. 1901.
144 *Fayetteville Observer*, North Carolina, 29 June 1863.
145 *Wilmington Journal*, North Carolina, 2 July 1863.
146 Note that the name reported on its first arrival was *Clyde*, not *Ad-Vance.*
147 William H.C. Whiting, commander of Fort Fisher at the mouth of the Cape Fear River.
148 James Sprunt, *Chronicles of the Cape Fear River 1660–1916*, Edward and Broughton Printing Company, Raleigh, 1914, p. 376.
149 State of North Carolina Archive, Zebulon Vance Letter Books. Letter to John White from Zebulon Vance, 10 July 1863.
150 The listing of Wyllie's nationality varies in reports and publications, many times being listed as 'English'.

Chapter Four

151 R.L. Gray, 'The famous Confederate Blockade Runner the *Ad-Vance*', *The Farmer and Mechanic*, Raleigh, North Carolina, 22 May 1905.
152 Bermuda Archives. Manifest, Inwards for steamer *Ad-Vance* at St George's, 27 July 1863.
153 National Archives of Ireland, Dublin. Agreement and Account of Crew for a Foreign Going Ship, Steamer *Lord Clyde*, 17 January 1865. http://census.nationalarchives.ie/reels/cl/007604195_00693.pdf .
154 State of North Carolina Archive, Bills of Exchange, Joannes Wyllie, 10 August 1863. From Vance Letter Books, Military Collection, Civil War, Box 67, Folders 3 and 9.
155 Wise, *Lifeline of the Confederacy*, p. 111.
156 *Weekly National Intelligencer*, 27 August 1863.
157 Thelma Peters, 'Blockade Running in the Bahamas during the Civil War', Tequesta: *The Journal of the Historical Association of Southern Florida*; 25, no. 1, 1946. http://digitalcollections.fiu.edu/tequesta/files/1945/45_1_02.pdf <accessed csp 24 March 2021>
158 Frank Everson Vandiver, *Confederate Blockade Running Through Bermuda, 1861–1865; Letters and Cargo Manifests*. University of Texas Press, Austin, 1947, pp. 116–17.
159 State Archive of North Carolina, Vance Papers, GP168.
160 Wise, *Lifeline of the Confederacy*, pp. 124–128.
161 John Wilkinson. *Narrative of a Blockade Runner*. Sheldon & Company, New York, 1877, pp. 199–200.
162 David Winfred Gaddy, 'John Baptist Smith', NCPedia, https://www.ncpedia.org/biography/smith-john-baptist . <accessed csp 24/03/2021>
163 The crew list for the *Ad-Vance* (dated February 1864) listed the first cook as J. Venerman, born in France. This could be the 'Frenchie' referred to in Smith's account.
164 John Baptist Smith, 'The Saucy Blockade Runner', *The Guildford Collegian* 9, no. 1, September 1896: 70–74.
165 Peter Anton, 'Risen from the Ranks: Captain Wyllie, the Great Scottish Blockade Runner', *The People's Friend*, July 1889: 454.
166 Captain Justus Scheibert, *Seven Months in the Rebel States During the North American War, 1863*, trans. by Joseph C. Hayes. Confederate Publishing Company, Tuscaloosa, Alabama,1958, pp. 147–151.
167 State Archive of North Carolina, Vance Papers, Military Collection, Civil War, Box 67, Folders 3 and 9.
168 'James H. Burton', National Park Service, https://www.nps.gov/hafe/learn/historyculture/james-h-burton.htm . <accessed csp 24/03/2021>
169 Walter Clark. ed, *Histories of Several Regiments and Battalions from North Carolina.* State of North Carolina, Goldsboro, North Carolina 1901, p. 341.
170 Diary of James H. Burton, Entry for 9 October 1863. CSA Armory website, http://www.csarmory.org/index.html . <accessed csp 24/03/2021>
171 *Ibid.*
172 State Archive of North Carolina, Vance Papers, GP 170, Steamer *Advance.*
173 Journal of the House of Commons of the General Assembly of the State of North Carolina, at its adjourned session, 1864. Governor's Message, Document 7. W.W. Holden, printer to the State, Raleigh, North Carolina, 1864), p. 5.
174 Daniel E. Sutherland and Georgia Toutziari, *Whistler's Mother: Portrait of an Extraordinary Life*. Yale University Press, New Haven, Connecticut, 2018, pp. 130, 215.
175 Richard W. Lobst, 'Thomas Morrow Crossan', NCPedia, https://www.ncpedia.org/biography/crossan-thomas-morrow . <accessed csp 24-Mar-21>
176 Myron J. Smith Jr, *Civil War Biographies from the Western Waters*. McFarland Books, Jefferson, North Carolina, 2015, p. 101.
177 State Archive of North Carolina. Vance Papers, GLB 50, Steamer *Advance.*
178 State Archives of North Carolina. John Julius Guthrie Papers. 'A Brief History of a Noble Life: Captain Guthrie's Service in the Navy' James Barron Hope, 1877.
179 State Archive of North Carolina. Vance Papers, GLB 50, Steamer *Advance.*
180 *Western Democrat*, 24 November 1863.
181 *Western Democrat*, 1 December 1863.
182 *O.R.N.* Series 1, Vol. XVII, p. 872.

183 Wise, *Lifeline of the Confederacy*, p. 157.
184 State Archive of North Carolina, Vance Papers, GLB 50, Steamer *Advance*. Letter to Power Low & Co from Governor Vance, 6 January 1864.
185 Bermuda Archives. Manifest, Inwards for steamer *Ad Vance* at St George's. 9 January 1864.
186 Wise, *Lifeline of the Confederacy*, pp. 236–237, 278–281.
187 John Baptist Smith, 'The Stranded Blockade Runner', John Smith Papers, Accession #7054, Special Collections, University of Virginia Library, Charlottesville, Va.
188 *Fayetteville Observer*, 1 February 1864.
189 National Archives of the United States, Washington, DC. Vessel papers for steamer *Advance*, Microfilm collection, M909 Roll 1. Invoice from Thomas E. Roberts to Power Low & Company, 1 February 1864.
190 *O.R.N.* Series 1, Vol. IX, p. 413.
191 *Glasgow Saturday Post*, 20 February 1864.
192 State Archives of North Carolina, Vance Papers GLB 50. Letter to Thomas Boykin from Governor Vance, 1 February 1864.
193 State Archive of North Carolina. John Julius Guthrie papers, Box 4 of 4. Officers and Crew List of the *AD. Vance.*
194 Eric J. Graham, *Clyde Built: Blockade Runners, Cruisers and Armoured Rams of the American Civil War*. Birlinn, Edinburgh, Scotland, 2006, p. 3.
195 Bermuda Archives. Manifest Inwards for steamer *Ad Vance* at St George's. 9 February 1864.
196 Wise, *Lifeline of the Confederacy*, p. 150.
197 This is the disbursement for the steamer without the inclusion of the 5 per cent commission charged by Hurst, which brought the total to £3,880 1s 8d.
198 State Archives of North Carolina. Treasury and Comptroller of North Carolina Collection, 26C Box 952c. Disbursements of the steamer *Ad-Vance*, 10 February 1864.
199 *Wilmington Journal*, 3 March 1864.
200 State Archives of North Carolina. Governor Vance Papers, GP177. Letter to Power, Low & Company from Thomas Boykin, Purser *Ad-Vance*, 10 May 1864.
201 State Archive of North Carolina. Governor Vance Papers, GLB 50. Letter to Power, Low & Company from Governor Vance, 1 February 1864.
202 *Western Democrat*, 16 February 1864.
203 State Archives of North Carolina. Governor Vance Papers, Guthrie Papers, Box 3. Letter to John Julius Guthrie from Governor Vance, 26 February 1864.
204 State Archives of North Carolina. Governor Vance Papers, GP 174. Letter to Thomas Boykin from Governor Vance, 29 February 1864.

Chapter Five

205 State Archives of North Carolina. Governor Vance Papers, GP 174. Letter to Joannes Wyllie from John Julius Guthrie, 29 February 1864.
206 State Archives of North Carolina. Governor Vance Papers, GP 174. Letter to Governor Vance from Thomas Boykin, 29 February 1864.
207 *Ibid.*
208 One of the items sold on at this auction has ended up in the collection of the State of North Carolina. It once adorned the interiors of the governor's mansion in Raleigh. With its carved dolphins and floral designs, its high luxury would indicate it was in the first-class passenger saloon. Why it, and all the other items on sale, had not been removed earlier to allow for greater cargo loads remains a mystery.
209 Wise, *Lifeline of the Confederacy*, p. 16.
210 Jim McNeil, *Masters of the Shoals: Tales of the Cape Fear Pilots Who Ran the Union.* Southport Historical Society, Southport, North Carolina, 2014, pp. 93–95.
211 *Ibid.*
212 State Archives of North Carolina. Governor Vance Papers, GP 175. Letter to Governor Vance from Power, Low & Company, 1 March 1864.
213 State Archives of North Carolina. Governor Vance Papers, GP 175. Letter to Power, Low & Co from Joannes Wyllie, 11 March 1864.
214 'Franklin Inge, Wilson' Dictionary of North Carolina Biography, https://www.ncpedia.org/biography/wilson-franklin-inge . <accessed csp 24/03/2021>
215 These were John Carrow, fourth officer; William H. Jones, boatswain; P.G. Gilligan, seaman; A. Scholar, officer's steward; and A.S. Scholar, storekeeper. All were from North Carolina. All identified from crew list of February 1864.
216 Frank I. Wilson, *Sketches of Nassau: to which is added the Devil's ball-alley, an Indian tradition.* Offices of the Raleigh *Standard*, Raleigh, North Carolina, 1864, p. 33.
217 State Archives of North Carolina. John Julius Guthrie Papers, Box 4. Letter to John Julius Guthrie from Frank I. Wilson, 6 April 1864.
218 Wise, *Lifeline of the Confederacy*, p. 146.
219 State Archives of North Carolina. Governor Vance Papers, GP176. Telegram to Governor Vance from Christopher Memminger, 13 April 1864.
220 State Archives of North Carolina. Governor Vance Papers, GP 175. Letter to Governor Vance from Captain Wyllie at Nassau, 21 April 1864.
221 State Archives of North Carolina. Treasury and Comptroller of North Carolina Collection, 26C Box 952c. Disbursements of the steamer *Ad-Vance*, 29 April 1864.
222 *Halifax Citizen*, Halifax, Nova Scotia, 28 April 1864.
223 State Archives of North Carolina. Governor Vance Papers, GP 177. Letter to Governor Vance from Joseph Flanner, London, 14 May 1864.

224 State Archives of North Carolina. Governor Vance Papers, GP 178. Letter to Governor Vance from Joseph Flanner, London, 11 June 1864.
225 *Manchester Courier and Lancashire General Advertiser*, 18 May 1864.
226 *Gore's General Liverpool Advertiser*, 19 May 1864.
227 State Archives of North Carolina. Treasury and Comptroller of North Carolina Collection, 26C Box 952c. Disbursement Account of the Steamer *Ad-Vance* at Liverpool, 30 June 1864.
228 There were several crew members listed with their first name beginning with C in a crew list compiled on 25 June 1864, just as the *Ad-Vance* was ready to sail from Liverpool. The most senior of these was Charles Harris, first engineer, but also C.Y. Neal (bo'sun), C. Roberts (sailor), C. McQuestin (oiler), and C. Aldrith (boiler maker).
229 National Archives of the United States, New York. Prize court documents from the steamer *A.D. Vance*. Letter from Charlie to an unidentified acquaintance, 11 June 1864.
230 State Archives of North Carolina. Governor Vance Papers, GP 178. Letter to Governor Vance from Joseph Flanner, London, 11 June 1864.
231 *Southern Reporter and Cork Commercial Courier*, Ireland, 1 July 1864.
232 State Archives of North Carolina. Governor Vance papers, GP 178. Letter from Joseph Flanner at Queenstown, Ireland, to Governor Vance, 29 June 1864.
233 Wise, *Lifeline of the Confederacy*, pp. 276–281.
234 *O.R.N.* Series I, Vol. X, p. 438.
235 Vandiver, *Confederate Blockade Running*, p. 137.
236 The Bill of Health and Clearance forms are found in the prize court documents of the *A.D. Vance* taken from the steamer after its capture. They are held at the National Archives of the United States, New York.
237 Diary of Mary White, in the James P. Beckwith Papers, #3853, Southern Historical Collection, the Wilson Library, University of North Carolina at Chapel Hill.
238 National Archives of the United States, New York. Prize court documents from the steamer *A.D. Vance*. Report and Manifest of the Steamer *Ad-Vance*, 19 August 1864.
239 State Archives of North Carolina. Governor Vance Papers, GP 179. Letter from John White aboard the S.S. *Ad-Vance*, to Governor Vance, 1 September 1864.
240 This is in reference to the famous horse race run at Epsom Downs, England. Barclay & Perkin was a famous brewery in England at the time.
241 Peter Anton, 'Risen from the Ranks: Captain Wyllie, the Great Scottish Blockade Runner', *The People's Friend*, July 1889, 454.
242 *O.R.N.* Series I, Vol X, p. 456
243 Clark, *Histories of Several Regiments and Battalions from North Carolina*, pp. 338–339.
244 Meriwether Stuart, 'Dr Lugo: An Austro-Venetian Adventurer in Union Espionage', *The Virginia Magazine of History and Biography*, 90, No. 3, July 1982: 339–358.
245 Journal of the House of Commons of the General Assembly of the state of North Carolina, at its adjourned session, 1864. Governor's Message, Document 1,W.W. Holden, printer to the State, Raleigh, North Carolina, 1864, pp. 2–3.
246 Anton, 'Risen', 454.
247 Ella Lonn, *Foreigners in the Confederacy*. University of North Carolina Press, Chapel Hill, North Carolina 2002, p. 306.
248 National Archives of the United States, New York. Prize Court Documents from the steamer *A.D. Vance*. Appeal Documented of Joannes Wyllie sworn before E. Delafield Smith, New York, 20 September 1864.
249 Details for these calculations are taken from the *Ad-Vance* prize court documents, the history of the *Santiago de Cuba* and the pay rates from the Act to Establish and Equalize the Grade of Line Officers of the United States Navy approved by President Abraham Lincoln on 16 July 1862.
250 Anton, 'Risen', 454.
251 National Archives of the United States, New York. Prize Court Documents from the Steamer *A.D. Vance*, Order of Judge Samuel Betts rescinding previous order to deliver gold chronometer to Captain Wyllie, New York, 23 September 1864.
252 Anton, 'Risen', 454.
253 *News and Observer* Raleigh, North Carolina, 1 January 1886.
254 Clark, *Histories of Several Regiments and Battalions from North Carolina*, pp. 470–472.

Chapter Six

255 Peter Anton, 'Risen from the Ranks: Captain Wyllie, the Great Scottish Blockade Runner', *The People's Friend*, July 1889, 454.
256 'Aitken and Mansel, ships built in 1864', Caledonian Maritime Research Trust, http://www.clydeships.co.uk/list.php?vessel=&year_built=1864&builder=7 . <accessed csp 24/03/2021>
257 Walter Clark, ed, *Histories of Several Regiments and Battalions from North Carolina*. State of North Carolina, Goldsboro, North Carolina, 1901, p. 379. https://archive.org/details/historiesofsever03clar .
258 Wise, *Lifeline of the Confederacy*, p. 158.
259 *Saunders's News-Letter*, Dublin, 18 November 1864, and William Pembroke Fetridge, *Harper's Handbook for Travellers in Europe*, Harper & Brothers,

New York, 1885, p. 92, https://archive.org/details/harperseuropeeast00fetr .

260 'Running the Blockade', *Cork Examiner*, 26 November 1864.

261 *Carolina Watchmen*, Salisbury, North Carolina, 21 January 1886.

262 Vandiver, *Confederate Blockade Running*, p. 144.

263 Clark, *Histories*, pp. 379–381.

264 Vandiver, *Confederate Blockade Running*, p. 146.

265 This is in reference to the paddle steamer *Stag* built by Bowdler, Chafer and Company of Seacombe (Liverpool) in 1864, not the 1853 Denny Brothers vessel of the same name.

266 These were the *Palmetto State*, *Chicora* and *Charleston*, which were scuttled and burned by retreating Confederate forces on the night of 18 February 1865.

267 Anton, 'Risen', 471.

268 Named for John Newland Maffitt, who surveyed this channel while working in Charleston harbour in 1854.

269 'Catskill I (monitor)'. *Dictionary of American Naval Fighting Ships, Navy History and Heritage Command*, https://www.history.navy.mil/research/histories/ship-histories/danfs/c/catskill-i.html .<accessed csp 24/03/2021>

270 *O.R.N.* Series I, Vol. 16, pp. 254–255.

271 *The New York Herald*, 28 February 1865.

272 Anton, 'Risen', 471.

273 Ranger is listed as 33 years old, born in Ireland and a resident of Nova Scotia as of 1865.

274 Anton, 'Risen', 471.

275 'Abraham Lincoln: Executive Order—Ordering the Arrest and Designation as Prisoners of War All Persons Engaged in Intercourse or Trade with the Insurgents by Sea', 14 March 1865. Online, by Gerhard Peters and John T. Woolley, *The American Presidency Project*. http://www.presidency.ucsb.edu/ws/?pid=70081.

276 Anton, 'Risen', 471.

277 Anton, 'Risen', 471.

278 *Boston Evening Transcript*, Boston, Massachusetts, 9 March 1865.

279 *The New York Herald* editions from around that date lists numerous steamers which could have been Wyllie's.

280 A full list of the ferries can be found on contemporary maps held by the New York Public Library. Lionel Pincus and Princess Firyal Map Division, the New York Public Library. 'New York city map', New York Public Library Digital Collections. http://digitalcollections.nypl.org/items/9ea0c39c-cad4-4cd3-e040-e00a18066f50 . <accessed csp 24 March 2021>

281 Edward S. Knapp, 'French's Hotel, New York City', *Stamps*, 14 October 1933, 72, and Wilson's Business Directory of New York City, 1 January 1864, pp. 242–244.

282 It is not known if this captain would be a passenger on the steamer, or just visiting. There is another ship master listed on the passenger list of the *United Kingdom*, 'Capt. Crabb', who could have been a Nicolas Gibbs Crabb, who was on board ships in the West Indies during the Civil War, but it is not known if he was a blockade runner in any context.

283 Anton, 'Risen', 472.

284 National Archives of Ireland, Dublin. Passenger List of the steamer *United Kingdom*, New York to Glasgow, 17 April 1865.

285 Anton, 'Risen', 472.

286 Lloyd's Captains Register 1851–1869, and Lloyd's List.

Chapter Seven

287 Wise, *Lifeline of the Confederacy*, p. 322.

288 Entry for R.A.S. Pittman, Lloyd's Captains Register, 1851–1869.

289 Maritime History Archive. Agreement and Account of Crew for a Foreign Going Ship, *Carolina*, 26 February 1866.

290 National Archives and Records Administration, Washington, DC. Quarterly Abstracts of Passenger Lists of Vessels Arriving at New Orleans, Louisiana, 1820–1875. M272. Passenger list of the *Carolina*, 2 April 1866. Quarterly.

291 *New Orleans Daily Crescent*, 14 April 1866.

292 *Liverpool Daily Post*, 5 June 1866.

293 National Museums Liverpool. *Liverpool Customs Bill of Entry*, 4 July 1866.

294 'Death of a Gallant Ex-Confederate', *Carolina Watchmen*, Salisbury, North Carolina, 21 January 1886.

295 *Newcastle Chronicle*, 25 August 1866.

296 *Cardiff Times*, 24 August 1866, and *Cardiff and Merthyr Guardian*, 19 October 1866.

297 'Large Cargo of Wheat', *Fife Herald*, 6 December 1866.

298 Wise, *Lifeline of the Confederacy*, p. 302.

299 *Freeman's Journal* Dublin, Ireland, 7 January 1865.

300 *Shipping and Mercantile Gazette*, London, 15 December 1864.

301 *Gore's Liverpool General Advertiser*, 1 June 1865.

302 Also known as the War of the Triple Alliance.

303 Leslie Bethell, *The Paraguayan War (1864–1870)*. Institute of Latin American Studies, London, 1996, pp. 1–10.

304 Entry for James Alexander Duguid, Lloyd's Captains Register, 1851–1869.

305 Graham *Clyde Built*, 126–127, and Lloyds Captains Register, 1851–1869.

306 *Cork Examiner*, Cork, Ireland, 20 March 1867.

307 Maritime History Archive, Memorial University of Newfoundland. Logbook of *Georgia Belle*, 27 March 1867.

308 *Fife Herald*, 7 March 1867.
309 *Cork Examiner*, 5 April 1867.
310 Maritime History Archive, Memorial University of Newfoundland. Logbook of *Georgia Belle* and Agreement for a Foreign Going Ship, 27 July 1867.
311 'Paddle Steamer *Stag*', *Clyde Ships*, Caledonian Maritime Research Trust, http://www.clydeships.co.uk/ <accessed csp 24/03/2021>.
312 *Liverpool Mercury*, 29 December 1865.

Chapter Eight

313 *Dundee Courier*, 18 June 1868.
314 *Farmer's Monthly Visitor*, 31 August 1843.
315 *Fife Free Press & Kirkcaldy Guardian*, 25 August 1877.
316 *Fifeshire Advertiser*, 9 January 1875.
317 Graham, *Clyde Built*, p. 159.
318 *Ibid.*
319 Colin Carlin, *Captain James Carlin: Anglo-American Blockade Runner.* University of South Carolina Press, Columbia, South Carolina, 2017.
320 National Records of Scotland, Edinburgh. 1877 Valuation Roll for Wyllie, Joannes (Valuation Roll VR002700006-/616 DYSART BURGH).
321 *Fife Free Press & Kirkcaldy Guardian*, 16 August 1890.
322 *Fife Free Press & Kirkcaldy Guardian*, 24 October 1884.
323 *Fife Free Press & Kirkcaldy Guardian*, 26 November 1892.
324 *Fife Free Press & Kirkcaldy Guardian*, 8 December 1894.
325 *Dundee Advertiser*, 18 November 1889, and *Fife Free Press & Kirkcaldy Guardian*, 30 November 1901.
326 *Fife Free Press & Kirkcaldy Guardian*, 21 December 1901.
327 *Fifeshire Advertiser*, 29 December 1883.
328 *Fife Free Press & Kirkcaldy Guardian*, 9 June 1894.
329 *Fife Free Press & Kirkcaldy Guardian*, 21 December 1895.
330 *Fife Free Press & Kirkcaldy Guardian*, 17 August 1872.
331 *Fife Herald*, 5 February 1874.
332 Glasgow Museums Collection. Letter from William Pirie to Donald Pirie, 6 September 1937 (T.2018.50).
333 *Fife Free Press & Kirkcaldy Guardian*, 8 March 1902.
334 Peter Anton, 'Risen from the Ranks: Captain Wyllie, the Great Scottish Blockade Runner', *The People's Friend*, July 1889, 404.
335 National Records of Scotland. Inventory of Joannes Wyllie, 1902. (SC20/50/84 Cupar Sheriff Court Inventories).

Conclusion

336 *Fife Free Press & Kirkcaldy Guardian*, 19 April 1902.
337 Wise, *Lifeline*, pp. 304, 285–328.
338 William H. Oliver *Blockade Running by the State of North Carolina.* Publisher unknown, New Bern, North Carolina, 1895, pp. 1–2.
339 *Fife Free Press & Kirkcaldy Guardian*, 19 April 1902.

Appendices

340 *Evening Mail*, London, England, 9 September 1857.
341 *Shetland Times*, 23 December 1872.
342 *Shipping and Mercantile Gazette*, 21 December 1877.
343 *Liverpool Daily Post*, 17 September 1860.
344 *Shields Daily News*, 23 February 1898.
345 *Algemeen Handelsblad*, Amsterdam, Netherlands, 31 October 1874.
346 *Evening Star*, Washington, DC, 26 September 1883.
347 *News and Observer*, Raleigh, North Carolina, 1 January 1886.
348 *Times Picayune*, New Orleans, Louisiana, 20 June 1889.
349 *Times-Democrat*, New Orleans, Louisiana, 11 November 1891.
350 *Ibid.*
351 *Glasgow Herald*, 22 December 1865.
352 American Lloyd's Register of American and Foreign Shipping 1873, https://research.mysticseaport.org/indexes/ship-registers/ . <accessed csp 24/03/2021>
353 Lloyd's List, 10 December 1872.
354 Memorial University of Newfoundland. Maritime History Archive. Crew List and logbook of *Georgia Belle*.
355 Appropriation book listing for *Stag*, http://www.crewlist.org.uk/ . <accessed csp 24/03/2021>

INDEX

More fantastic titles from Whittles Publishing

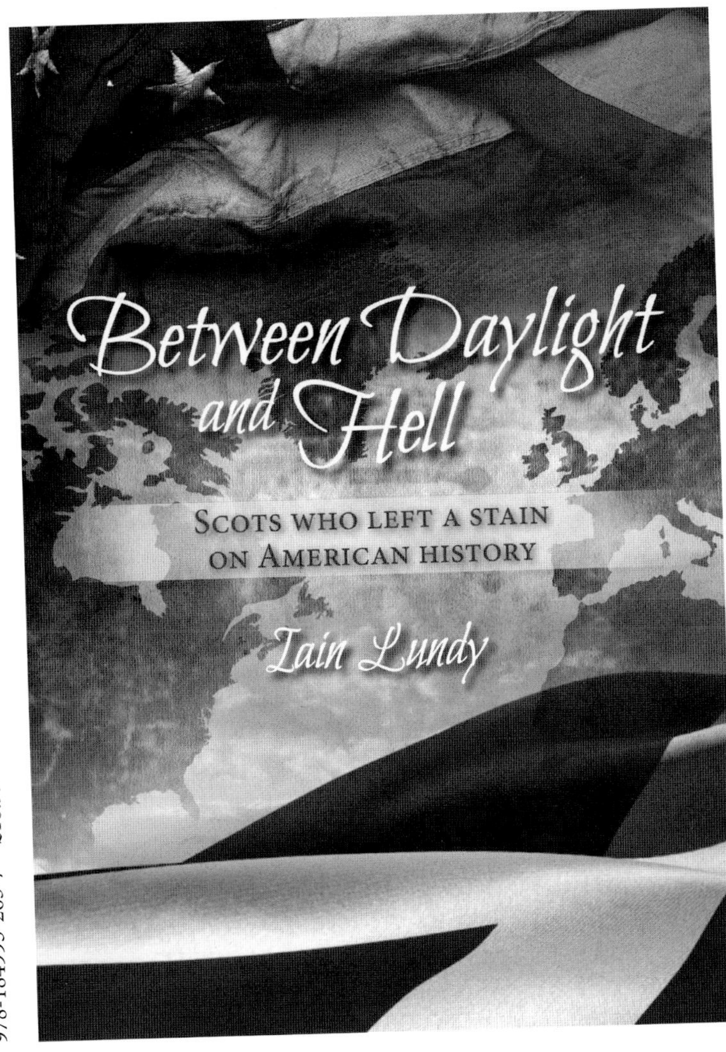

978-184995-263-7 £18.99

'...a well-written and beautifully researched book that explores the lives of 16 Scots who settled in America and whose deeds earned them infamy rather than fame... ...for a book looking at the darker side of the Scots abroad you won't find a better tome'. ***Scottish Field***

'...Scots have always been one of the most outward-looking and widely-travelled of races ... Many of those who left Scotland to make new lives elsewhere achieved great things ... But it is perhaps inevitable that, by the law of averages, some of those who left these shores made their names for altogether less positive reasons. The book's cover reports that "everyone loves a good 'baddie' and this book is full of them". It is, and their stories are fascinating'. ***Undiscovered Scotland***

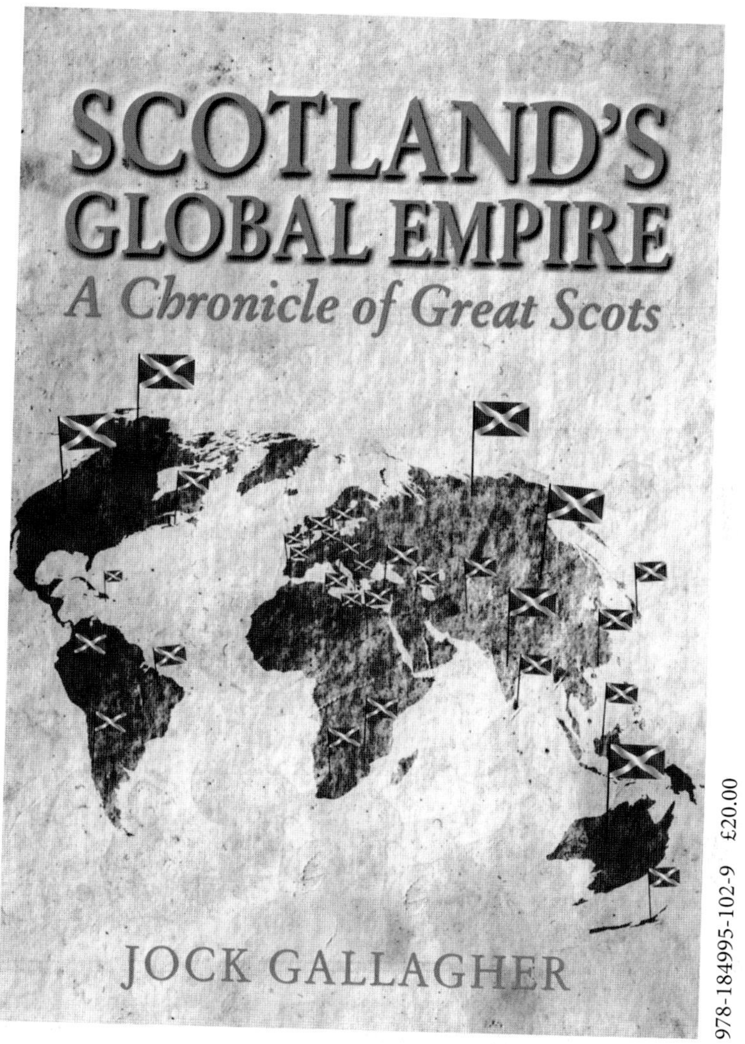

SCOTLAND'S
GLOBAL EMPIRE
A Chronicle of Great Scots
JOCK GALLAGHER
978-184995-102-9 £20.00

'...Gallagher brings together a heady mix of vision, creativity, energy, skill and, more often than not, sheer doggedness. It's an absorbing read with more than one revelation, including heroes from the American Civil War, sporting and showbiz superstars and prolific writers whose prose would inspire, amuse and enlighten'. ***The Scots Magazine***

'...Jock Gallagher truly shows us the power and influence of Scotland's global empire. A sturdy, informative, meaty volume for your bookshelves; and eye-catching not least for its excellent typeface, paper quality, and (for the true Scot) inspiring cover; a map of the world bristling with Scottish flags!' ***Journal of the Chartered Institute of Journalists***

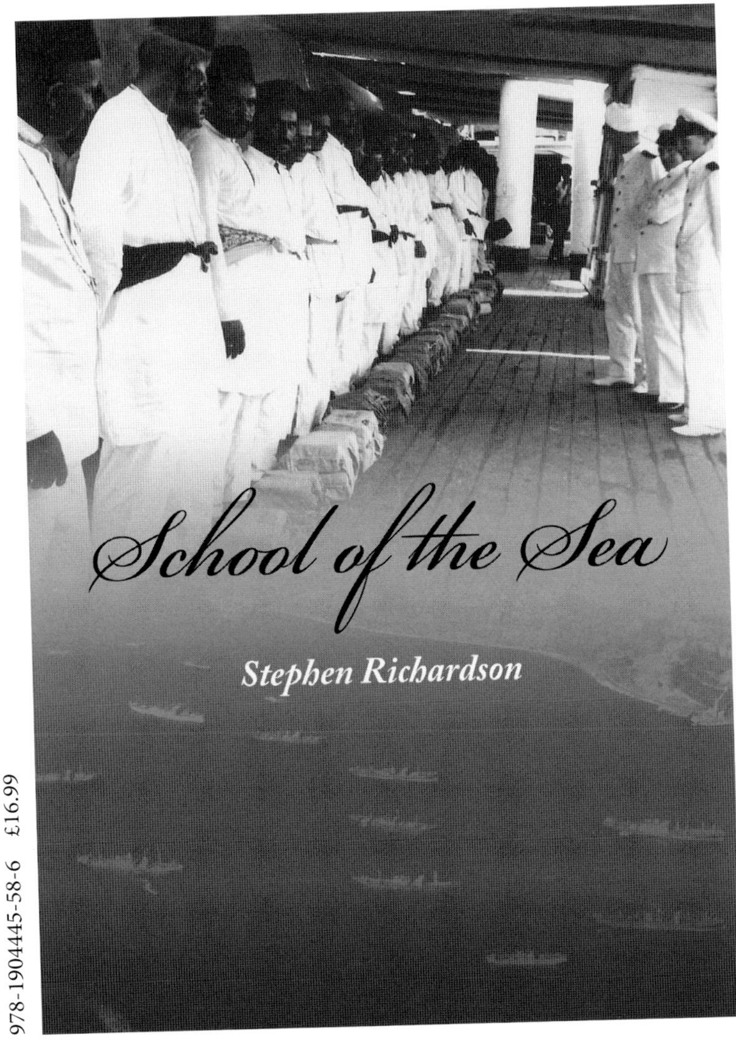

978-1904445-58-6 £16.99

'...a gem beyond price... his ability to convey his experience in vivid and eminently readable prose. Reading his book was a great privilege, and I cannot imagine that anyone with an interest in twentieth-century shipping, maritime ethnography, or merchant service during World War II would not want to own it'. ***International Journal of Maritime History***

'...tells the story in a very personal and moving way of the life of a Merchant Seaman from a 16 year old Indentured Apprentice in 1937 through to Master Mariner in 1964. ...vividly portrays a style of life and on the job training... ...The style of writing is unique... ...he is a natural and gifted writer'. ***Royal Naval Sailing Association Journal***

From **Whittles Publishing**, Dunbeath, Caithness, Scotland KW6 6EG, UK

+44(0)1593 731 333 info@whittlespublishing.com www.whittlespublishing.com